上海外国语大学校级重大科研项目“外国人讲述中国故事的理论建构和范式研究”阶段性成果

Phased Progress of SISU's Key Research Project of "Foreigners Telling China Stories: Theories and Paradigms"

◎跨文化视角下的中国：

外国专家的中国文化故事

第二辑

A CROSS-CULTURAL PERSPECTIVE ON CHINA: FOREIGN EXPERTS' CHINESE CULTURAL STORIES

张红玲 梁晓雪 主编

上海外语教育出版社
外教社 SHANGHAI FOREIGN LANGUAGE EDUCATION PRESS

图书在版编目(CIP)数据

跨文化视角下的中国：外国专家的中国文化故事. 第2辑：汉英对照/张红玲，梁晓雪主编.
—上海：上海外语教育出版社，2021
ISBN 978-7-5446-6788-3

I. ①跨… II. ①张… ②梁… III. ①中外关系—文化交流—文集—汉、英 IV. ①G125-53

中国版本图书馆CIP数据核字(2021)第061615号

出版发行：上海外语教育出版社
（上海外国语大学内） 邮编：200083
电　　话：021-65425300（总机）
电子邮箱：bookinfo@sflep.com.cn
网　　址：http://www.sflep.com
责任编辑：梁瀚杰

印　　刷：上海宝山译文印刷厂有限公司
开　　本：890×1240 1/32 印张 9.125 字数243千字
版　　次：2021年9月第1版 2021年9月第1次印刷

书　　号：ISBN 978-7-5446-6788-3
定　　价：30.00元
本版图书如有印装质量问题，可向本社调换
质量服务热线：4008-213-263 电子邮箱：editorial@sflep.com

Contents

目 录

Preface I
To Tell the Story of China and Make China's Voice Heard

Zhang Hongling

In 2001–2002, I studied at the University of Minnesota as a Fulbright Scholar, living in Minneapolis for almost a year. As a researcher of cross-cultural studies, that year was for me about learning and research as well as an opportunity to put my theories about cross-cultural studies to practice. I gained many insights from my time in Minneapolis. There was an American friend of mine in her fifties, who had a successful career and happy family life. She had just resigned from her job and returned to academia to pursue a Master's degree.

We shared certain courses and often went to class or studied together, becoming friends. She often invited me to her home; I grew close to her and her husband. They were kind, warm people, and avid readers. However, after many conversations I realized that they had a very limited, even skewed, picture of China. They could not understand my decision to leave behind my husband and child to study in America alone — for them it was "proof that 'Red China' was interested only in revolution and not human rights." Not long after I returned to China, I invited them to Shanghai on holiday. The moment they stepped in to my home, they were gasping nonstop in amazement: "What? You actually have a wooden floor, a piano and fresh flowers?!" The China of their imagination was one of a country stuck in the feudal, autocratic, backwards era, where the ordinary people could not possibly afford such luxuries. After that, I was frustrated by a question: why was so many Americans' understanding of China so skewed from what we Chinese had expected? How could stereotypes be changed?

After more than three decades of economic and political reform, China has become the world's second largest economy. As China enjoys increased international influence, the international community hopes that China will take on more responsibility internationally. Meanwhile, China also desires to play a more active role in creating understanding and learning between countries, nations and cultures around the world. Since the 18th CPC National Congress, President Xi Jinping has on numerous visits abroad emphasized the necessity for mankind to see its symbiotic destiny. This and cooperation for mutual benefit have become an important part of Chinese diplomacy. The "One Belt One Road" initiative, AIIB and other strategic measures have put into practice these diplomatic ideals.

Bringing together individuals and minds is an important way to ensure success in mutual benefit cooperation and symbiotic destiny. Each culture has developed against a particular environment and historical context, and has its own distinct character. This has allowed human civilization to become as rich and varied as it is. Chinese culture is both ancient and profound. To quote President Xi, "Observing and understanding China requires a knowledge of both history and the present, of the material as well as the spiritual. Chinese history is unbroken, from the beginning of Chinese civilization over five millennia ago, through the struggles of the Chinese people over the past 170 years, the endeavors of the Communist Party of China over the past 90 years, the development of the People's Republic of China over the past 60 years, and the explorations of the Reform and Opening-up of the past three decades. A proper understanding of China is incomplete without understanding Chinese history, culture, the spiritual realm of its people, and the profound changes the country has undergone."

Xi Jinping has also emphasized that "China needs to make significant efforts in promoting itself globally, using innovative new methods. Our country needs to focus on combining Chinese and international ideas and expressions, in order to tell the story of China and make China's voice heard."

In summary, to tell the Chinese story by improving international understanding of China and promoting traditional Chinese culture is an extremely important but challenging task, and one worthy of study. In the past, there has been a focus on conscious, organized efforts by government offices, cultural groups, NGOs, and educational institutions to inform about and promote Chinese culture. In recent years, with growing recognition of the importance of public diplomacy, the public has played an increasingly central role in cultural transmission. These developments can be summarized as the "Going Global" move in Chinese culture.

Another effective means to inform the world about China is to "invite" the world in. This refers to the role played by international students, tourists and foreign workers in China. This group is important for two reasons. Firstly, international students and professionals in our country can relate their experiences in China to their compatriots back home. Secondly, by informing us of their impressions, we can gain another perspective on ourselves and improve.

As an elite institution that is comparatively open to the outside world, Shanghai International Studies University (SISU) recruits over a hundred foreign experts from more than 30 countries around the world each year to teach or undertake research. Some of them stay for shorter periods (one to three months), while others stay here for the long term (half a year to a year, or even more than a decade). They leave their mark not only in the classroom and around the university: because of their interest in our country and its culture, in addition to the duties of their work, they often explore the snaking alleyways of Shanghai, travel around the country, and see both urban and rural areas. China viewed from their perspective is surely instructive for us.

"China in My Eyes" began as a task in the Cross-Cultural Communication course at Shanghai International Studies University's Institute of Intercultural Studies in the 1990s. Students on this course from all over the world have been required to complete this task, so that they can reflect on their experiences and record those events which have had a particularly strong impact on them cross-culturally. Furthermore, by sharing their experiences with those around them and learning about those of their peers, these students gain a better understanding of cross-cultural experience and learn about adapting in different cultural contexts.

Inspired by the Cross-Cultural Communication course, the "China in My Eyes" project asks foreign experts working and living in China to share their China stories, in order to discover issues of particular relevance and see our country from their point of view. These university-employed foreign experts are of a high caliber, are idealists, and have come to China not just to pursue teaching and research but also to learn about our country. When SISU's foreign experts learned about our project, the vast majority expressed a keen willingness to take part. This is how, in just four months after we issued a call for submissions, we received dozens of essays from our international faculty. These stories cover a wide range of topics and forms. They include prose, novels, poetry, and speeches, covering (amongst other topics) history, philosophy, language, literature, cuisine and travel. Some contributions offer a macroscopic view, taking a broad look at China's history and development and its interaction with other countries; others focus on a particular experience, seeking to describe the experience of work and life in China through intricate personal stories. Others still remark with wonder and praise at the pace of development in our country, or provide some criticisms of the less positive aspects of our society.

Of those foreign experts who submitted contributions, some had only been in our country several months, still overwhelmed by a sensory bombardment, which means that their stories are like a first impression of China. A larger number of essays have been written by those who have lived and worked in China for several years, some of whom have even married and started families here and who speak fluent Chinese. For this reason, their understanding of our country is more nuanced than simple stereotypes or attempts to speak Shanghainese.

These foreign experts come from all over the world. Each individual has a different culture, family background, level of education, faith, and set of values. Coupled with their unique experiences, they have an immense scope of different perspectives between them. Nevertheless, having lived and worked in China for a time, the great majority of foreigners will agree on the richness of Chinese culture, the complexity of its society, and the tremendous changes sweeping the nation. These are not something that an individual foreigner can comprehend in a short period of time; the complications and uncertainties in our country form a part of the challenge and pleasure of the Chinese experience. To quote a French expert in *Making Sense of China*: "To me, France is becoming increasingly stagnant, closed on itself, intolerant towards non-Europeans. As opposed to the predictable, sanitized, standardized comfort of France which tames my senses (I will admit an exception for the cheese and wine), China awakens your senses and makes you feel alive and forces you to have feelings. Chinese people have an attitude that makes everything seem possible, while the French are nowadays pessimistic and resigned. China is alive and France is asleep. For some foreigners this is just too much to take in, but for me this daily thrill keeps me awake and alive. For many foreigners their relationship with China is a love-hate relationship. For me it is the constant buzz, changes and contradictions described above that I miss when I am not in China. As I spend more time in China, I find myself gaining understanding and becoming more knowledgeable, yet growing increasingly confused and at ease with this confusion."

This European foreign expert's words will resonate with many international residents in China. When we work with foreigners, we discover that those with a passionate curiosity for Chinese culture, who are willing to explore new things, and who are willing to step outside their comfort zone, are often better at adapting to their new environment. By contrast, those unwilling to broaden their horizons, refuse to connect with or understand Chinese culture, tend to have a less positive experience. Fortunately, the vast majority of our international faculty belong to the former group: they endeavor to learn Chinese and about our culture, getting involved socially, trying Chinese food, and travelling all over the country to experience the local cultures. Despite the inevitability of difficulties or the odd unhappy experience, most of their China experience is unique and unforgettably positive.

Against the backdrop of globalization, more and more people are leaving their hometowns behind and choosing to live elsewhere. To quote the Song dynasty poet Su Shi, "I cannot see what Mt. Lu looks like really, because I am standing there." Having grown up with them, we Chinese may have dulled our senses to our surroundings. These foreigners, however, can both stand "on" and "at a distance from" the mountain, thus gaining a clearer picture. Their sensitive rediscovery of details overlooked by us for so long is therefore all the more fascinating and precious. The greatest value of this book lies perhaps not so much in the details of each foreigner's China experience, but in how we can discover "another" China that we do not know or understand.

A Cross-cultural Perspective on China is a book series dedicated to foreigners in China sharing cultural stories and communicating the Chinese culture. It is listed as one of the projects under the Peak Discipline (Foreign Language and Literature) Development Program, as well as SISU's key research project of "Foreigners Telling China Stories: Theories and Paradigms".

Staff of the Office of International Cooperation and Exchange, as well as faculty and students of relevant SISU schools and departments helped with soliciting and translating. To all of the above-mentioned people, I wish to extend my sincere gratitude.

ZHANG Hongling

Director, the SISU Intercultural Institute (SII)

August 2016, Shanghai

Revised in June 2021, Shanghai

序一
讲好中国故事，传播好中国声音

张红玲

2001至2002年间，我作为富布赖特学者在美国明尼苏达大学研修，在明尼阿波利斯这个美国中西部城市生活了近一年。作为一名跨文化研究学者，这一年对我来说既是学习和研究的一年，也是跨文化探索和实践的一年，可谓成果丰硕，感悟深刻。记得当时我有一个美国朋友，她年过五旬，事业有成，家庭幸福，当时刚辞去工作，回到学校攻读硕士学位。我们有共同修读的课程，经常一起上课、学习，于是便成为朋友。我经常受邀到她家做客，与她和她丈夫非常熟悉。他们善良、热情，喜欢阅读。然而，在多次闲聊过程中，我惊讶地发现他们对中国的了解相当有限，甚至偏颇。在他们看来，我远离丈夫和孩子，独自一人在美国生活学习，不可思议，“这就是‘红色中国’只讲革命、不讲人权的一个例证。”我回国后不久，邀请他们来上海旅游。他们从踏进我家大门那一刻起就接连发出惊叹：“啊，你们家竟然用的是木地板，有钢琴，还有鲜花！”在他们的印象里，中国还停留在封建、专制、落后的时代，普通百姓的生活怎么可能如此讲究！

由此，一个问题时时缠绕在我心头：为什么很多美国人对中国的理解与我们的期待如此大相径庭？他们对中国的刻板印象如何才能改变？

经过30多年的改革开放，中国已经发展成为世界第二大经济体。随着国力的不断增强，世界期待中国承担更多国际责任，中国也希望在促进世界各国、各民族、各文化之间的沟通理解、交流互鉴方面起到更加积极的推动作用。十八大以来，习近平主席在多次出访演讲中积极倡导构建人类命运共同体，合作共赢和命运共同体成为我国对外交往的重要理念。“一带一路”和亚投行等国家重大举措，就是这些理念的具体体现。

人文交流与心灵相通是实现合作共赢、构建命运共同体的重要保证。每个文化都有其发展环境和历史渊源，具有各自的特点，人类文明因而丰富多彩。中国文化源远流长，博大精深。正如习近平主席所说：“观察和认识中国，历史和现实都要看，物质和精神也都要看。中华民族5000多年文明史，中国人民近代以来170多年斗争史，中国共产党90多年奋斗史，中华人民共和国60多年发展史，改革开放30多年探索史，这些历史一脉相承，不可割裂。脱离了中国的历史，脱离了中国的文化，脱离了中国人的精神世界，脱离了当代中国的深刻变革，是难以正确认识中国的。”习总书记还强调：“要精心做好对外宣传工作，创新对外宣传方式，着力打造融通中外的新概念新范畴新表述，讲好中国故事，传播好中国声音。”

综上所述，如何让世界了解中国、认识中国，如何传播中国文化、讲述中国故事，这是一项意义重大又极具挑战的任务，是一个值得研究的课题。通常我们更关注的是，如何通过政府机构、文化组织、非政府组织、教育机构等有意识的组织行为去进行中国文化的介绍和传播。近年来，随着公共外交理念不断推广，公众参与文化交流和传播的积极性越来越高。这些可以概括为中国文化传播的“走出去”模式。

让世界了解中国的另一个有效途径是“请进来”，即充分发挥留学生和在华旅游、工作的外籍人士的作用。这里包含两个层面的意义。第一，在华外籍学生和工作人员可以将他们在中国的所见所闻、亲身感受带回国，与同胞分享；第二，他们对中国的印象反馈给我们，有助于我们更好地认识自我、完善自我。

上海外国语大学作为一所国际化水平较高的大学，每年聘请来自世界30余个国家的百余名专家来校任教或从事科学研究。他们或在上海短期停留（一个月至三个月），或长期生活（半年至一年，甚至十余年），他们的足迹不仅集中于课堂、学校，出于对中国和中国文化的兴趣，他们还常常会在工作之余，利用节假日去上海的大街小巷，去中国的东南西北、城市乡村，走一走看一看。以他们的视角来审视中国，一定会给我们带来新的发现。

“我的文化故事”是上海外国语大学跨文化研究中心教学团队自20世纪90年代以来在“跨文化交际”课程中一直坚持的一项学习任务，来自世界各地修读本课程的学生都必须完成这项作业，目的是让学生回顾和反思自己的人生经历，记录和讲述自己印象深刻或对自己产生重要影响的跨文化经历，同时通过与其他同学分享、交流各自的文化故事，达到增强跨文化意识、提升跨文化能力的目的。

“外国专家的中国文化故事”项目借鉴“跨文化交际”课程教学的经验，利用外国专家在华生活和工作的机会，请他们讲述自己的中国文化故事，以期从中发现他们对中国的关注点，了解他们眼中的中国。实际上，高校外国专家群体素质高，有思想，他们来中国除了教学科研之外，本来就有探索中国、了解中国的希望。当我校的外国专家了解这个项目时，大都表现出极高的热情和参与愿望。因此，征稿通知发出仅四个月，我们就收到了几十封来稿。这些稿件内容丰富，形式各异。体裁方面，有散文、小说、诗歌、演讲等；内容涉猎广泛，有历史、哲学、语言、文学、美食、旅游等。有的从宏观角度出发，纵论古今、横贯中外；有的从微观小事入手，以个体的细腻笔触，描绘自己在中国工作和生活的心路历程；有的对中国经济的飞速发展表示惊叹、赞美，也有的对中国社会的不良现象提出批评。撰稿外教中，少数人刚到中国数月，尚处于各种新鲜事物的感官“轰炸”之中，因而笔下叙述更多的是对中国的“第一印象”，而更多的撰稿者在中国工作、生活已有数年，个别甚至已经在中国结婚生子，会说流利的汉语，对中国的熟悉早已超出看“东洋镜”或“会讲上海话”的层面，因而他们笔下的中国又是另一番图景。

这些外国专家来自世界各地，每个人的文化及家庭背景、受教育情况、宗教信仰、价值观往往迥异，加之他们独特的人生经历，导致他们看待事物的角度非常之多元。尽管如此，大多数外国人在中国生活和工作一段时间以后，都会达成一个共识，即中国文化之博大精深，中国社会之错综复杂，中国发展之天翻地覆，绝不是一个外国人一朝一夕就能真正理解领悟的，而这其中的矛盾和不确定性也恰恰是生活在中国的挑战和乐趣所在。援引一位法国专家在《解读中国》一文中的话：“……法国正在日益变成一个停滞不前、自我封闭、对外来人愈加严苛的国家。法国可预见的、洁净的和标准的舒适很容易麻痹人的感官……相反，中国却让你的感官觉醒，让你感到自己是活着的，它强迫你去感受。中国人有一种‘万事皆有可能’的心态，而当今的法国人却变得日益悲观消极。中国是生机盎然的，而法国却在沉睡。对有些外国人来说，中国实在有点难以消化。但对我来说，每天的感官刺激让我能保持清醒和活力。对很多外国人来说，他们对中国的感情是爱恨交织。对我来说，它是连绵不断的喧闹、矛盾和变化，当我不在中国时，就会想念这一切。随着在中国生活的时间越来越长，我发现自己对中国的理解和认知也日渐加深，同样，我的困惑也越来越多，但我已经逐渐学会用泰然处之的心态面对它们。”

这位来自欧洲的外国专家道出了很多在华外国人的心声。事实上，我们在与外国人打交道的过程中常会发现，那些对中国文化抱有强烈好奇心、乐于发现并探索新鲜事物、敢于走出自我心理舒适区（comfort zone）、勇于尝试的外国人，往往更容易适应当地环境；反之，那些不愿意敞开心胸，抗拒接触或理解当地文化的外国人，往往有很糟糕的文化体验。令人欣慰的是，我们从绝大多数外国专家的来稿中感受到的是前者：他们努力学习汉语和中国文化，积极扩大社交圈子，兴致勃勃地品尝中国美食，前往中国各地体验当地的风土民情。尽管他们在中国免不了遇到挫败和不快，但总体来说，在中国工作、生活的经历对他们来说绝对是独一无二、永生难忘的。

在当今全球化的背景下，越来越多的人离开故乡，选择“生活在别处”。“不识庐山真面目，只缘身在此山中。”作为中国人，我们对身边的一切也许已经习以为常，感官趋于迟钝，而这些外国人既在“山外”，又在“山中”，他们能够重新发现我们长期忽视的细节，充满感性的认识也因此显得更加有趣和弥足珍贵。此书最大的价值或许不是这群外国人在中国工作、生活的点滴，而是在于从他们那里，我们会发现还有一个我们不熟悉、不了解的“别样中国”。

《跨文化视角下的中国》是一套外国人讲述中国故事、传播中国文化的系列丛书，得到了上海外国语大学I类高峰学科建设项目及校级重大科研项目“外国人讲述中国故事的理论建构和范式研究”的资助。

上海外国语大学对外合作交流处和相关院系师生参与了本书的组稿、翻译等工作，对他们的付出，在此谨致以衷心的感谢。

张红玲

上海外国语大学跨文化研究中心主任

2016年8月，上海

2021年6月二稿，上海

Preface II
The Value of Cultural Stories in Context

Steve J. Kulich (U.S.A.)
Proofread by George Fleming

"Who are you? Who am I? What connects us, or distances us, or then helps build bridges when we meet new situations, or each other in new cultural contexts? Who am I culturally and how can I relate meaningfully in a new culture? Or who do you think I am, or expect me to be?" These are some of the questions that begin to emerge when we cross over into new cultures. The things that we previously took for granted about ourselves or assumed about our comfortable "home" cultural patterns can suddenly feel uncomfortable, lack support, or seem to be questioned.

As noted in a previous SFLEP Volume (*Intercultural Research, Vol. 4*), in each of our own familiar cultural contexts, we generally exercise a basic need or desire to associate with sameness (as "birds of a feather flock together", or like "a fish in water", swimming instinctively with its school in known waters). But it is often differences and our encounters with "Other" that become starting points for fostering at least an awareness of the need for cultural sensitivity (Kulich, 2012, pp. 33–35).

"Own-culture awareness" is an important first step toward becoming more intercultural. As the pioneer of what later became the "intercultural training" field, Edward T. Hall noted:

> *Culture hides much more than it reveals, and strangely enough, what it hides, it hides most effectively from its own participants. Years of study have convinced me that the ultimate purpose of the study of culture is not so much the understanding of foreign cultures as much as the light that study sheds on our own. (Hall, reprinted in Bennett 1998, p. 59)*

This has been one of the core components and unique features of the intercultural communication (IC) teaching and research program that we have undertaken at SISU for the last two decades. Starting from when I offered the first intercultural orientation courses at the Overseas Preparatory Department in 1994 and continuing with my colleague Zhang Hongling through our co-teaching and research partnership in undergraduate and post-graduate courses since the late 1990s, our team has been asking participants to write and reflect on their "cultural stories" in our courses and training designs.

Through taking time to examine the cultural elements or influences that have shaped each of us, explore the cultural differences we're observing in new contexts, and reflect on the ways that cross-cultural experiences might be impacting us or others, each of us gains greater insight into the complex web of relationships, values, hopes, and aspirations that link us to cultural communities. Thus, writing such "cultural stories" can be a wonderful self-discovery and cultural exploration and adaptation process for ourselves. The process of exploring our cultural roots, influences, socialization, or *modus operandi* often helps us depart from essentialized or monolithic assumptions about "our culture" because we realize that we too are complex cultural beings, made up of the fusion of unique strands, backgrounds, histories, or narratives of origin. Such exploration and reflective writing makes us open to other cultural variations that we might observe or interact with.

The tool is even more developmental when we start to share these "cultural stories" with others, read or hear their perspectives, and mull over the diverse lenses through which each of us views our unique cultural orientations, expectations, or experiences. This is precisely what the first volume of the series compiled by Prof. Zhang Hongling and her staff at the SISU Office for International Cooperation does for us. As she details in her Preface, this is an important way of both telling "Chinese stories" and experiencing them through new and fresh eyes and dynamic encounters.

As she further suggests, when we bring "together individuals and minds" there is greater opportunity and chance for success in our common endeavor to realize President Xi Jinping's vision for "mutual benefit cooperation and symbiotic destiny" of the world. The recording and compiling of cultural narratives or "Chinese stories" told from overseas viewpoints and varied experiences helps us begin to realize the rich diversity of ways that each one perceives the culture they grew up or live in, even among those who thought they had "similar backgrounds" or good cultural preparation before coming to China.

With Zhang Hongling, our team and I have used this "cultural story" exercise in many contexts and forms, including as a key start-up step in our international MOOC course with FutureLearn (www.futurelearn.com/courses/intercultural-communication), which in its multiple runs since 2015 has attracted over 65,000 enrollees from over 180 countries and regions. But this new book series brings a welcome addition and new inspiration to that legacy, asking learners to describe "China in My Eyes." As each of the stories in the first volume shows us, reflecting on the China that each of us encounters as a specific cultural context stimulates wonderfully insightful Chinese stories and enhances the potential for greater cross-cultural understanding.

Thus, we are very pleased that coinciding with the 10th anniversary of the establishment of the SISU Intercultural Institute (SII, launched on September 23, 2006 and legally structured on January 23, 2007), Professor Zhang's first book in this series was published (December 2016)! It contributes to the documentation of our institute's commitment to explore cross-cultural encounters and gain insights relevant and helpful for bridging cooperation in Chinese contexts. This book series is a very tangible illustration of how exercises in "own culture awareness" and "understanding cultural Others" (whether as explorations of identities, values, negotiated meanings, communication styles, or adaptation preferences) serve as an impetus for our work together over the last decade, and how it can continue to be in the coming years.

SISU is exemplary in the interdisciplinary collaboration experienced across the university! This is evident not only in work among our various research institutes, centers, schools, and departments, but also through the over 200 international faculty members that come to work with us each year through global partnership and exchange efforts initiated or maintained by the Office of International Cooperation.

As Director Zhang Hongling and her team have strengthened SISU's internationalization in these ways, this volume shows what a welcome initiative it also is to ask each foreign expert to contribute their personal view on "China in My Eyes." We can only hope and expect that as each new group of international experts comes to work at SISU these volumes will likewise inspire them to draft their own accounts as a key contribution to this continuing series of personalized "Chinese stories." Though a diverse set of accounts, as she notes in her Preface of the first volume, most "agree on the richness of Chinese culture, the complexity of its society, and the tremendous changes sweeping the nation", and that "Chinese people have an attitude that makes everything seem possible…".

Our Chairman, Dr. Jiang Feng already at the start of his tenure in April 2014 (in his closing remarks at the 2nd Intercultural Disciplinary Development Forum we hosted) cast his vision for SISU, saying: "Interpret the world, translate the future."

In line with that spirit, Prof. Zhang's team entitled the *2013–2014 SISU Annual Review*: "Bridges & Beyond."

Together, we drafted the caption describing SISU as "A Multicultural and Dynamic University Dedicated to Holistic Human Development." (Cover of *SISU 2015*, Shanghai International Studies University). That is truly what we hope our university, programs, and people aspire to!

This volume of "Chinese Cultural Stories" is an inspiring embodiment of that vision and aim. It not only helps us better tell important stories in new ways, but as Professor Zhang notes, allows us to "discover 'another' China that we do not know or understand." Through others' vantage points, challenges, and insightful breakthroughs, may we each grow in greater intercultural understanding and awareness.

It is our sincere hope that this *A Cross-cultural Perspective on China* book series will continue to fulfill the SISU vision to take us over new "bridges beyond" and further "interpret and translate China's future" and that of those nations represented in these writings as we interact globally and interculturally!

Steve J. Kulich, Shanghai International Studies University (SISU)
President, the Intercultural Academy of Intercultural Research (IAIR) (2019–2021)
Director, the SISU Intercultural Institute (SII)

序二
文化故事的价值

顾力行（美国）
衷苾璇　译
梁晓雪　审校

“你是谁？我是谁？是什么拉近了彼此的距离，抑或将彼此疏远？又是什么在我们遇见新事物或新的文化环境时，为我们搭建了桥梁？我的文化身份是什么？我如何与新的文化建立联系？你眼中的我是怎样的？你期望我是什么样子？”这些都是我们在过渡到新文化中会出现的问题。突然间，我们对原以为理所当然的事情产生了不自信、犹豫，甚至开始质疑我们自身的文化。

我曾在上海外语教育出版社“跨文化研究”系列丛书第四辑中写道，人在自身文化环境中通常会表现出与同类为伍的基本需求或愿望（就像鸟以类聚、鱼以群居）。然而，文化差异和与“他者”的碰撞往往成为培养文化敏感的起点（Kulich，2012，第33–35页）。

“拥有文化自觉”是在跨文化道路上迈出的第一步。跨文化培训领域先驱爱德华·霍尔指出：

> 隐藏的文化因素远比显露出来的更多，奇怪的是，越是在该文化中成长的人，越难以察觉文化中隐藏的部分。多年的研究使我深信，与其说文化研究的最终目是理解其他文化，不如说这些研究是对我们自身文化的启发。（Bennett主编，1998，第59页）

这是过去20年来上外跨文化研究中心开展教学和科研

的核心和特点之一。自1994年我在上外海外合作学院开设第一门跨文化培训课程，到20世纪90年代末与我的同事张红玲为本科生和研究生共同授课、合作科研，我们的团队一直要求学生思考并撰写他们自己的“文化故事”。

通过花时间审视影响自身的文化印记及因子，在新环境里探索我们所观察到的文化差异，反思对自己或他人产生重要影响的跨文化经历，每个人都将更深入地了解我们所处的复杂关系网络、价值观、希望及追求——正是它们将我们联系起来，让我们形成文化群体。因此，撰写这样的“文化故事”可以是自我发现、文化探索及自我文化适应的绝佳方式。对我们的文化根源、所受的影响、社会化的方式（即处事方式）进行探索的过程，常常能让我们摆脱对“我们的文化”的某些概括化或单一化假设，让我们明白，我们同样是复杂的文化生物，是由多种独一无二的因素、背景、历史和起源叙事融合而成的。这样的探索和反思性写作，也使我们能够包容我们观察或接触到的其他不同文化。

当我们开始与他人分享这些“文化故事”，阅读或倾听他们的观点，并琢磨我们通过各色各样的镜头看到的独特文化取向与经历时，这一方式会更加有效。这正是张红玲教授及其对外合作交流处的团队编写《外国专家的中国文化故事》（第一辑）的目的。正如她在第一辑前言中提到的，如何讲述“中国故事”并以新的视角和多样化体验呈现“中国故事”，是非常重要的课题。

她进一步提到，促进“人文交流”和“人心相通”有助于进一步实现习近平主席所倡导的“合作共赢和命运共同体”。通过记录和收集来自世界各地的人们所撰写的“中国故事”，我们逐渐认识到不同的人对于自身成长过程所处文化的不同见解，这甚至包括那些自认为有着和中国“相似的背景”或来中国前已经做好准备的人。

我、张红玲教授以及我们跨文化研究中心的团队成员在许多情况下充分利用了我们的“文化故事”素材，例如将其作为我们在FutureLearn平台的国际慕课课程（www.futurelearn.com/courses/interculturalcommunication）中的重要起步素材。自2015年上线以来，我们的慕课课程已经吸引了来自180多个国家和地区的65 000多名注册学生。本系列著作让学习者讲述他们眼中的中国，给慕课课程带来了有益借鉴和新的灵感。正如第一辑书中所展现的那样，每个人都处在中国这个具体的文化背景中，对自身经历的回顾能催生出很多精彩而又深刻的中国故事，增进跨文化理解。

因此，在上海外国语大学跨文化研究中心成立十周年之际（中心于2006年9月23日启动，正式成立于2007年1月23日），由张红玲教授主编的《外国专家的中国文化故事》（第一辑）于2016年12月出版，令我们非常高兴。它承载了我们中心在探索跨文化交流中，对中国文化走出去所做出的努力。这一丛书是我们在过去十年来对“自我文化意识”和“理解多元文化”（无论是身份认同、价值观、交流意义、沟通方式还是跨文化适应）方面所做出努力的生动诠释，也是鼓舞我们继续协同合作的动力。

上海外国语大学是跨学科合作的典范。这不仅体现在学校各研究机构、学术中心和院系，还体现在国际教职工身上。在对外合作交流处的支持下，每年有200多名外国专家和访问学者通过校际合作协议来上外进行教学和科研。

张红玲教授及其对外合作交流处团队通过种种举措，

致力于推进学校的国际化水平。邀请外国专家讲述“他们眼中的中国”就是举措之一。随着一批批外国专家的不断加入，我们希望以这一系列丛书作为引子，启发他们写出自己的中国故事，为后续作品增添丰富素材。张红玲教授在她的第一辑序言中提到，大多数外国人“都会达成一个共识，即中国文化之博大精深，中国社会之错综复杂，中国发展之天翻地覆”，以及“中国人有一种‘万事皆有可能’的心态”。

校党委书记姜锋博士在其2014年4月任职开始之际（在第二届跨文化学科发展论坛闭幕致辞中）讲了上海外国语大学办学理念：“诠释世界，成就未来”。

按照这一精神，张红玲教授及她的团队将2013–2014年度《上外年鉴》的主题定位为：“桥梁与未来”。

上海外国语大学的目标之一是“建设多元校园文化，服务人的全面成长”（《上外2015年鉴》封面语）。这是我们对上外和上外人的期待。

《外国专家的中国文化故事》是这个愿景和目标的体现。正如张红玲教授所言，它不仅以创新的方式讲述重要的故事，还让我们“发现一个我们不熟悉、不了解的别样中国”（第一辑序言）。通过他人的视角、挑战和突破性见解，我们每个人都可以培养跨文化理解和思维。

最后，希望《跨文化视角下的中国》丛书继续贯彻上海外国语大学的愿景，帮助我们搭建新的桥梁，在跨文化的语境中，更好地解读中国，诠释世界，成就未来。

顾力行，上海外国语大学
国际跨文化研究学会（IAIR）会长（2019–2021）
上海外国语大学跨文化研究中心主任

Cultural Tapestry　多元融合

Clash of Cultures or Fusion of Horizons? The Hermeneutic Challenges of a Travelling Scholar

Inge van de Ven (Netherlands)

Proofread by George Fleming

Written on the Wall at West Forest Temple

From the side, a whole range; from the end, a single peak:

Far, near, high, low, no two parts alike.

Why can't I tell the true shape of Lushan?

Because I myself am in the mountain.

— Su Shi, trans. Burton Watson

This poem by the famous Chinese poet Su Shi was brought to my attention by Liang Wenbo (Kate), one of the students on the course "Hermeneutics in the Information Age: from Close to Distant Reading" that I co-taught at Shanghai International Studies University in April 2017. It reflects my experiences as a visiting scholar in an unfamiliar cultural setting quite splendidly, as it holds that vision is dependent upon one's perspective. Just as I cannot fathom the "true shape" of the mountain, for I am in it, I cannot perceive my own cultural make-up. To my mind, the poem stands as an image for the method of dialogical hermeneutics we operationalized with the students in this course, while trying to make sense of the transcultural phenomenon of Shanghai Disneyland. In a broader sense, it stands for the cultural perspectives and prejudices that I myself inevitably brought to Shanghai with me.

In what follows, I share some of the confrontations (or "hermeneutic challenges", De Mul, 2011) that resulted from this, and how in the end they broadened my horizon and made our familiar way of doing things in Tilburg, strange.

Hermeneutic challenge #1

Somewhere on my Western cultural horizon, there was the expectation that Chinese universities would be marked by strictly hierarchical relations between different levels of staff and students. Upon arrival, this expectation was immediately shattered when we were welcomed by a mixed group of staff members of the Department of Intercultural Communications, from secretary to ex-student and from teachers to the head of the Office of International Cooperation and Exchange. All were equally encouraged to share their research interests and stories. The praise bestowed upon each individual scholar by their colleagues was heart-warming. The sense of pride for one another's talents and the highly democratic atmosphere that was conveyed at this meeting proved characteristic of the vibe at the department.

Hermeneutic challenge #2

If, when asked if they have understood everything you just explained, students politely nod; this does not necessarily mean that they have actually understood. Sometimes they are just being polite.

Hermeneutic challenge #3

When you are attending a show by a noise act called Torturing Nurse, consisting of one guy ramming on a keyboard and another smashing his guitar to pieces, do not expect to end up in a loud, smoky basement with befuddled, unshaven, stinky "crusties". Expect a clean-looking bunch of youngsters sitting on chairs in a well-lit, atmospheric venue (Chair Club), politely applauding, and feasting on champagne and oysters (!). It will make for a memorable night.

Hermeneutic challenge #4

One cannot assume *anything* about the level of exposure to Western cultural influences on the part of the Chinese student. In this regard, there is no "typical" Chinese student. Setting out the course from the presupposition that Shanghai Disneyland brings together two worlds or horizons — the one of Chinese culture, and the other the horizon of Disney and its stock characters and symbols — proved erroneous. Whereas one student states that they had "grown up with the exposure to the Disney culture since my childhood. I watched the cartoons from the TV and read the fairy tales from the books," another describes Disney as "something from the remote country, the United States. It is totally different from our culture." Any attempt at forming a generalizing statement about these influences, we learned, was futile. What united us all in the end, since some things are universal, was a love for *Titanic*.

Hermeneutic challenge #5

When invited to give a keynote lecture at a conference in China, do not expect to be the only one, or even among a small group. It might very well be that a whole day has been reserved for keynote lectures by international scholars. As said, the Chinese are *very* polite. Do expect to be asked to pose for pictures with audience members. Go with it, and feel like a rock star.

Hermeneutic challenge #6

One would imagine that the experience of living in a vibrant metropolis like Shanghai would make boredom a thing of the past. One shouldn't. Judged by the eagerness with which I was clung to for dear life by inebriated Western expats and reeled in as "new meat" in the bar area of the French Concession, life can get lonely and monotonous when working abroad. Even in Shanghai.

Hermeneutic challenge #7

Whereas back home in Tilburg, I am one of the lucky few who still manage to get through life without a Smartphone, the idea of pulling this off in China is preposterous. Not only is one totally defenseless without a Smartphone, one is powerless *with* one if there's no WeChat app installed on it. The Chinese equivalent of Facebook, Twitter, WhatsApp, Tinder, and numerous other services, Wechat is media convergence 2.0. It allows you to pay contactless when shopping, going for dinner, getting a cab, booking a holiday, or buying tickets for concerts. And in order to use it, you need to have a Chinese telephone number. Do not expect to accomplish *anything* without it. Being without WeChat in China, however, does grant one an experience of feeling excluded that has become rarified in an age of global connectivity.

Making the familiar strange

Interpretation would be impossible if expressions of life were completely strange.

It would be unnecessary if nothing strange were in them.

— Dilthey, 1914–2005, Vol. 7, p. 225

All these hurdles were productive, as in the end, the dialogical fusion of horizons renders the familiar (our own codes and traditions) strange. Hermeneutics can offer us insight into other cultures that are unfamiliar historically or geographically, which is an important condition for reaching a critical distance from our cultural context, from what we take for granted, and what seems fixed and unchangeable. For "one's encounter with the otherness of the other is an encounter with oneself" (Marotta, 269). I can certainly say that my time in Shanghai has defamiliarized my habitual way of seeing things. To give one example, differences between the Chinese and Western educational systems asked for a flexible attitude. I have learnt to offer students more space and time for questions and reflection, and to build in repetitions in the classes. These are insights I took with me in my teaching in Tilburg.

Luckily, in overcoming all these challenges I was all but left to myself: first and foremost, I express my gratitude to the incomparable Zhong Bixuan and Angie, who were so helpful and accommodating. The same goes for the inspiring Steve Kulich and the rest of the staff at SISU, such as Alex English, Grace Leung, Zhang Hongling, Wang Xin, and visiting scholar Michael Steppat. I thank aforementioned mediator and translator Kate for all her interesting stories, and the other students, such as Doris, David, Zhao, and all the rest. And the students from Online Journalism who participated in an ethnography project and sat with me and my colleague in a coffee shop for hours, explaining Chinese history to us:

Scarlett, Vilen, and Emily. All of you have made my time in Shanghai unforgettable.

References

Dilthey, W. (1900). *Die Entstehung der Hermeneutik.* New York, NY: Cornell University.

De Mul, J. (2011). Horizons of hermeneutics: Intercultural hermeneutics in a globalizing world. *Frontiers of Philosophy in China, 6* (4), 628–655.

Marotta, V. (2009). Intercultural hermeneutics and the cross-cultural subject. *Journal of Intercultural Studies 30* (3), 267–284.

About the author:

Inge van de Ven, Dutch, is Assistant Professor of Online Culture at the Department of Culture Studies at Tilburg School of Humanities, the Netherlands. She holds a PhD in Comparative Literature from Utrecht University, where she also completed postdoctoral research on creativity in education (Education for Learning Societies). She was a lecturer at the Comparative Literature department at Utrecht University and in Film and Literary Studies at Leiden University. She held a visiting scholarship at Harvard University (2013). Her articles have appeared in journals such as *European Journal of English Studies*, *Between*, *Image & Narrative*, and *Journal for Creative Behavior*, and she is currently finishing a monograph titled *Big Books in Times of Big Data*.

Inge was a visiting scholar at Shanghai International Studies University in March and April 2017, when she co-taught a course at the Department of Intercultural Communications titled *Hermeneutics in the Information Age: From Close to Distant Reading*. This research stay was funded by the program "Outgoing Scholarship for Training" from the Erasmus Institute for Public Knowledge.

文化冲突还是视野融合？
——荷兰访问学者的诠释性挑战

Inge van de Ven（荷兰）

梁晓雪　译

唐钰昀　审校

题西林壁

苏轼

横看成岭侧成峰，远近高低各不同。

不识庐山真面目，只缘身在此山中。

2017年4月，我在上海外国语大学与同事合授一门课程“信息时代的诠释学：从精读到遥读”，一位叫梁文波的学生介绍了中国著名诗人苏轼的这首诗，引起了我的注意。这首诗贴切地反映出我作为一个访问学者在陌生文化中的体验。这首诗指出，一个人的视野是由他的视角所决定的。正如我自己就在山中，因而无法领会山的“真面目”那样，我也无法感知我自身文化的组成。在课上，我与学生一起用对话诠释学来理解上海迪士尼的跨文化现象，在我看来，这首诗就像镜子一样，反映了我们所使用的研究方法。从广义来看，它代表着我到上海时，伴随我而来的文化视角与偏见。

接下来，我会分享一些这些视角与偏见所导致的文化冲突（或者“诠释性挑战”，德·穆尔，2011），以及它们最终如何拓展了我的视野，反而使我对在蒂尔堡所熟悉的做事方式感到陌生。

诠释性挑战#1

以我的西方视角来看，我对中国大学的预期是不同层级的教职工及学生之间有着严格的等级关系。而当我一抵达中国，这个预期便被打破。迎接我们的是跨文化研究中心的一群人，有秘书，有毕业生，有老师，也有对外合作交流处的领导。在座的每个人都分享了他们的研究兴趣和背景经历，而每位分享者都获得了同事的真诚赞赏与鼓励。团队的每个人都对彼此的才能感到骄傲，这次会谈还体现了一种高度的民主氛围，我想这正反映了这个团队的氛围特色。

诠释性挑战#2

当问到学生是否理解你已解释的内容，他们会礼貌地点头，但这并不一定代表他们真的理解了——有时他们只是出于礼貌。

诠释性挑战#3

当你在“折磨护士”乐团[1]的噪音演出现场，看到一个人在键盘上疯狂击打，另一个人把吉他砸得粉碎时，不要以为演出场地会是一个人声鼎沸、烟雾缭绕的地下室，也不要以为身边的人会是酩酊大醉、不修边幅、散发着恶臭的“脏皮士”。实际上，演出场地Chair Club[2]光线充足、富有情调，观看演出的是一群干干净净的年轻人，他们坐在椅子上，礼貌地鼓掌，尽情地享受香槟与生蚝（！）。这是一个难忘的夜晚。

诠释性挑战#4

你无法预设西方文化对中国学生的影响程度。从这个角度讲，没有“典型的”中国学生。这门课原本的设定是上海迪士尼将两个世界或者两种视野（即中国文化与迪士尼人物及象征）连接在一起，但这样的设定完全失败了。一位学生说：“我从小就接触迪士尼文化，我在电视上看迪士尼动画片，在书中阅读迪士尼故事。”而另外一位学生则把迪士尼描绘成“来自遥远的美国，与我们的文化完全不同”。我们认识到试图对这些影响做出概括性的总结是徒劳的。只有普世的东西才能将我们最终联结在一起，比如我们对电影《泰坦尼克号》的普遍热爱。

---

1 “折磨护士”为上海一噪音乐团。

2 上海一酒吧。

诠释性挑战#5

当你收到邀请，去在中国举行的一场会议进行主旨演讲，不要以为你会是惟一的发言者，或者寥寥数位中的一个。其实，有可能一整天的时间都预留给了国际学者做主旨演讲。正如前文所述，中国人非常礼貌。因此，你要准备好被邀请和参会者合影留念。不要犹豫，拿出摇滚明星一样的气场去做吧。

诠释性挑战#6

人们可能会觉得，居住在上海这样一个充满活力的大都市，“无聊”一词将是过去式。其实不然。当年法租界的酒吧区里，醉醺醺的西方人拼命靠近我，把我当成酒吧新手来搭讪。由此可见，即使在上海，生活也可能寂寞而单调。

诠释性挑战#7

在我的家乡蒂尔堡，我是为数不多的能不靠智能手机过活的幸运儿。然而这在中国却是绝对行不通的：没有智能手机，一个人会无计可施；而手机没有安装微信，一个人则寸步难行。微信是中国版的脸书、推特、WhatsApp、Tinder以及无数个其他的应用，它代表了融媒体2.0时代。它能够让你在购物、吃饭、打车、旅游、买演出门票时统统实现移动支付。你需要一张中国的电话卡才能使用微信。如果没有微信，你就什么也做不了。尽管身处全球化时代，但在中国，如果没有微信，你将会体验到少有的与世隔绝的感觉。

从习以为常变得陌生

假若生活的表达全然陌生，那么诠释就绝无可能。

但如果没有任何陌生的东西，那么诠释就毫无必要了。

——狄尔泰，1914–2005，第7卷，第225页

所有的这些障碍都有好处，因为最终，对话的视野融合会将我们熟悉的东西（我们自己的文化编码与传统）变得陌生。诠释学能够提供一种视角，让我们观察其他历史或地理上不熟悉的文化，从而构成一个重要的环境，使得我们能够批判性地看待自身的文化

语境、我们认为理所应当的事物和那些看似固定无法变更的东西。“人们与他者相异性的相遇其实就是与自我的相遇。”（马洛塔，269）我可以很确定地说，在上海生活的这段日子使我看待事物的习惯性方式陌生化了。举个例子，面对中国与西方教育系统的差异，我需要有一个变通的态度。我学习到要给学生留下更多提问与反思的空间与时间，同时需要在课堂上不断重复。我将这些经验带回了蒂尔堡。

幸运的是，在克服这些挑战的过程中，我并非孤身奋战：首先，我想对衷苾璇和张安琪表示感谢，她们是如此随和、乐于助人。同样我要感谢鼓舞人心的顾力行教授以及上外的其他教师，例如Alex English、梁晓雪、张红玲、王欣以及访问学者Michael Steppat。感谢前文提到的诗歌译者梁文波，谢谢她有趣的故事。也感谢其他学生，如Doris、David、Zhao等。感谢来自国际新闻专业的同学参与到民族志的项目中，感谢他们花费数小时在咖啡厅为我和同事讲解中国的历史，他们是Scarlett、Vilen和Emily。你们所有人都让我在上海的时光变得难忘。

作者简介：

Inge van de Ven，荷兰籍，荷兰蒂尔堡大学人文学院文化研究系在线文化助理教授。她持有乌得勒支大学比较文学博士学位，之后在那里完成了关于教育创新（学习型社会教育）的博士后研究课题。她曾是乌得勒支大学比较文学系与莱顿大学电影与文学研究讲师。2013年，她在哈佛大学担任访问学者。她的文章曾被刊登在《英语学习欧洲学刊》《之间》《图像及叙事》《创新行为期刊》等期刊。目前她正在撰写专著《大数据时代的巨著》。

2017年3月至4月期间，Inge在上海外国语大学担任访问学者，合授跨文化交际方向研究生课程“信息时代的诠释学：从精读到遥读”。此次研究访学由伊拉斯姆斯公共知识研究院的“出国培训奖学金”项目资助。

Chinese Dining Etiquette

Ben Keegan (Ireland)

Proofread by George Fleming

Part of my job as an English teacher with Shanghai International Studies University is to teach culture. Part of this task involves pointing out the mistakes students should try to avoid when eating at the dinner table. I explain how to hold cutlery correctly, how to eat without offending anyone with the sight or sound of your masticated food and generally how to comport yourself in a restaurant. By the end of ninety minutes the students will be well equipped to handle themselves appropriately when eating in a formal situation.

My own education in Chinese dining etiquette has been much more haphazard, and has seen me commit every Chinese dining faux pas equivalent that I warn my students against. When I first arrived in China, planting my chopsticks firmly into the mound of rice in my rice bowl seemed an eminently sensible way to avoid leaving them lying on the sometimes grubby dining surface when I needed my hands free. Unfortunately, I now know this is a major faux pas as it evokes the imagery of leaving a sacrifice of burning incense at an ancestor's grave. Because chopsticks naturally look like a pointer, I also used to use them to make my verbal points or to indicate things around the table: both of which, I now know, are as rude as using a fork and knife to gesticulate. Chopsticks, being slender pieces of wood, are not obviously sharp and blunt ended, so I have also often used them the wrong way round, which I'm sure made me look as foolish to hawk-eyed locals as a Chinese person using a knife or fork in that fashion.

In the West it is good etiquette to always make sure your plate and bowl are flat on the dining table. So, for several years in China, I followed this rule and made sure not to lift my rice bowl nearer to my mouth. Unfortunately, I was also following the Western dining rule of sitting as straight-backed as possible, so the result was that a trail of rice was always left between my bowl and the edge of the table. This, I'm sure, is akin to leaving strands of spaghetti between yourself and your plate in Italy.

One instance in which I made a faux pas while trying my best to ingratiate myself, was a meal with my future in-laws. One rule I've always tried to follow is to eat at least a little of whatever is provided by your host. So when my mother-in-law served up river fish, I waved away my girlfriend's protests that this would be too difficult for me to eat due to the number of small bones it would contain. Biting confidently into a piece of the fish as my future wife's relatives all smiled at my bravery, I quickly managed to get a piece of bone lodged in my gum. In trying to free this with my tongue I only made matters worse, and when blood started trickling over my bottom lip my in-laws thought they had surely killed me — or at least caused me grievous injury. But after hurrying from the table to the bathroom and cleaning myself up, I returned to the table and tried another bit of fish to save their face and mine. My in-laws smiled again at this bravado, before turning back to their own conversation and politely turning a blind eye to the trail of rice I then started leaving between my rice bowl and myself, while gesticulating with my chopsticks at the food I appreciated and then planting my chopsticks in my rice bowl to show I was finished.

About the author:

Ben Keegan, Irish, English teacher and aspiring novelist. He has been working for SISU Overseas Training Centre since September 2010.

中国的餐桌礼仪

Ben Keegan（爱尔兰）

梁晓雪　译

我在上海外国语大学担任英语老师，西方文化是教学内容的一部分，这其中就包括指出学生在餐桌上吃饭时应该避免的错误。我教他们如何正确使用刀叉，如何在咀嚼食物时不发出声音并且保持端庄的吃相以避免冒犯他人，以及在餐厅吃饭的礼仪等。通过90分钟的课程，学生们能够掌握如何在正式场合得体用餐。

然而，我自己在中餐礼仪方面的知识就非常混乱，因此我屡屡犯下餐桌礼仪的种种大忌——恰恰是我告诉学生要避免的类似错误。我初到中国时，我常常在需要腾出手时把筷子直直地插在饭碗里，这样就避免将筷子放在油乎乎的餐桌上，似乎很合理。然而，我现在才知道这一做法是大忌，因为它会让人联想到把焚香插在祖先坟头的画面。另外，因为筷子很像教鞭，我说话时会时不时挥舞筷子来阐明我的观点，或用筷子来指点周围的事物——现在我知道，这两种行为就如同在西方的餐桌上挥舞刀叉一样粗鲁。由于筷子是用木头做的，没有哪一端特别尖锐，因此我之前常常拿反，我想这肯定让我在目光犀利的本地人眼中显得愚不可及，正如把刀叉拿反的中国人在西方人眼中的那种形象。

在西方，将盘子和碗平放在餐桌上就餐是一种礼貌的行为。因此在中国的头几年，我谨遵这一规则，在就餐时从不把饭碗举到嘴边。不幸的是，由于我同时也谨遵"吃饭时肩背挺直"这一条西方餐桌礼仪，所以我的碗和桌沿之间总会留下一串米粒。我确信，这就如同吃意大利面时将面条洒落在盘子外面一样。

有一次同准岳父母吃饭，我拼命想讨好他们，却犯了大忌。我遵循的一条准则是把主人准备的每样菜都吃一点。当我未来的丈母娘将一盘河鱼端上来的时候，我女朋友提醒说鱼刺太多，对我来说难度太大。对此我置之不理，自信满满地咬下一口鱼肉。未婚妻的家人们对我这一英勇行为纷纷投来赞许的目光，然而，很快就有一个鱼刺卡在了我的牙龈里。我用舌头拼命舔啊舔，试图把刺弄出来，但情况却越来越糟——血顺着我的下嘴角流了下来，我的准岳父母肯定以为他们"谋杀"了我，或至少使我受到了严重的伤害。在我匆忙离席到洗手间清理干净后，我又回到餐桌，为了挽回他们和我自己的颜面，我又夹了一块鱼。我未来的家人们再次对我的勇敢投以微笑，但很快他们就转开头继续聊天，假装看不到我在碗周围洒落米粒、挥舞着筷子点评菜肴以及将筷子插在碗里以示吃完等种种行为。

作者简介：

Ben Keegan，爱尔兰籍，英语教师，渴望成为小说家，自2010年9月起任教于上海外国语大学出国培训部。

"All's Well That Ends Well": My First Wedding That Never Was

Kizito Tekwa (Canada)

Proofread by George Fleming

My experience working in China began in late 2003 when I landed in Beijing as a young adventurous 29-year-old single man. My initial intention had been to vacation in China for a month and return home to the translation job I had with a Montreal-based translation firm. Little did I know that I would entirely immerse myself into Chinese society for the following five years without glancing back. My first gig was in Shanghai for a little over a year, before moving to Guangdong Province. I had found myself a school in Dongcheng District, Dongguan and quickly settled down in this less bustling, hotter and charming city.

During my stay in Guangdong, I made many friends from all parts of China and, of course, the world. I soon noticed that there was a huge community of Brazilians whose love for soccer no one dares to dispute. I joined one of their many soccer teams and we regularly had, first the soccer tournaments, then the beer and barbecues. I met people from Romania, Pakistan, Ireland, England, Scotland, Ghana, Australia and the U. S. But most of all, I made friends from China — all parts of China. I soon noticed that in China, everybody lived everywhere. As a teacher in a mostly adult training centre, I had the opportunity to see lots of people come and go. Gradually, I noticed that people from different geographical locations had different sorts of problems learning English, especially the pronunciation component. For example, it was quite difficult for my Guangdong students to pronounce a word with a "b" and "r" written together. If there was the letter "z" a little down the road, that really made matters worse. A word like "Brazil" was a pronunciation nightmare for some of them.

One day, after I finished my lessons, my boss called me into his office and told me he had had a phone call from a prospective student with special needs we would have to accommodate. When I heard "special needs" I thought he was referring to a physical, or perhaps a mental disability. But no, he was not. He was referring to a student who was too busy to be chauffeured to class so I had to be chauffeured to his office to give him lessons. And the student lived in Hengli, one of the thirty-two towns that make up the greater Dongguan area at that time. Hengli was about 45 minutes away from Dongguan city centre.

I had a rather shocking experience on my first day in Hengli. I had been informed that the boss himself was to come with his driver to pick me up. However, when the SUV showed up, I noticed that the driver was alone.

The taciturn young man in his late twenties with a rough beard informed me that the boss was busy and could not make it. However, he assured me that by the time we got back, he would be ready and waiting. When we got to Hengli, he took me to a hotel lobby where his boss was waiting. Generally, when a nearly 30-year-old man is hired to drive a man he calls his boss, most people would expect the boss to be older, occasionally chubbier and with a professional demeanour about him. That was almost the exact antithesis of the person I was introduced to and who was waiting for me. He was younger, thinner, shorter and there was something of a "playboy" about him. He came up to me and we greeted each other. His English was not good but he managed to pull off a carefully rehearsed greeting. When the conversation got deeper, he gave up the effort to carry on in English. However, as I could communicate pretty well in Chinese, I thought using the language he was comfortable with would make for a good opportunity to better understand his needs and figure out the best way to help him. He invited me to have dinner before the class and the pleading that it was always business before pleasure for me fell on deaf ears.

I asked for steak and turned down all other invitations for snacks, drinks, etc. After dinner, he asked me to come with him. I thought we were heading to the classroom. No. He invited me to get into the car and his driver took us through the downtown into the suburbs, then even more suburbs and then into a huge open area. It was the site of a quarry. It was calm because there was no work going on but there was evidence of the amount of action that went on there during working hours. He pointed at it and said, "You see, this is all mine." I stared at him for a while, then asked, "How old are you?" He told me he was 25. He had, indeed, just turned 25.

I was completely lost. I was wondering how on earth a 25-year-old kid could possess what looked like a life-time of property. When did he start working? How could he have acquired this? Did he inherit it from a family member? Was it a gift from his father? I was not too sure of what to say next but I understood the need not to ask further questions. I did not want to display my bewilderment. At the same time, I did not want to ask too many questions for fear of embarrassing him or myself. But in my mind, there were of course tons of questions that needed answers. From the machines and other structures at the quarry, one could tell that it had been functional for a long time. So, when did Gary set all these up? When he was 20? When he was 18? When he was 15? I was genuinely curious to find out the enigma behind this story.

It was not until about a month later that the mystery was unravelled. I had come to teach him as usual and after the lesson, I stood in the yard chit-chatting with him and his fiancée who had also joined the class. She was his high-school classmate and, as a couple, they got along pretty well during the lesson, often helping each other finish off sentences, spell out difficult words but also share jokes about yesteryear. As we stood talking, a man walked up to us. He was probably in his late fifties. He was not particularly tall but he looked healthy and quite down-to-earth. He casually greeted me in Chinese and began talking with my student. At the end of their conversation, Gary turned to me and said, "This is my dad," with a smile. "Huh? You got a dad?" I asked with my eyes wide open.

It was as if a heavy burden had suddenly been lifted off my shoulders. Here, finally, was the answer to the mystery — so simple, so bare, so logical. To me, at least, it was simply unfathomable how a son could, while his father was still alive, claim ownership of his property. Apparently, the quarry, the hotels and everything I had been made to believe belonged to the son, actually belonged to his father. My understanding was that you don't inherit your parents' estate until they bequeath it to you in their will. But here was a man that was alive and well, and by all indications, would be alive for the foreseeable future, having his estate already wrestled away from him by his young son. That was simply unthinkable. It was simply shocking. The kid had not even mentioned, when he introduced the estate to me, that he had a father. Did he consider his father an afterthought? What gave him such an abundance of confidence? Why could his sister, for he had one, be so completely side-lined? Could it be he had seen his father's will? Or maybe his father had showed him? Or maybe his uncle or mother had told him everything in the will? Something was certainly wrong somewhere, so I thought. I did finally learn, to my utter amazement, that in China, it was customary for the male offspring to continue the family lineage including taking over and controlling the family estate, sometimes even before the parents actually passed away. For daughters, being married off to another family technically ended their lineage as they moved on to help other families procreate.

The second very weird activity that happened while I was teaching Gary was his wedding. He had told me that he was engaged shortly after we initially met; then, during the course of teaching him, things progressed really rapidly. He told me one day in class that his wedding was coming up in about a month. I, of course, congratulated him and his fiancée and asked how the lessons would be impacted by the wedding. He informed me that he was taking the week prior to and the wedding week itself, off. Then he said he wanted me to come to the wedding. Of course, I was happy to go because I had wanted to observe how weddings were organized and celebrated in China. I had not been to any wedding before and that only helped to intensify my curiosity. He told me the date and I was a little taken aback. It was a Wednesday. I was thinking, "who the hell celebrates a wedding midweek?" Besides, I worked six days a week and Wednesday was a perfectly good example of an odd day to party. Gary had not explained to me the line-up of activities on that day so when I showed up, I had no idea what he had in store for me.

As he had instructed, I arrived in Hengli around twilight hoping to see a crowd of people waiting for the official ceremony to commence. What I instead saw was a group of people, around 25 in total, idling around and looking so unprepared for anything. They were not dressed for a celebration; everything looked casual — it felt like it was business as usual. That was the first surprise. I did notice, however, a line of cars parked conspicuously along the road — and they were all expensive cars. I could not immediately find Gary. He was still inside his newly bought and decorated house making final preparations for the evening. When I finally saw him, I wanted to know immediately why there were not many people and especially where the bride-to-be was. He told me she was at her parents' house and we were about to go over. I had thought the wedding was certainly going to be in her fiancé's hometown, not Hengli. After waiting for another hour or so, we set out in a convoy. It was about 50 kilometres away and since we were in a long convoy, it took well over an hour to get there. I had insisted on driving my own car since I had no idea how long the ceremony was to last. I was also working the following day and wanted to be in total control of my time and actions.

When the convoy finally pulled over and people started virtually hopping out of their cars, I was certain we had arrived at our destination. But what was conspicuous was the utter darkness that shrouded us. I asked one of the invitees where we were and he said we had arrived. I thought he was insane.

"Where is the compound?" I asked.

“Right there,” he replied, pointing to the silhouette of a single home.

“Yeah, but there’s nobody there. It’s an empty house,” I retorted. The whole thing was now seeming like a joke to me. How could we drive for over an hour to an uninhabited dark house? What was going on? As we did not seem to understand each other, the young man moved away. I was left on my own to watch and guess what was happening in the darkness. For the first time, I noticed that almost everyone in the convoy was either a boy or a man. And then I really began to think there was something seriously amiss. How could anyone describe what was going on as a wedding? Then I noticed that the men were talking to each other in low tones much in the same way dark nimbus clouds consult each other prior to an Amazon-style torrential downpour. After about a quarter of an hour of meetings and apparent deadlocks and meetings again and again, what happened came as an utter shock to me.

A group of men, about eight of them in total, charged towards the door in an attempt to tear it open. As the effort yielded no fruit, they walked back and orchestrated another calculated charge. The second surge was as fruitless as the first. By this time, I was more than convinced there must be something criminal going on. First, there was the cover of darkness and now, what appeared to be a burglary in full swing. I tried to find out the meaning of what was happening but nobody paid attention to me. They all seemed glued to the action of the select group of men. They were watching in earnest for when the hinges of the door would finally give up their stubbornness and send the door crashing inwards. Well, it took a while. After battling for about half an hour, the men were covered in sweat and they retreated. Another group immediately took over the charge. With fresh energy, the door didn’t hold out for too long before it crumbled inward with a deafening bang. The convoy of men swarmed in trampling on each other and on everything in their path. I was curious to see what they were looking for so I hurried in after them. Once in, they turned on the light and, yes, there were people in the house. Lots of people, actually. The bride-to-be was seated on a centrally decorated seat surrounded by several other women. They all seemed richly clad in what looked to me like traditional regalia. There were many other women in the living area of the house. They had kept an utter silence while the vandals wreaked havoc on the door. I thought there would finally be peace after Gary had, at long last, found his woman. Unfortunately, peace wasn't going to come that soon. Actually, this was only the beginning of more chaos.

After the aggressors broke in, they spent no time on civilities. Even Gary had no time for his wife. The visitors instinctively knew their next task. For me, I was waiting for kisses and laughter and jollity; well, in vain. Before I could familiarize myself with the surroundings and the bodies in the room, the group of men had started to ransack every visible object in the house. They pulled drawers, turned armchairs and sofas upside down. Some went straight into the kitchen and began opening every container they laid eyes on and thrashing the contents while others dashed into the bedrooms, turned over mattresses, tore through the wardrobes and pulled down clothes, sheets, boxes and everything. There was chaos everywhere.

"What the hell is going on," I inquired. "What is missing? What are they looking for? Why are they doing this?" I asked.

"The shoe," a woman responded.

"The shoe? Whose shoe?" I went on.

"The girl's, his wife's," came the answer.

"What happened to the shoe? Why did she hide it?" I continued then quickly realized there wouldn't be a question-and-answer session. When

I looked, I noticed that the bride-to-be only had one shoe on. I figured out that until the other shoe was unearthed, she was going nowhere. Actually, nobody was going anywhere. Well, first I wanted to get out of there as soon as possible and secondly, I was hoping the craze would stop once the shoe was found. So, I joined in the search making sure not to vandalize property. I hadn't searched for long when someone shouted, "I got it, I've found it!" The voice was coming from the attic. "Vicious people," I thought. How did they come about with the idea to hide the shoe up in the attic?

The journey back to Gary's home did not begin till after another forty-five minutes. As I walked out, I noticed that a bricklayer was putting the door back in place. "Fair enough," I thought. Nobody wants to sleep with the door open. By this time, it was about midnight and the journey back to Hengli was just about to begin. I was very tired. I had worked all day and needed to work for most of the following day. Also, I had no idea what time the convoy (now even longer) would make it to Hengli that night. When I finally had the chance to speak to Gary, I asked how long it would take to get back home. I was shocked at what I heard. They would spend the rest of the night travelling back home. In other words, they were not to get to Hengli till dawn. That was impossible to fathom. That was a journey of fifty kilometres to be covered in six hours, by car not on foot.

Well, as it turned out, it was worse than trekking. We had driven less than ten minutes when the convoy, now with more than double the number of cars, stopped. Gary and his fiancée came out, together with lots of other people, for the first "station of the cross." As had been planned, the next one kilometre was to be done on foot with Gary partially carrying his fiancée on his back. The convoy was moving at a snail's pace and that had led to an unprecedented traffic jam. The honking of cars and noise from people increased the insanity. After they finally got back into the cars, there was another 10-minute drive and out they came again for the next lap. This time, Gary was asked to walk on his knees, carry his girl on his back and walk another distance with blindfolds. Despite what appeared to me as human abuse, everybody seemed to be enjoying the event and, actually, having lots of fun. Gary bore the suffering with all the jollity anyone could only imagine. He was constantly laughing as he responded to the multiple jokes from his many friends. His fiancée loved the attention she was receiving and reveled in subjecting her willing "victim" to her whims and caprices. Apparently, the events of the day had appalled only me.

When we got to the first major road junction, I branched off onto the highway. There had been greetings when I arrived but there was to be no leave-taking. I had had enough and in the unending confusion that had been the masterpiece of the evening, I had forgotten to hand the wedding gift — a coffee machine — I had bought for Gary. The only consolation was that the actual wedding had to take place the following Saturday and I could have the opportunity to present my gift to the bridegroom. That Wednesday night, however, I had taken part in a wedding that was everything a wedding should not be. But as far as the invitees had enjoyed the destruction, the vandalizing of property, the sixes and sevens, and now the laborious procession back to Hengli, I thought, all's well that ends well. And that was my first real encounter with Chinese culture.

About the author:

Kizito Tekwa holds a PhD in Translation Studies from the University of Ottawa, Canada. He has worked at various institutions of learning in Canada and China as a translator or teacher of English as a foreign language. He has been teaching at the School of English Studies and the

Graduate Institute of Interpretation and Translation, Shanghai International Studies University since September 2016.

皆大欢喜——我参加的第一个中国婚礼

Kizito Tekwa（加拿大）
梁晓雪　译
唐钰昀　审校

我在中国的工作经历始于2003年末，那时我还是一个29岁的单身汉，初到北京，充满冒险精神。我最初的想法是在中国休假一个月，之后就回到位于蒙特利尔的翻译公司继续我的翻译工作。当时的我并不知晓在接下来的五年里我会义无反顾地留在中国。我的第一份工作是在上海，干了一年多，然后我就搬到了广东省。我在东莞市东城区一所学校找到一份教职，随后便迅速在这座不那么繁华，但同样炎热而充满魅力的城市安定下来。

我在广东结识了很多朋友，他们来自五湖四海、世界各地。不久我便发现了一个庞大的巴西人社团，他们对于足球的热爱无人能敌。我加入了他们众多足球队中的一支，定期参加足球联赛，然后一起喝啤酒，吃烧烤。我遇到不同国家和地区的人，他们来自罗马尼亚、巴基斯坦、爱尔兰、英格兰、苏格兰、加纳、澳大利亚、美国，但更多的还是中国人，他们来自中国的四面八方。我很快发现在中国，每个人都来自不同的地方。作为成人培训中心的一名老师，我发现周围的面孔在不断变化。我逐渐意识到来自中国不同地区的人在学英语时会有不同的问题，尤其是在发音方面。比如说，广东学生很难发出“br”这个音，如果单词里又带字母“z”，情况会更糟糕。像“Brazil”这样的单词发音简直就是一些人的噩梦。

一天课后，老板把我叫到办公室，告诉我他接到一个潜在学生客户的电话，这个学生有一些特殊的需求，要我们照顾一下。乍听到“特殊需求”，我还以为这位学生有身体或者心理方面的缺陷。然而并非如此。事实是这位学生实在太忙，无法亲自来教室上课，因此我会被接到他的办公室给他上课。这位学生所在的横沥是当时东莞市下辖的32个镇街之一，离东莞市中心大概45分钟车程。

在横沥的第一天我就经历了一件奇事。我事先得到的消息是这位老板本人会同他的司机一起来接我。然而当接我的车到了之后，我看到车里只有司机一人。这位快30岁的年轻人留着粗糙的胡须，沉默寡言，他说他的老板很忙，没能一起来，但他保证等我们抵达时，老板会在那里等着我们。到了横沥，司机带我来到一个酒店的大堂，老板正在那里。一般来说，一个将近30岁的司机所称的老板应该比他更年长，也许体型稍胖，举止专业。但恰恰相反，这位老板比他的司机更年轻、更瘦、更矮，而且给人一种“花花公子”的感觉。他走了过来，我们彼此打了招呼。他英语并不好，但还是说出了明显事先准备好的一句问候。随着我们的交谈逐步深入，他索性不用英语说了。不过我中文很好，就用中文和他说话，因为使用他所擅长的语言能更好地理解他的需求，进而找到最好的教学方法。他邀请我在上课之前共进晚餐，对我“先办正事再娱乐”的请求充耳不闻。

我点了一份牛排，谢绝了甜点和酒水。吃好晚饭，他让我跟着他，我以为要去教室了，但并非如此。他邀我上车，司机带我们开过城区驶向郊区，又到了更偏远的郊区，最终抵达一大片开阔的场地。这是一个采石厂。由于当时没有工人作业，现场十分安静，但是仍旧能看出平日相当大的工程量。他指着采石厂说：“你看，这些都是我的。”我盯着他看了一会儿，问：“你多大了？”他告诉我他25岁。他确实刚满25岁。

我完全懵掉了，思索着：一个25岁的小伙子究竟是如何拥有别人一辈子才能赚得的资产的？他何时开始工作？如何得到这些的呢？是从家族继承的吗？是他父亲的馈赠？我不确定接下来该说什么，但我明白自己不应刨根问底。我不想表现出自己的困惑，同时也不想追问过多，让彼此尴尬。然而，我的心里确实有千万个未解之谜。从采石厂的机器及其他构造来看，这里已经运行了相当久了。那么，加里（该学生的英文名）是从什么时候开始创立这些的呢？20岁？18岁？15岁？我真的很好奇，想解开这背后的谜团。

约莫一个月后，这个秘密才得以解开。那天，我像往常一样去给他上课，下课后，我站在院子里跟他和他的未婚妻闲聊，她也一起跟着上课。他们是高中同学，作为一对恋人，他们在课堂上十分默契，经常帮助对方完成句子、拼出难词，同时也经常调侃过往的趣事。我们正站着聊天，一位快60岁的男人向我们走来。他不是特别高，但看上去健康而务实。他随口用中文和我打了招呼，然后开始跟我的学生讲话。聊到最后，加里转向我，笑着介绍道："这是我父亲。""啊？你有父亲？"我吃惊地睁大了眼。

突然间我如释重负。谜团终于被解开了——如此简单直白，合乎常理。至少对于我而言，我无法理解一个儿子怎么可以在他父亲尚在人世的时候拥有财产的所有权。不过显然，这个采石厂、酒店以及所有我误认为属于加里的财产都是他父亲的。我之前的理解是，只有父母在遗嘱中把财产赠与子女，他们才能够继承财产。然而这个父亲尚且健康在世，并且明显还有很长的人生之路，但他的财产竟然已经被儿子据为己有，这简直令人费解和惊讶。这个儿子在给我介绍这些财产时甚至都没有提到他有父亲。他已经将自己的父亲抛诸脑后了吗？他为什么如此自信？为什么他的妹妹（他有一个妹妹）完全靠边站了呢？有没有可能是他已经看过他父亲的遗嘱了呢？又或许他父亲已经给他看过自己的遗嘱了？要么就是他的叔叔或者母亲告诉了他遗嘱的一切内容？所以我觉得肯定有哪里不对劲。最终，我极度惊讶地发现，中国的传统习俗便是男孩理所当然地继承家族血脉，包括接管与掌控家庭财产，有时，这一切甚至在父母去世之前就开始了。对于女儿而言，嫁到另一个家庭基本上就终结了原生家族的血脉，因为她们要为另一个家庭繁衍后代。

第二件奇事发生在加里的婚礼上。我们认识后没多久，他便告诉我他已经订婚了。在教他的过程中，他的婚事进展迅速。有一天在课上，他告诉我一个月后他就要举行婚礼。我自然向他和他的未婚妻表达了祝贺，并询问课程将如何调整。他告诉我婚礼那一周及前一周的课程都将取消。然后他邀请我出席婚礼。我当然很乐意参加，因为我一直很想看看中国人是怎样举办婚礼的。在这之前，我从未参加过任何中式婚礼，这也让我变得越发好奇。他告诉我婚礼是在周三，我有些吃惊，心想："谁会没事儿在一周的中间那天举办婚礼呀？"况且我一周要工作六天，周三去参加聚会实在奇怪。加里没有跟我解释婚礼当天的安排，因此当我到达时，我对将要发生的事情一无所知。

按照他的要求，我在黄昏时到达了横沥。我本期待看到一群人聚集在那里等待着仪式正式开始，然而我只看到大概25人毫无目的地四处游荡。他们并没有特意为婚礼着装，一切看上去都很随意，让人觉得这与平时并无差别——这是令我感到惊奇的第一件事。不过我确实注意到，路边停靠着一排很显眼的车——都是豪车。我没看到加里，他还在刚装修好的新房里做最后的准备。当我终于看到他时，我想立马搞清楚为什么这里看不到什么人，尤其是看不到新娘。他告诉我，新娘在她的父母家，我们也即将过去。我猜想，婚礼一定将在她未婚夫的家乡举办，而不是横沥。大概又等了一个多小时，我们随着车队出发了。路程大概50公里，而由于我们有一个很长的车队，大概花了一个小时才到。我坚持开自己的车，因为我不知道婚礼会持续多久，而我第二天还要工作，所以我必须完全掌控自己的时间与行动。

车队终于停下来了，人们陆续从车上下来，我确信我们已经到达了目的地。可举目所及都是漆黑一片。我问其中一个客人我们在哪儿，他告诉我我们已经到了。我觉得他疯了。

“结婚场地在哪里？”我问道。

“就在那里。”他指着一幢院子的黑色轮廓答道。

“好吧，但是那里一个人都没有，那是间空房子。”我反驳道。这整件事情在我看来就像是个玩笑。我们开了一个小时的车，就只到了这幢无人居住的空房子？到底发生了什么？因为我俩无法很好地交流，那个年轻人便走开了，留下我一个人待在那里，独自猜想黑暗之中正发生着什么。就在那时，我才发现车队里所有人都是男性。我真的开始觉得不对劲。有人能解释一下到底发生了什么吗？随后，我发现男人们都在窃窃私语，就如同亚马逊雨林猛烈的暴雨来临之前，天上乌云滚滚，连成一片。大家大概反复讨论、协商了一刻钟，接下来发生的事才真正震惊了我。

一群男人，大概八个，冲向了那座房子，试图撞开大门。尝试无果后，他们往回退一点，重新策划下一次进攻，而第二次同样失败了。到此时，我几乎确信这些人在犯罪。在夜色的掩护下，一起入室抢劫似乎已全面展开。我试图搞清楚到底是怎么回事，但是没人理我。他们都紧紧盯着那群男人，热切地盼望门的铰链断掉，门被撞开。当然，这花了好些时间。战斗了大约半个小时后，这群男人大汗淋漓地回来了，另一群人立马接替了他们。新的战斗力加入后，大门没过多久就支撑不住了，伴随着一声震耳欲聋的响声，门终于被撞开了。人们争先恐后，蜂拥而入。我很好奇他们在找什么，所以也跟了进去。一进去，人们便把灯打开了，是的，确实有人在房子里，而且有挺多人。新娘坐在中间一把装饰过的椅子上，被几个女人围绕着。她们都衣着华丽，在我看来就像是宫廷盛装。房子的客厅里还有很多别的女性，在那些破坏者撞毁大门的时候，她们都保持着绝对的沉默。我想，既然加里已经找到了他的妻子，事情应该要告一段落了吧！不幸的是，事实并非我所想的那样，实际上，这只是更多混乱场面的前奏。

进入房间之后，这群入侵者并没有花时间客套，甚至连加里都没有时间跟他妻子说话。他们本能地知道自己的下一个任务是什么。我以为会有亲吻和欢笑，然而并非如此。我还没来得及熟悉周围的环境和人，那群男人已经开始搜查房子里每一个可见之物。他们拉开抽屉，把椅子和沙发颠倒过来。有些人直接走到厨房掀开所有锅碗瓢盆查看，还有些人干脆冲进卧室，把床垫翻了个底朝天，并在卧室里翻箱倒柜——到处都是一片狼藉。

“到底怎么回事？”我询问道，“有什么东西丢了吗？他们在找什么？为什么要这样做？”

“鞋子。”一个女人回答我。

“鞋子？谁的鞋子？”我继续问。

“那个女孩，他妻子。”这便是答案。

“鞋子怎么了？为什么她要藏起来？”我接着问，但是这时已经没人顾得上我了。我观察之后，发现新娘只穿了一只鞋。我猜想，在找到另一只鞋之前，新娘不能去任何地方。事实上，所有人都不能走。一方面，我想尽早离开这里；另一方面，我又希望鞋子找到之后这一切混乱就能平息。于是我也加入搜寻的行列，并确保没有损坏财物。我没有搜查多久，便听到有人叫道“找到了，找到了！”声音是从阁楼传来的。“狡猾的人啊！”我心想。他们到底是怎么想到要把鞋子藏到阁楼上的？

45分钟后，我们终于可以返回加里的家了。走出来时，我发现工匠已经把门装回原处了。“很好，”我心想。没有人能够开着门睡觉。此时已经是午夜，而返回横沥的行程才刚要开始。我很累。我已经工作了一天，而且第二天还要上班。我不知道返回到横沥还要花多久时间，毕竟车队更长了。当我终于有机会和加里说话的时候，我问他返程需要多久。他的回答让我震惊：要花整个晚上。也就是说，天亮才能抵达横沥。我完全无法理解：50公里的路程，居然要开六小时，又不是步行！

事实证明，开车比步行更糟糕。现在的车子数量已经是来时的两倍，我们才开了不到十分钟，便停了下来。加里和他的未婚妻走出来，跟随着很多人，开始经历第一“关”。按照事先计划，接下来的一公里，加里需要背着他的未婚妻走。车队以蜗牛般的速度前行，造成了前所未有的交通拥堵。车喇叭声和人群的吵闹声更增加了疯狂的程度。当他们终于回到车上后，又开了大概十分钟车，他们又走出来接受下一个任务。这一次，加里需要背着他的新娘，蒙着眼睛，跪着行进一段距离。在我看来这纯属虐待。可其他人看上去都很享受，并且乐在其中。就连加里的喜悦也是溢于言表。他回应着朋友们各式各样的打趣，不停地开怀大笑。他的未婚妻也很喜欢获得关注的感觉，沉迷于随心所欲地折磨她心甘情愿的“受害者”。显然，在这所有的活动中，大家都很尽兴，除了我。

当我们到达第一个主道口时，我拐到了高速公路上。虽然我到达时受到了问候，但我决定不告而别。这一切已让我筋疲力尽。在整晚的混乱中，我竟然忘记了给加里送新婚礼物——一台咖啡机。还好真正的婚礼下周六才举行，届时我还有机会把礼物送给新郎。然而在这个周三的夜晚，我所经历的一切都超出了我对一场婚礼的认知。但是，只要所有人都享受了这一切大肆的破坏、财物的损毁、乱七八糟的状况和返回横沥的艰巨旅程，我觉得结局就算皆大欢喜。这就是我第一次真正领略中国文化的经历。

作者简介：

Kizito Tekwa，加拿大籍，渥太华大学翻译学博士。他曾在加拿大和中国的多家教育机构担任英语翻译或教师，自2016年9月起在上海外国语大学英语学院和高级翻译学院任教。

Successful Tales in an Intercultural Marriage

Alex English (U.S.A)

Proofread by George Fleming

Often times I am asked, "Do you speak English or Chinese with your Chinese wife?" I really don't know how to answer, because we have developed our own language *Chinglish* but with a twist. My spouse and I have been together for almost four years and we met at Toastmasters International, an organization dedicated to helping people communicate effectively. While we would both be considered highly effective communicators, it is sometimes the case that conflicts may arise. Some friends say they may because of cultural differences, others often tell us, "If you don't fight, then you are not really married." And yes, we may argue but as successful communicators we've developed several tips that we'd like to share.

Early in our relationship, my spouse and I would quarrel over miniscule issues ranging from: when we should go out for dinner, what transport we should take, how to dress or even when we should wash our clothes. There's one argument that signaled a major turning point in our relationship, that while gruesome and challenging, was also an important and positive experience as it helped us grow.

It happened in Northeastern China, during the Chinese New Year vacation in 2015. We had been out for the day skiing and both of us had skipped lunch; we were completely exhausted. Our dinner arrangement had been set for 7 pm but I had wanted to quickly wash my shirt. Immediately my spouse started yelling at me that we wouldn't have time. I knew I had enough time because I only needed 10 minutes to wash my shirt. I had always been pretty quick at washing clothes. My spouse continued to yell at me and I decided to forget it. I knew I'd wash my clothes another time.

On our walk over to her family's house, we started discussing the issue in the middle of the street. I almost felt like one of those Chinese couples who would yell at each other in public. I was hungry and tired and just wasn't in the mood to discuss the topic. Suddenly we stumbled upon a shop that was selling *roujiamo* (Chinese hamburger). I stopped in and bought two, one for her and one for me. We hadn't eaten all day! After eating the burger, our mood suddenly changed. It was finally the perfect scenario to discuss our major complication today. I told her directly how I felt. I wanted some space and just wanted to wash my shirt so I could have it dry by the morning. From her perspective, she was thinking I had planned to wash multiple clothes and knew it would take more than ten minutes. We had an exhausting day that meant our moods were irritable. We had not eaten all day, but after eating the snack, we both had become more receptive, more understanding and more compassionate. We agreed that from that day on, we would resolve our conflicts in three major ways: 1) eat before arguing or discussing major topics; 2) ensure both of us are properly rested; 3) communicate clearly and directly so both of us are clear on each other's meaning.

In my opinion, an intercultural marriage requires a lot of tender loving care and a lot of efforts on effective communication and trying to understand your partner's perspective. Our communication style has changed a lot since this major fight. It was an important turning point for us and helped us to become more aware of the other person. Since that day, we've grown closer and now have an acute ability to recognize the other person's feelings, thoughts and even their emotional well-being. While we are still in the "honeymoon phase" of our new life together, it is without a doubt the most exciting time in our life. There may be ups and downs, but that's like in any relationship. It's all about meeting in the middle and making sure we have eaten before addressing problems.

About the author:

Dr. Alex English, American, obtained his Ph.D. in Cultural Psychology from Zhejiang University in 2016. He has lived in China for ten years and previously lived and worked in Shenzhen and Hangzhou. He has been a research fellow at the SISU Intercultural Institute since September 2016.

跨文化婚姻的成功秘诀

Alex English（美国）

梁晓雪　译

经常有人问我："你和你太太之间说英语还是中文？"我真的不知道如何回答，因为我们历经曲折，已经发明了我们自己的中式英语。我和太太在一起快四年了。最初，我们相识于Toastmasters国际演讲俱乐部，这是一个致力于帮助人们有效沟通的组织。尽管我们两人都算高效沟通人士，但仍时不时会产生冲突。有些朋友说可能是因为文化差异，另一些则告诉我们："如果不吵架，那就不算真的结婚了。"是的，我们可能会吵架，但是作为成功的沟通者，我们在此愿意分享一些建议。

在我们的关系初期，我俩经常会为一些鸡毛蒜皮的小事争吵，诸如何时吃晚饭、坐什么交通工具、穿什么衣服，甚至何时洗衣服等。其中有一次争吵成为我们关系的转折点，尽管此事很不愉快且充满挑战，但它是一次重要且积极的经历，帮助我们成长。

那是2015年的春节，我们在中国东北过年。我们出去滑雪，一整天下来，两个人都没有吃饭，筋疲力尽。晚饭安排在傍晚七点，但我想赶快洗掉我的衬衫。顿时，我的太太开始朝我大喊大叫，说已经没时间了。我知道我来得及，因为我只要10分钟就可以洗好衬衫——在洗衣服这件事上，我向来动作很快。但她不依不饶，继续冲我发火，于是我只好算了，打算之后再洗。

在去我太太家的路上，我们又开始在大街上讨论此事。我觉得我们和那些在公众场合大吵大闹的中国夫妻没什么两样。我又累又饿，完全没有心情继续争执下去。这时，我们无意间走到了一家卖肉夹馍（即中国式汉堡）的店，我进去给我们两人各买了一个。

我们已经一整天都没有吃东西了！填饱肚子后，我们的心情突然变好了，正好可以讨论刚才发生的重大分歧。我坦白说出了自己的感受，说我需要一些空间，并且我只是想洗好衬衫，这样它明早就可以晾干。而从她的角度来看，她以为我打算洗很多件衣服，并且会远远超过10分钟时间。这一整天我们都很疲惫，加上饿着肚子，坏情绪很容易一触即发。但是吃完东西后，我们两个都变得更愿意倾听，更理解对方，也更有同理心。于是我们决定，从那天起，我们将用三种方式解决彼此之间的冲突：1）在争论或者讨论重大问题之前，先吃饱喝足；2）保证两个人事先有充分的休息；3）表达清楚，直截了当，确保彼此完全了解对方的意思。

在我看来，跨文化婚姻需要很多细微的关爱，双方需要付出很多努力，以实现有效沟通及互相理解。自从这次争吵后，我们的沟通方式有了极大的转变。这对于我们来说是一个重要的转折点，让我们更加关注对方。那天之后，我们之间变得更为亲密，并且能够敏锐地察觉对方的感受、想法以及情感需求。目前，我们仍然处于婚姻生活的"蜜月期"，这毫无疑问是我们人生中最美好的时光。生活中难免有跌宕起伏，但所有的关系都是如此，重点是双方学会各让一步，海阔天空，拥有良好的心理状态，而且在处理问题前，先填饱肚子。

作者简介：

Alex English，美国籍，2016年获得浙江大学文化心理学博士学位。他在中国已居住十年之久，曾经在深圳、杭州工作和生活。他从2016年9月开始在上海外国语大学跨文化研究中心担任研究员。

China in My Eyes: My Chinese Cultural Story

Roop Rani Luthra (India)

Proofread by George Fleming

My cross-cultural journey of China started developing in my brain when I got my teaching assignment. I got so much input about China and Shanghai. Frankly speaking, I had known about this country, Chinese food, Chinese martial arts and had a fair idea about the recognition of

Chinese language.

Everything was new for me as I had got married just before the new assignment. I took it as a challenge to adjust with my new life partner as well as teaching the Indian language to Chinese students in China, whose language and culture are unfamiliar to me. My colleague hosted a dinner in our honor but I could not eat much as I was used to homemade vegetarian food. He gave me guidelines and showed me the nearby shops and supermarkets. This is how my cross-cultural story started.

The first thing I noticed was that people here walk and drive on the right side which is opposite to my country. We walk and drive on the left, and our vehicles have steering on the right side. But in China the driving sense is wonderful and the Chinese drivers respect the pedestrians. They also obey the traffic laws, generally. I admire and salute them. The first word I learnt was "*ni hao*" like any other foreigner. I find that the handshake is the most common form of greeting with the foreigners, whereas in our culture females especially prefer to greet with "Namaste" rather than shaking hands. Though I am still not familiar with the language, I readily take the help of the call centre 962288, which is a boon for cross-cultural people like me. Though I find that half of the new Chinese generation have some command of English and are helpful, product labels are mostly in Chinese language, making it difficult to do any shopping.

Like any other foreigner, the first thing which fascinated me, and still does, is the typical Chinese face, especially men's haircut. I find their haircuts in funny styles, especially the young crowd. Chinese teenagers' dress sense is also unique and they look like fashion models. They don't wear as much jewelry as Indians. Indian women look beautiful in saris and jewelry. Indian marriages are very expensive and lavish. Teenagers wear kurta jeans or kurta (long shirt) payjami (tight leggings). Both

Indian and Chinese teenagers are simple, smart, healthy, fit and above all cheerful and bursting with laughter. Chinese kids and teens are really cute and wear nice, sometimes silken dresses. Females are more dominating than males in many spheres and China has more working females as compared to India, which is a plus point for a stable society and a nation.

I have been a keen observer of Chinese eating habits and cuisine, which are totally different from Indian foods. We cannot even imagine eating all kinds of animals, birds and reptiles. The Chinese prefer to entertain in public places rather than in their homes especially when entertaining foreigners, whereas the Indians prefer to entertain in public places as well as their homes. Giving a bouquet of flowers is considered friendly in India which I don't think is the case in China where many associate it with funerals. Gifts are exchanged in both cultures at the new year, weddings, births and birthdays. Giving a fruit basket or a box of sweets as a gift is preferred in India when you visit friends and families. It is considered a great honor in both our cultures if you are invited to somebody's home. It is considered polite to explain if there is conflict in your schedule in both cultures. Arriving on time and eating well is considered good to demonstrate that you are enjoying the food in both cultures. Removal of shoes is not necessary before entering houses in Indian culture, except in some houses. The guest of honor is asked to sit on the right-hand side of the host and not facing the door, as in China. The guest is asked to begin eating first in India, unlike China where the host offers the first toast. It is not necessary to try everything in Indian homes as compared to Chinese hospitality. Chopsticks and bowls are used in China for eating whereas Indians use spoons and plates along with small bowls. It is necessary to finish all food on your plate in Indian dining etiquette whereas it is not necessary in China. Making slurping or belching sounds is considered bad manners whereas in China it indicates that someone is enjoying their food. Chinese eat dumplings whereas Indians eat chapaties (a flat pancake). Chinese generally eat boiled and steamed food, which is not the case in India. Indians are fond of fried food. Indian food is spicier than Chinese food. In China, lightly sweetened desserts are preferred, whereas in India desserts tend to be more heavily sweetened. Alcohol is not a fundamental part of Indian culture whereas in China it is part and parcel. Mostly Indian women do not drink alcohol as compared to Chinese women. However, tea is the common beverage in both cultures though the preparation methods are different. Indians use CTC (crush, tear, curl) tea whereas Chinese tea is orthodox. Mostly Indian men do not cook food in the home and it is considered women's job.

India is one of the most religiously diverse nations in the world, with some of the most deeply religious societies and cultures. Religion plays a central and definitive role in the life of many of its people. India is also a land of many languages but Hindi is the national language and Hinduism is the main religion besides Islam, Sikhism, Jainism, Christianity and Buddhism; in China, the main faith is Buddhism, and Chinese is the main language.

To sum up, both Indian and Chinese culture are ancient and different from how they are perceived by Westerners. They have their own rich heritage, language, music, festivals, culture and religion. Both are progressive and modern.

You only need wide-open eyes to see, experience and believe.

About the author:

Roop Rani Luthra, Indian, from the Indian Council for Cultural Relations (ICCR), taught Hindi language at the School of Asian and African Studies at SISU from April 2014 to July 2016.

中国之我见——记我的中国文化轶事

Roop Rani Luthra（印度）
梁晓雪　译

我在中国的跨文化之旅始于我的中国任教经历，它让我对中国和上海有了许多新的认识。说实话，在来到这片土地之前，我只对中国美食、武术和汉语有些许的了解。

在被外派到中国教学前，我刚刚结了婚。我既要适应婚后的二人生活，又要在中国教授印地语，应对陌生的语言和文化，于我而言，这一切是新起点，也是新挑战。中国同事设宴招待我们，但因我是一位素食主义者，所以我吃得不多。他还递上了一份生活指南，里面详尽地介绍了周边超市等信息。我的跨文化之旅就此拉开序幕。

我在中国注意到的第一件事就是，人们都靠马路右侧行走或驾驶。而在印度，恰好相反：我们靠左行驶，机动车的方向盘设在右边。不过，中国的司机都遵守规则，也会礼让行人。在这里，我学会的第一句话就是“你好”，就像其他外国人一样。在这里，握手是最常见的打招呼方式；而在印度，女性常用双手合十来打招呼。因为我中文不太好，我就拨打962288热线求助，这条热线对我这样的外籍人士帮助很大。尽管不少年轻人都能说几句英语，而且乐于助人，但是商品的标签几乎全是中文的，让我望而却步。

和其他外国人一样，我对中国人的脸部特征很感兴趣，尤其是男士的发型。很多年轻人的发型很“潮”，他们的穿衣风格也很独特，看起来就像模特儿。相较而言，印度人则更喜欢穿戴首饰，印度女性喜欢佩戴美丽的莎丽（用以裹身的长巾）和首饰，印度婚礼也极尽奢靡；年轻人们喜欢穿有地方特色的库尔塔牛仔裤或库尔塔长衫和紧身裤。两国青年们都是那么单纯、聪慧、健康，最重要的是他们都积极乐观，总能在路上听见他们银铃般爽朗的笑声。中国青少年们很可爱，着装好看，有时穿丝质衣服。我发现与印度相比，中国女性在许多领域比男性具有更大的影响力，工作场合也有很多女性员工，这有利于中国的和谐与稳定。

我对中国的饮食文化也充满着好奇。它与印度饮食完全不同，天上飞的，地上爬的，应有尽有，超乎我们的想象。中国人喜欢到餐厅饭馆里设宴招待外宾，而印度人除了去外面吃，有时也会在家里招待。在印度，上门做客带上一束花那是再好不过了；但在中国，人们通常在葬礼仪式上献花。无论是新年、婚礼还是生日，中印两国都讲究礼尚往来。在印度，拜访亲朋好友时一般会带上一个水果篮或者一盒糖。在两国文化中，受邀去别人家里都是莫大的荣幸。时间上若有不便，也不妨直说。准时抵达别人家，尽情享用食物，这都会让主人倍感荣幸。去印度人家里做客，一般不必脱鞋。在印度，客人坐在主人的右边，而且和在中国一样，不面向大门就座。在印度，主人要邀请客人先用餐，而在中国则是以主人敬酒开始。在印度，不一定要尝遍宴席上的每一道菜，而在中国可能盛情难却。中国人就餐常用碗筷，而印度则喜欢用勺子、碟和小碗。在印度习俗中，我们应吃完碟中所有的饭菜，而在中国，则可以剩余一些。在印度，喝东西发出啧啧声或吃东西时打饱嗝都是不礼貌的，而在中国一些地方，这是对主人厨艺的赞美。中国人喜欢吃饺子而印度人喜欢吃薄饼。中国人喜欢吃蒸煮的食物，而印度人喜好吃煎炸的食物。印度的食物更为辛辣。甜点方面，印度的口味更重一些。酒在中国文化中占了很重要的地位，而印度则不然。此外，印度的大部分女性都不饮酒。两国人民都喜好喝茶，但制作工艺不同。中国茶叶采用的是传统工序，而印度则采用CTC工序，即压碎、撕裂、揉卷三个步骤。大部分印度男人不会进厨房做饭，他们认为这是女人的事情。

印度是世界上宗教最为多元的国家之一，拥有一些最虔诚的宗教社群和文化，宗教在许多人生活中起着决定性的作用。印度有很多语言，但印地语是官方语言；印度教是主流宗教，此外还有伊斯兰教、锡克教、耆那教、基督教和佛教。在中国，最多人信仰的是佛教，汉语是主流语言。

总的来说，两国都有着源远流长的历史文化，西方人对其的看法往往不准确。两国都拥有宝贵的文化遗产，如语言、音乐、节日、文化、宗教等，都是迅速发展、日益现代化的国家。

你要做的，就是睁大双眼，去发现，去体会，去相信。

作者简介：

Roop Rani Luthra，印度籍，2014年4月至2016年7月由印度文化关系委员会外派至上海外国语大学东方语学院印地语系任教。

The First Day in Shanghai

Ahmad Rezaei (Iran)

Translated by George Fleming

We finally arrived at Shanghai Pudong Airport after a long-haul flight. It was ten in the morning, a three-and-half-hour time difference with Tehran. It took a fair while getting through the airport, and we had been on the road since the day before. We were absolutely exhausted, particularly as we were bringing our two children Parsa and Pedram. Parsa did his best to help out, and my wife was looking after both of them. Pedram looked like he had caught a cold. Next we got our hold luggage back — we had so much of it! Very few passengers take so much as we did that day. We finally cleared the last round of customs and exited to see crowds of people waiting to pick people up. Some held cards with passengers' names written on them that could be seen from a long way off.

There was surely someone among them waiting for us — yes, at the end of the line was a lady waving to us. In her hand she held a card with my name on it — we had found an acquaintance in the crowd. We walked over to her and she introduced herself, saying her Farsi name was Susan. She was very young — I thought she might be a final year Farsi student as her Farsi was very good. I quietly marveled at her fluency and thought to myself: what an excellent student. She must have lived in Iran for many years to speak such excellent Farsi.

Susan gave us a very merry welcome before helping the driver to load our luggage into the car, before we set off into the unknown and towards our new home. Pedram was a bit down — he had clearly caught a cold on the plane and we were worried about him. As the car slowly joined the motorway, the air was full of dust. It seemed like the whole city was shrouded in dark clouds. We were in a very strange place, but things are like that: whenever you go to a new environment, everything is unfamiliar and novel. We sat there quietly, taking in the surroundings. Perhaps for every newcomer to the megacity of Shanghai, the crisscrossing network of overpasses catch their eye.

As we moved away from the airport, the city gradually came into view. Before we came to Shanghai, I had read many articles about the city online, particularly those about its roads and skyscrapers. For this reason, from the first moment, we were looking for these great towering buildings. Finally, half an hour after we left Pudong Airport, these buildings began to come into view. They are now a status symbol of Shanghai; I had previously read that Shanghai is known as "Little New York".

We passed road after road, finally arriving at an ancient looking structure that stood between two overpasses: an ideal location. Once we had unloaded our baggage from the car, we were met by a lady at the entrance. She told Susan that our room was on the first floor. I was surprised we'd have to move our luggage up there ourselves! The two security guards at the entrance didn't help us either, which really shocked me. As guests from afar, we expected a bit of help.

Well, no matter. After we had checked which room we were in, we carried our bags up, and then I took Parsa with me to the university to handle our registration. On the way we crossed a river that was really polluted — it was filthy. Still, everything around us was new to me and I tried to take it all in and get my bearings.

We arrived at the university and went to the first floor of Building No.1, where Susan introduced me to a lady named Grace, whose English was excellent. I had been in contact with Grace for a while by email; she had been helping me sort everything out for our arrival. I had expected her to be a rather strict, middle-aged woman, but to my surprise I found a warm, friendly young lady with a smile on her face. Grace took me through the program for the following day carefully. These first impressions led me to conclude that the women of this country were much friendlier than its men; at least, that's how I felt in the period immediately after my arrival.

We left the university and went back home. Susan said goodbye and left us, by which time it was nearing dusk. Pedram began to cry; everyone seemed very down. After all, we had just come to a completely new place and would have to get used to an unfamiliar city and its people. Outside our brand new home were new people of whom I knew nothing. We decided to take a walk outside and cheer ourselves up. We ambled along the pavement. We soon discovered a serious problem: nobody here could speak English. We looked at them, and they looked back at us, occasionally saying something completely unintelligible. Some people were very interested in our children, but because of the language barrier, we were like aliens. We just watched them. We decided to go back. That was our first night in Shanghai.

I don't remember when we got to sleep that night, but I awoke very early the next morning, as I normally do. It was as if nothing had changed. I put on some clothes and went out. There wasn't a single person about and it was very quiet. I paced slowly along, but before I had got very far I heard a rustling sound from somewhere. What could that be, so early in the morning? I continued ahead. It was a cleaner, sweeping the streets in the dark. The rustling sound came from his rhythmic sweeping. He must have been the earliest riser in all Shanghai, focused on his work and uninterested in anyone or anything, as if he was doing the most important thing in the world at that moment. I walked up to him but had no means of communicating with him. The cleaner glanced up at me, noticed I didn't look like your average Chinese, and was rather surprised. He smiled and said something to me that was still unintelligible, but I could feel his happiness and goodwill to me through his smile. I smiled back. A smile is the true universal language of mankind: it shows integrity and honesty. Nothing compares to it. I really wanted to extend my respect to him in some way, but I didn't know what to say. I believed he could understand my feelings through my smile, just as I could read his.

After that, the cleaner became my friend. He was the first person in Shanghai to extend a silent welcome to me, with his warm and friendly smile. Even now, I can see him working from early morning until evening, living his own life with each rustle of his broom.

I don't know how many days and nights it took us, but now we are part of this city. We have learned a lot here, and made many friends — especially Susan! She is no longer a student but "Ms. Wang", my colleague at the university. Thanks to her friendly welcome, we were never lonely in our first moments in Shanghai.

About the author:

Ahmad Rezaei, Iranian, Associate Professor of Persian language and literature. He taught for SISU from 2015 to 2018 at the Persian Language and Literature Department.

在上海的第一天

Ahmad Rezaei（伊朗）

张谦　译

王振荣　梁晓雪　审校

在经历了漫长的航程之后，我们终于抵达了上海浦东国际机场。此时已是上午十点，与德黑兰有三个半小时的时差。在机场内办理手续花费了不少时间，而从昨天起我们就一直在路上。我们已经疲惫不堪了，特别是还要带着两个孩子：帕尔萨和佩德拉姆，妻子负责照看他们。帕尔萨一直在努力帮忙，而佩德拉姆似乎有些着凉。接着我们取回了托运的行李箱，我们实在有太多行李了！很少有旅客会像我们这样随身携带如此多的行李。终于过了最后一道海关，出口处有很多接机的人，一些人还举着写有旅客名字的姓名牌，远远就能看到。

其中一定有人在等待着我们，是的，在熙熙攘攘的人群尽头有一位女士冲我们挥手，她手里还举着一块写着我名字的牌子，我们找到了认识我们的人。我们向她走去，她自我介绍道，她的波斯语名字叫苏珊。她很年轻，我以为她是波斯语专业高年级的学生，因为她波斯语说得很好。我还在心里默默赞叹：多么优秀的学生啊，一定在伊朗生活过很多年。

苏珊（王振荣）热情地欢迎我们的到来，并和司机一起帮我们把行李放入了车内，带着我们向未知的新家驶去。佩德拉姆心情有些低落，很显然他在飞机上着了凉，我们也很担心他。汽车慢慢驶入了高速公路，空气中弥漫着烟尘，似乎整个城市都被乌云所笼罩。我们依然在一个惊奇的状态里，这也是情理之中：每每进入一个新的环境，所有的一切好像都是陌生的、新奇的。我们都静静地坐着，向四处张望着。也许对于每一个第一次来到上海这座超级都市的人来说，他们的目光都会被层层叠叠的立交桥所吸引。

离开机场后，城市的面貌慢慢展现在眼前。来上海之前，我在网上看了很多关于上海的报道，特别是关于上海的交通以及高楼大厦的。因此从一开始我们就在寻找着高楼，并终于在离开机场半个小时后，渐渐看到了这些摩天大楼。它们已经成为上海这座城市的身份象征，我还曾读到，上海因此有着“小纽约”的美名。

驶过一条条道路，到达了我们的落脚之地。这是一幢古老的建筑，在高架桥之间，位置很理想。取下了汽车里的行李后，我们就在大楼入口的接待处看见一位女士，她告诉苏珊我们的房间在二楼。我们竟然要自己动手，把这些沉重的箱子搬到二楼！尽管在门口有两位保安模样的先生，但他们没有帮助我们，这让我震惊，毕竟我们是远道而来的客人，希望得到别人的帮助。

不过无所谓了！在确定房间后，我们自己把行李搬了上去，随后我带着帕尔萨跟随苏珊去学校办理相关的手续。路上我们经过了一条河，河水很脏，污染严重。然而周围的事物对我来说都是全新的，我努力观察，稍微熟悉了下环境。到了学校，我们去了一号楼的二楼。苏珊把我介绍给了英文很好的格蕾丝女士（梁晓雪）——她一直同我进行邮件往来并帮我处理好来上海的各项手续。我还以为她是一位做事严格的中年女子，结果她竟是一个热情友善、笑语吟吟的年轻人。她将我第二天要做的事情仔细讲给我听。这让我觉得这里的女性普遍要比男性友善得多，至少在我到达之后的一段时间里我是这样想的。

离开学校后，我们回到家里，苏珊在同我们告别后也离开了。此时已接近黄昏。佩德拉姆哭了起来，全家人看上去都很压抑，毕竟，我们刚刚来到一个全新的地方，要面对一个陌生的城市和一群陌生人。全新的家周围是全新的人，而我对他们一无所知。为了改变心情，我们走出家门，在附近的街道上慢慢走着。很快我们发现了一个很大的问题：这里没有人懂英语。我们看着他们，他们也观望着我们，偶尔还说着一些我们完全听不懂的话。有些人对我们的孩子表现得很热情，然而语言不通，我们像是外星人一样，只能看着他们。最后我们还是回家了，这是我们在上海度过的第一个夜晚。

也不记得是什么时候睡着的，但我醒得很早，跟从前一样，好像一切都没发生变化。我穿上衣服后就出了门，大街上没有一个人，到处都静悄悄的。我在街上慢慢地踱着步，没走几步就听到了一阵沙沙声持续不断地传来。在如此早的清晨，这会是什么声音呢？我继续前行几步，发现了一位在黑暗中扫大街的环卫工人，那沙沙声就是他在打扫时发出的有节奏的声响。他一定是这个城市里最早醒来的人，沉浸在自己的工作中，不去关注任何人、任何地方，像是在做着全世界最重要的事情。我走近他身边，但是没有办法同他交流。环卫工人抬头看了我一眼，发现我长得有些不一样，略微有些吃惊。他笑着向我说了句什么，我依然没能听懂，但是我能感受到他的笑容背后的愉快与善意。我也向他露出了一个微笑。微笑才是人们共同的语言，它展示着正直与诚信，没有什么可以与之媲美。我好想向他表达我内心诚挚的敬意，但不知要说什么。我想他应该可以从我的微笑里读懂我的感受，正如我能够读懂他的微笑一样。

从此之后，这位环卫工人成了我的朋友，他是上海这座城市里第一位用无声的语言欢迎我的人——用他那热情的微笑。直到现在我每天都还能看到他从清晨劳作到晚上，用他那沙沙的扫地声谱写出一首首生活的赞歌。

不知经过了多少个日日夜夜，我们也已经融入了上海这座城市。在这里我们学到了很多，也交到了很多朋友，特别是苏珊女士。她已经毕业，成了我的同事。正是她的友善，让我们在到达上海的那一刻并不孤单。

作者简介：

Ahmad Rezaei，伊朗籍，波斯语语言文学副教授，于2015–2018年在上海外国语大学波斯语专业任教。

"The Students Will Love You!": Soaking up the Warmth of SISU Students

Brian Charles Lewis (U.S.A.)

Proofread by George Fleming

I arrived here at SISU as a Fulbright Scholar in 2017 to spend one academic year teaching American Literature. During the fall semester, I taught a postgraduate Short Novels course and an Honors course in Classic American Literature. I had heard many sorts of stories about Chinese students prior to coming to China. The most common among them was that they could not write very well and that they might not understand me. I was worried that communication would be difficult, particularly considering that, when I came here, I spoke almost no Chinese at all. All I could say was "*ni hao*." So I was very nervous about this.

Nonetheless, my friend Yanmei, who had once taught at SISU, assured me otherwise. "The students will love you!" she asserted. I was still skeptical, but I tried to feel reassured.

On my first day of my postgraduate Short Novels class, two students met me at the School of English Studies to take me to the class. One carried an umbrella to shield me from the sun, and the other carried my briefcase. I reveled in the royal treatment. There are NO students at my home institution who would do this! Anyway, the girls and I were walking around, and one of them received a message on WeChat that we were going to the wrong classroom. So I found out 10 minutes before my class started where the class was actually being held, which struck me as very strange. Back home, they scheduled the classes and the rooms about nine months in advance.

They took me to a huge lecture hall. I was expecting to see 20 students, but I counted 87 STUDENTS IN THE ROOM. I thought to myself, "What am I going to do?" I still introduced myself, walked around the room, and let them ask me some questions. The first student asked what Americans thought of Donald Trump; the second asked what I thought of feminism; and another asked me if I knew how to use chopsticks before I came here. They were fun questions more than serious ones, but they broke the ice a bit. I then talked about the class, and decided to forego my plan to have them sign up for presentations. I figured this was pointless at the moment. I kept alluding to the fact that the class was so large, and at one point they all began to laugh. "What is it?" I asked. "Professor, today we are just observing. We are not registered yet," one young woman with a British accent sitting in the front row explained. "Ohhhh…" I replied. They all laughed. I had no idea, obviously, and wished that someone had explained this to me. I went on to lecture a bit on the novel as a genre, and then collected brief "intros" from them about their name, why they were here, and questions they had. I decided not to grade these or anything, though, until I had a better sense of who was in the class.

After class, about 10 students surrounded me. "Please professor," one implored, "would you open up more seats in your class?" "Do you all want to take my class?" I queried. "Oh yes," they replied, and nodded their heads. "I'll see what I can do," I said. Later, I e-mailed Professor Wang Xin, asking if she could increase the enrollment to 30. I thought this was fair considering that I had only 15 in the other class at that point, and SISU has been very, very kind to me so far. On the way to the School of English Studies, I said to Jin, one of the young women who led me around initially, "I hope they liked the class." "Yes! They think you are nice!" She replied. Later on I was inundated on WeChat with messages from students telling me how wonderful they thought I was. "I think you are lovely," proclaimed one. "Today you are just like a super star! Every student likes you. Hope you enjoy your life and work here," Jin wrote me later on WeChat. WOW. I began to realize how much I was going to like these students!

This WeChat conversation with Jin enabled me to learn the importance of WeChat as a means of communication in China: it's really a means of community-building with students. All semester long, I used WeChat to make announcements, answer their questions, or even encourage them. They would respond with cute little stickers, such as little panda bears or kittens that blew kisses, which they were forever trying to teach me how to use properly. One day, on the way to class, a student stopped me, and asked, "Are you American?" "Yes," I replied. He went on about America and how he wanted to go there, etc. I introduced myself and he did the same. "Will you be my friend on WeChat?" he shouted after me when I was going into my class. But he didn't stick around to let me friend him, though. However, it's interesting to see how WeChat is used just as a means of getting to know someone. In America, we wouldn't walk up to random strangers and ask, "Will you be my friend on Facebook?"

As I mentioned, the semester began by having the students in both my classes write introductions to me. I was a bit put off at first when one of them, in her introductory paper, wrote, "Have you ever thought about losing weight? Just kidding!" But I was reminded by the fact that, in China, mentioning weight isn't such a big deal; it may even be a way of getting to know me better. In fact, I've found that most people in China comment on my weight and then offer to feed me more. Furthermore, many of the comments on the first Honors American Literature paper said things like, "I think you are a very nice teacher!" and "I like you and your class and I hope I can have a good time!" Many of the students apologized for their "poor handwriting," which I found so unusual — it would be very rare for American students to apologize for such a thing.

Weekly, I assigned written response papers: the undergraduates had to write one page per week, and the postgraduates two. Once the response papers started coming in, the high quality of the written work stunned me. I even informed my Honors undergrads that they wrote better than my students did back in the United States. They were equally surprised. "Aren't you going to say 'but'?" one of them asked. They kept expecting insults rather than compliments. However, I assured them of the high quality of their work. Consequently, they became even nicer to me. They laughed at my corny jokes and even applauded me when I counted to ten in Chinese. I felt like I was four years old again, but I appreciated their encouragement.

Even by the end of the semester, the students were still fond of me.

Here are some comments that I received via e-mail from the Short Novels students when they submitted their final papers:

"Many thanks to you for this semester's class. I really enjoyed it. You are the best teacher I have met in SISU. I wish you a happy winter holiday and happy every day."

"Heartfelt thanks for everything you have done for us and this course.

I do enjoy every second of it.

Wish you all the best in 2018!

Wish you all the best in China!"

"Thank you very much for your lessons this semester! Hope you like your staying in China! My advice is that you try more local food, and go to different cities in China! I'm sure you will find them amazing! It's so nice to meet you and it's my pleasure to be one of your Chinese students! You are a great professor! Hope you will have good health and a fantastic life!"

After reading comments like this from them, I realized how blessed I was to be teaching at SISU. It's wonderful to feel so appreciated and so loved by such amazing students! I learned how much it can make a difference to me when I'm treated in such a gracious way. I do have some wonderful students back in the United States, but they are much less effusive in their praise of either me or the class. Liking school just isn't "cool." But here, I noticed a definite change. Whether a class is successful depends just as much on the students as it does on the teacher. A class can work well with students who are excited about the learning process. While I have the privilege of being here, I will continue to soak up the warmth this university and its students have to offer, and I hope to return again someday.

About the author:

Dr. Brian C. Lewis is a Fulbright U. S. Scholar for the 2017–18 academic year at SISU. He teaches American Literature courses at the School of English Studies and the Honors College, covering Short American Novels, Classic American Literature, and American Literature and Culture: 1900–Present.

“学生们会很喜欢你的！”——感受来自上外学生的浓浓暖意

Brian Charles Lewis（美国）

梁晓雪　译

2017年，我作为富布莱特学者来上海外国语大学任教一年，教授美国文学。第一学期，我负责给研究生上短篇小说课程，并且在上外的卓越学院教授美国经典文学。来中国之前，我听说了很多关于中国学生的趣闻轶事。其中最多的便是，他们的英语写作能力薄弱，以及他们很可能听不懂我讲话。我很担心和他们会有交流上的困难，尤其是我自己除了“你好”之外一句汉语都不会说。因此我忧心忡忡，惴惴不安。然而，我有一位朋友曾在上外教过书，她告诉我不用担心，“学生们会很喜欢你的！”对此，我半信半疑，不过，我还是努力试图宽慰自己。

给研究生上短篇小说课程的第一天，有两位学生在英语学院门口迎接我，她们一个为我打伞遮阳，一个为我拎包，我感觉自己像是受到了国王般的待遇。在美国，没有一个学生会这样照顾老师！

她们带着我四处熟悉了一下，忽然一位学生收到一条微信，说是换教室了。于是，我在离上课仅十分钟的时候才找到正确的教室，这让我感到非常奇怪。在美国，课程和授课地点往往会提前九个月安排好。

她们把我领进了一间很大的教室。我原以为只有20来个学生，可是我一数，居然有87个！我心想：天啊！这是什么情况？我做了自我介绍，在教室里来回走了几圈，请他们提问。一位学生问我美国人都是怎么看待川普的；另一位学生问我对于女性主义的看法；还有学生问我在来中国之前会不会使用筷子。当然，这都是一些有趣、轻松的问题，但也调动了氛围。接着，我谈了谈我的课程计划，并放弃了让学生们一个个上台演讲的安排，因为感觉没有必要。讲解期间我一直向学生们暗示上这门课的人数之多，他们终于忍不住大笑起来。“怎么啦？”我不解地问道。“老师，我们今天只是过来旁听，我们还没有选课呢。”坐在前排的一位女生用一口英式英语回答道。“哦……”我回答道。大家顿时哄堂大笑。我不明白这是为什么，真希望有人能给我解释一下。接着，我简单介绍了一下小说这种体裁，然后让学生们每人做一段简短的自我介绍，包括他们的名字，他们来旁听的原因，以及他们想问的问题。当然，在学生尚未正式选这门课之前，我是不会给他们打分的。

下课后，大约十个学生围住了我。其中一个问我：“老师，您的课程能增加选课人数吗？”“你们都想上我的这门课吗？”我问。“是的！是的！”他们点头答道。“好的，那我就想想办法吧。”之后，我给王欣老师发了邮件，询问她是否可以将我的上课人数增至30人。我觉得这对我来说是完全可以接受的，因为我的另一门课只有15人，并且上外对我那么好。在回英语学院的路上，我对先前带我去教室的金同学说：“我希望大家喜欢我的这门课。”“当然啦！他们都觉得你特别友好！”她说道。不一会儿，我便接二连三地收到学生发来的微信，他们纷纷告诉我，我是多么的棒。其中一位学生写道："我觉得您真的太好了！"晚些时候，我收到了金同学发给我的一条微信："今天您就像个大明星！所有同学都很喜欢您。希望您在这里工作顺利，生活愉快！"哇！我发觉自己将会越来越喜欢这群学生！

和金同学的微信聊天让我意识到，在中国，微信是一个多么重要的通讯工具：它的确是与学生们沟通的绝佳方式。整个学期，我都用微信发通知，解答学生的疑问，甚至鼓励他们。有时，学生们会用可爱的表情包回复我，比如熊猫呀，发飞吻的小猫呀，等等。学生们也一直在教我如何恰当地使用这些表情包。一次，在去上课的路上，一位学生拦住了我，问道："你是美国人吗？""是呀。"我说。于是，他便开始表达对美国的赞美和喜爱，以及对去美国的向往。随后，我们俩进行了简单的自我介绍。在我马上要进教室时，他从背后朝我大喊："我能加你微信好友吗？"但是，还没等我加他，他已经走了。不过，通过这件事，我发现微信也可以用来结识新朋友，这真的很有意思。在美国，不会有人对陌生人说："我能加你的脸书吗？"

正式上课之前，我让两个班的学生每人都写一份自我介绍。有一位学生写道："你有没有想过要减肥？开个玩笑而已。"一开始，这让我感到有些不开心，不过随后我发现，在中国，体重并不是一个敏感话题，聊聊体重甚至可以增进彼此的了解。我发现很多中国人都会谈到我的体重，但仍然会让我多吃点。除此之外，卓越学院美国文学课的学生在他们的第一份作业中还说道："我觉得您是位特别好的老师！""我非常喜欢您还有您的课，希望我能收获满满！"还有很多学生会对自己"糟糕的英文书写"表示歉意，这也让我感到很惊讶，因为很少会有美国学生为此道歉。

每周，我都会要求学生写读书报告：本科生一页，研究生两页。作业收上来之后，我对学生们的写作水平惊叹不已。我甚至告诉卓越学院的本科生，他们的写作水平比我的美国学生还要好。对此，他们也很惊讶，有一个学生还问道：“您在赞扬之后不打算说‘但是’吗？”他们总觉得我会批评而不是表扬他们。我向他们保证，他们的作业确实完成得极好。结果，学生们待我越来越亲了。当我讲了老套的笑话，他们会捧腹大笑；当我用汉语从一数到十时，他们甚至会为我鼓掌。那一刻，我感到自己又变成了四岁的小孩，但是我很感激他们对我的鼓励。

学生们对我的喜爱与日俱增，甚至到了学期末也毫无消减。很多学生在给我发期末论文的邮件中写道：

“很感谢您这学期给我们上课。我非常喜欢这门课，收获很多，您是我在上外遇见的最好的老师。祝您寒假愉快，开心每一天。”

“对您这学期为我们所做的一切表示最衷心的感谢。我享受这门课的每一秒钟。祝您新年快乐！在中国生活愉快！”

“非常喜欢您这学期为我们上的课。祝您在中国度过愉快的时光！您可以多品尝品尝我们的特色美食，多到不同的城市转转，一定会有很多意外的收获！很高兴能够认识您，也很荣幸能成为您的学生，您真的是一位非常棒的老师！祝您身体健康、生活愉快！”

看到学生们写的这些话，我由衷地为自己能来到上外教学而感到幸运。有这么多优秀的学生喜欢我，赞赏我，我感到多么地开心和自豪！通过这一学期的授课，我明白到，当学生们用亲切友好的方式对待我，会对我产生良好的影响。当然，在美国，我也有一些很优秀的学生，但是他们很少表达赞美，不管是对我还是对我的课程，因为他们觉得这样一点也不“酷”。然而，在这里，情况却大相径庭。一门课程的成功与否不仅取决于老师，还取决于学生，学生的积极参与是一门课成功的重要因素。当我有幸在上外教学时，我将继续享受来自学校和学生们的温暖，我希望有朝一日还能再回到这里。

作者简介：

Brian Charles Lewis博士，美国富布莱特学者，于2017–2018学年在上海外国语大学英语学院和卓越学院教授美国文学课程，包括美国短篇小说、美国经典文学、美国从1900年至今的文学与文化。

China Travelogue　中国纪行

The City

Boris Lopatinsky (France)

Translated by George Fleming

When we talk about the city, in a sense, we are talking about culture. Every country or region has its own particular customs and ideas about the city and how it should be organised. Asia is a particular case in point because of the number of memorable cities. No capital of Asia would be complete without some connection to dreams or aspirations. The poet

Hérédia has spoken of *Cipangu* (Japan) and her distant mines, evoking the emotional baggage Westerners have when it comes to Asia. The conquistador is not just the Man of the New World; he is also by definition the man who shrouds himself in death and desolation. It is funny that nobody has made an explicit comparison between the proud conquering nations that were the United Kingdom, France, the Netherlands and Spain, and the Four Horsemen of the Apocalypse (a thoroughly Western image, which is perhaps why one can understand the metaphor was never made).

What it comes down to is this: although we cannot deny these countries had certain strengths, above all military, astonishingly, they played no role in the making of the Asian city. It would certainly be foolish to deny that the "skyscraper" is a Western invention. Careful, they tell us, the temple towers in Xi'an or Suzhou are there to demonstrate to us that in ancient China there existed a sort of willingness to ascend to vertical heights, but these are not like the "vernacular buildings" in the West as certain architects dare to pompously call these buildings. We could add to the title that "culture is like jam: the less one has, the more one spreads". If "vernacular" was referring to a language, such as the local terms for animals, the word in fact means a local language. To simplify, and for the benefit of linguists, we might call them "regionalisms". But there is nothing like that for architecture; more so is the case for a town, particularly in its opposition to all forms of religious architecture.

The Chinese town — now there's something fascinating that draws you in. Defined by its layout, it conjures associations of hopscotch. We are talking about ancient towns where the layout has remained pretty much the same for a long time. Those towns that do not follow this plan are on the whole those constructed over the past two hundred years or by foreign nations. All things considered, these towns exude rather a sort of austere grandeur, reminding us of how China was already at the time one of the greatest civilizations in the world. Otherwise, one discovers a sort of organised anarchy, of the sort that brings a smile to the face of a Westerner, until they are confronted with such a reality. Rather, this apparent anarchy is often the result of a Western scheme, conforming to the austere plan of imperial towns.

At the roots of this variety of different accounts of architecture from the colonial period, one might well ask: is Western architecture, in this regard, anarchic? Yes, indeed, if one considers for example Shanghai, and the various former foreign concessions. At any rate, are these not the most promoted, to the family who comes here on holiday — to see us, to be amused by little comparisons, which serve to contrast the modern and the ancient, organised with genteel and obvious anarchy, hiding the sombre reality of government of districts and police checkpoints in the concessions? Happily, times have changed; China knows how to show the world that it needs no models to follow in order to find its way. Of course, one hears here and there certain voices of protest, calling for copying of established norms. But are these norms better?

In China, urbanisation and infrastructure are more advanced than in Europe. Take for example the network of high-speed rail connecting one province to another — in Europe we may have such infrastructure in several countries, but nothing comparable to China's system. The majority of public transport in China is more developed and tends to be improved with every passing year. In Europe, public transport is being neglected: one cannot rely on the free market at the same time as taking responsibility for the modernisation of infrastructure. Such an idea goes against the rule that there is no need for rules. Yes, I realize the West is a paradox; a little anarchic, like its towns. It has been a long while since towns took it in hand to switch taxis to natural gas and the buses to greener fuels. Only a few towns have managed to escape these constraining regulations that are nevertheless required in order to improve the quality of our daily lives.

On closer inspection, the Chinese town is far larger than its European counterpart. China is home to the world's largest municipality, Chongqing (London is but the 24th and Paris the 29th largest in terms of population, worldwide). What is astonishing is the ratio in Chinese towns: huge. One wonders how they manage to put it all together, while everything around is changing all the time. We won't fool ourselves about the decreasing youth population of Europe, but the Chinese aren't doing so badly in this respect. Although the birth rate has fallen with increased economic growth and there has been a consequent rise in living standards in the cities, in the countryside families continue to swell, presaging a future change in the original urban landscape. One doesn't hear whether dialects here or there are being replaced by new ones, themselves the product of urban sophistication.

So many regrets, which linger on the disappearance of such and such a quarter, or such and such a dialect, have nothing to do with the life of the city, which remains an engine of progression, lights the way, and, confident in its technological superiority, as Spengler put it so well, continues to whir until its collapse. "The city is dead, long live the city!" In reality, the city does not die — it transforms, remodelling itself time and again. It invents itself, at the risk of sometimes repeating itself and in the same way. Urbaneness, which populates or leeches off this strange modern Hydra, is constantly pretending to be something else — sometimes becoming part of the collective imagination, sometimes viewed as possessing an infinite amount of knowledge, proclaiming it to whoever will listen: I am the Man of the Future — of Modernity.

The future is not necessarily a sign of modernity. The rural folk, who in the end may prove to have a grain of truth, are often ridiculed because of their superstition. Our friends the dinosaurs knew something about that. In essence, urbanity is sure only of its certainties: certain that it holds the keys to its own destiny. As will be observed, the city is not without a sense of humour, but overall it is modest. Therefore, if tomorrow the countryside should cease to produce essential resources, the result would be that far from having its destiny in its hands, the city would find itself once more (as during every decline) the plaything of forces (for the superstitious) or factors (for the rational), which take it towards its doom, supernatural or otherwise.

But to return to the topic, and bring these dreamlike thoughts to a halt for an instant. Is the Chinese town attractive? Not at first sight for an innocent Candide of an observer, be he a Chinese farmer or a foreigner like me. The Chinese city is large, noisy, full of cars and everything seems unaffordable. Such an ecosystem requires a length of time to adjust. Therefore, unlike other ecosystems, the city can eat you up or reject you. It can also accept you, so you need to show patience and the ability to adapt. The rules of the city change from place to place. In this part of the country, or even the region, any provincial capital is seen as uninhabitable by those who do not live there. Adaptation is therefore the rule; twice rather than once. Can one prepare oneself? Certainly not, because every city is different and one must conform to the customs of a particular place. However, in the cultural domain, the city is a magnifier at both the macro and micro level. What well-meaning spirit we attach to the heart of civilization, which shapes our opinions and values!

Nevertheless, nothing is simple. The culture of which we speak is perishable, impermanent and certainly not confined to our own civilization.

Nowadays, as the Americans would put it so well, we live in an interconnected time where communication is at the centre of our thoughts. It is communication which illustrates to us the ubiquity; it is Buddha who would have been happy to live in our time. Boundaries of space-time have dissolved. Your boss can reach you twenty-four seven, and there is no longer anywhere, in the cities or anywhere else on the planet, that somebody cannot reach you in a second. What a great feeling.

But I said that we wouldn't talk about dream-world troubles and would get back to the main topic. Imagine we were to take a journey two millennia into the future. What would remain of our super communications and our city? To get an idea, imagine Shanghai without a single person: empty of its people or parasites. There would be nothing but buildings, as far as the eye could see — and that's assuming these were built in a reliable and coherent way, because otherwise there would be nothing but simple traces. We have to thank our ancestors for avoiding the folly of constructing buildings out of biodegradable materials and therefore leaving us Roman, Greek and Chinese buildings. Does the true urban ecology not reside in the construction of solid and almost indestructible structures? Certainly there are some who would rush at the opportunity to work in a building more than two millennia old. I imagine Robert saying to Ginette: "… and I'm the twentieth generation to work within these walls…" One senses a certain patrimony behind this sentence.

Despite all our certitudes, in the end nothing will remain except the traces of thousands of kilometres of cabling; archaeologists in the future will wonder: what purpose could these cables have served? They will conclude that we lived in underground cubes (car parks) or immense square or rectangular structures (department stores), which had to be defended, and that we lived in an equal and strata-less society. They will certainly add that this state of affairs was the product of the delinquency of a society based on property, a fact apparently supported by the remains of villas, and explaining the transition towards a model more adapted to the evolution of civilization. The construction of such unions, the villas, will be interpreted as outdated in view of the concentration of the populace in structures that would have effectively destroyed the idea of different social classes (let us leave the archaeologists of tomorrow there).

To speak of the city is to speak of culture. When one takes a closer look, it is evident that our culture is founded on nothing more than elements that will one day run their course, leaving no trace on the planet. We can now be sure that our culture will completely disappear in the future, allowing us to make good our bet about disappearing without a trace. This means that at its heart, our civilization, however modern it may be, will be judged by the standard of its successes in knowing nothing concrete — because everything will have disappeared.

About the Author:

Boris Lopatinsky graduated from the School for Advanced Studies in the Social Sciences (EHESS) and teaches at the School of Asian and African Studies at SISU. He is assistant researcher at the Laboratory of Philtext Research at the Free University of Brussels, assistant researcher at the Mediterranean and Byzantine Studies Laboratory at College de France, Paris 4, archaeology specialist at the French Association of National Archaeology (Paris), editor of the *Crusades from 11th to 13th Century*, and assistant professor at the Department of Art and Archaeology at Antananarivo University, Madagascar. He was part-time researcher at the French Ministry of Defence (War and Defense Research), assistant researcher at the Institute of Arabic Studies in Damascus, and political advisor specialising in French Polynesia at the Association du Hereaia.

城市随想

Boris Lopatinsky（法国）

张茜茹　译

很多时候，城市和文化息息相关。每个国家或地区对于城市及其规划都有自己的习俗和看法。在这点上，亚洲很值得一谈，因为亚洲的传奇城市特别多。亚洲国家的首都多多少少都与梦想或壮志相关。法国诗人埃雷迪亚曾描绘过遍地金山的日本国，使西方人产生了成见与欲望，并带着它们来到亚洲。说好听些，西方殖民者是发现新世界的探险家；说难听些，他们其实是杀戮者和毁灭者。奇怪的是，竟从没有人指出英国、法国、荷兰、西班牙这四大殖民国和圣经启示录里的四骑士[1]何等相似，大约是西方人不愿打自己耳光的缘故。

如果说这些征服者有什么强项，那恐怕也仅限于军事上。在亚洲的城市建设方面，他们毫无建树。也许你会说，如今在亚洲城市比比皆是的摩天大厦难道不是西方的发明吗？其实不然。西安和苏州保留下来的古佛塔明确地告诉我们，中国古人在建筑时早已有对垂直高度的追求。然而西方某些建筑学家却生造了“民间风格建筑”一词来形容这些建筑，估计也只是因为这个说法很新颖，分外夺人眼球。这好像正应了法国的一句俗语：“文化就像果酱，越是少，就越要铺，越要张。”“民间风格”本是用来形容语言的，就是“方言”之意；简化来说，从语言学家的立场看，他们用这个词是为了体现语言的“地域性”。谁知怎的，就被建筑学家借去。但

1　启示录里说到，在世界终结时，书卷的七个封印解开，将唤来骑着白、红、黑、绿四匹马的骑士，将战争、饥荒、瘟疫和死亡带给接受最终审判的人类，届时天地万象失调，日月为之变色，随后便是世界的毁灭。

在建筑方面没有这回事，特别是在排斥各种宗教建筑的城市里。

再说到中国的城市，那的确是极其诱人，极其令人向往的。方方正正的古城，总让人情不自禁地想到儿时的游戏“跳房子”。不过，这种横平竖直的条理也仅限于历史相对久远的古城。近两百年来建起的或由他国规划的城市则完全不按此条理规设。如果说古城是规整的、庄重的、雄伟的，象征着中国璀璨悠久的文明，那么殖民城市的布局则可以称为“有组织的混乱”。这种说法大概会让一个西方人觉得可笑。然而事实正是如此：这种混乱是西式方案所致，它与帝国城市简朴的规划相符。

我们也许还要问，伴随殖民而移植到中国城市的西方建筑，真有那么混乱吗？可惜，答案不容置疑，只要看看被近代各国租界割得支离破碎的上海便足矣。奇怪的是，每当家庭组团来上海旅游，大家的第一反应肯定是带他们去看旧租界，去看现代与古旧的对比。殊不知，旧租界才真是一盘无局之棋——各国只管自己那方寸之地，哪个租界不是关卡重重，守卫森严。让人高兴的是，这已然成为过去。今天的中国向全世界表明，它已找到自己的路，不必继续跟在别人后面亦步亦趋。当然，聒噪的声音还是存在，总嚷嚷着要让中国学习别人。可是别人的就一定好吗？

和欧洲相比，中国的基础设施和城市建设显然走在了前面。举个例子，连接各省的高铁网运作良好，而欧洲仅有几个国家拥有这样的铁路网，但也都无法和中国的规模相提并论。中国城市的公共交通更发达，且一年比一年好。欧洲的城市公交则在走下坡路，其问题在于：自由市场经济和基础设施的现代化建设相互冲突。这就和自由市场经济不需要规划的说法相冲突了。我看西方就是这么个矛盾体，有点乱糟糟的，和西方的城市一个样。中国许多城市的出租车都改用天然气，公交车改用环保燃料，例外的是少数。这些强制措施也是为了提高人们的生活质量。

进一步说，中国的城市也比欧洲城市大很多。世界最大的城市重庆就位于中国。论人口，伦敦排在24，巴黎只排到29。中国城市的规模让外人惊叹，不知如何才能管理这么大的地方，这样多的人，这般日夜不息的生活。欧洲人口老龄化严重，而中国在这方面情况还好。确实，随着经济增长，中国的出生率开始下降，城市的生活水平提高，但农村的人口依然不断增长，预兆着未来城市景观的变化。人们没有讨论各地的方言有没有被新的语言取代，它们本身就是城市复杂性的产物。

对于旧城区的消失或方言的衰退有很多惋惜之声，但这些都与城市本身无关。城市只在乎进步，只在乎前进，只为技术的日新月异而欢欣鼓舞。虽然斯宾格勒[1]预言，技术和文明最终要走向没落，然而亦有言："城市死去，而后复生。"其实，城市是不死的，它只是在不断变化，不断自我塑形，周而复始。它不断更新自己，冒着重蹈覆辙的风险。城市就像希腊神话里的七头巨兽，都市风潮如同它身上的寄生虫，想要装成别的东西：有时成为集体想象的一部分，有时好像拥有无限的知识，声称自己代表着未来，代表着现代。可未来不一定就是现代的象征。人们可能最终会被证明掌握了真理，但又常因迷信而愚昧。我们的朋友恐龙就上过这一课。说到底，都市人的自信是盲目的，"我的明天我做主"不过是他们的一厢情愿。城市具有一定的幽默感，但归根结底是普通的，因此，如果农村颗粒未收，城市就无法掌握自己的命运，就像历史上的每次衰落一样，而最终的结论依然会是：自己不过是玩物，受制于某些力量（按迷信的说法）或因素（按科学的说法），而结局总还是饿死，不管是迷信还是科学。

我们的话题似乎扯得远了点，那还是言归正传。中国城市让人

---

1 奥斯瓦尔德·斯宾格勒（Oswald Spengler, 1880–1936），德国历史学家，代表作为《西方的没落》。

喜欢吗？第一眼看上去，往往是不喜欢。我这话，是站在初来乍到的农村人，或者初次来中国的“老外”的立场上说的（比如我第一次来中国的时候）。中国的城市那么大，那么吵，到处都是车，什么都看似很贵。城市就像生态系统，是需要时间去调整的。但城市又不同于生态系统，它可以把你吞没，也可以排斥你。当然，它也可以接受你，只要你有足够的耐心，还是会适应的。每个城市都有自己的法则。在这个国家甚至地区，任何一个省会城市在外地人眼里都难以立足。适应似乎是唯一的办法，不适应也得适应。更麻烦的是，前一次的适应经验未必适用于下一个城市，因为城市和城市之间太不一样，有其自身的风俗。城市就是文化的放大镜，无论是宏观还是微观层面。城市是文明的中心，我们认为其具有美好的精神，其塑造了我们的思想和观念。

不过，也没那么简单。我们所说的文化是可消逝的，非永久的，不仅限于我们自身的文明。美国人自豪地说，我们的时代是伟大的通信时代。通信无处不在；佛陀要是再世，想必也会庆幸生活在这样的时代。时空界线不复存在。一周7天，一天24小时，老板随时能传唤你。不管在地球何处，只需一秒钟，就能联系上你。真是幸福。

一不小心又跑题了。好，假如时光加速，我们一跃来到2000年后，我们如此引以为豪的通信技术和城市会变成什么样呢？想象一下，空无一人的上海，或者换个角度说，失去所有“寄生虫”的上海。假如上海的建筑足够坚固，那么兴许还能留下些随处可见的楼和房；否则，除了这些痕迹就真的啥都不剩了。古希腊、古罗马、古代中国都能留下些建筑，这还多亏了古人用的是不易腐烂分解的建筑材料。而今日的生态材料，能够建起坚固持久的建筑吗？一定有人很想在屹立2000年不倒的建筑里工作。我想象小明对小红说：“……我是在这栋建筑里工作的第二十代人……”说这么一句话，祖上是有真古迹。

可以肯定的是，各种延绵数千公里的通信缆啊数据线啊，倒是能留下些痕迹。未来的考古学家会对着它们抓破头皮：这么多缆啊线啊，究竟是干什么用的？他们会说，2000年前的人（也就是现在的我们）住在需要守卫的地下大方块里（地下车库），或者住在四四方方的大屋子里（大卖场）；看来2000年前的人是没有阶级之分的，众生平等。假如还有私家别墅的遗址，又作何解释？他们还会说，以私有财产为基础的社会正在瓦解，文明正走向更高的阶段。而考虑到这些体现阶级平等的大片方块建筑，独幢而立的私家别墅是落后的……（剩下的话还是留给未来的考古学家去说吧）。

回到文章最开始的那句话，很多时候，城市和文化息息相关。如果仔细观察，就会发现构建文化的元素终会消失殆尽，不留痕迹。所以我们的文化最后也全会消失不见，一丝痕迹也不留。也就是说，让我们如此骄傲的现代文明，到最终却也还是落了个啥也不剩的命。

作者简介：

Boris Lopatinsky，法国籍，上海外国语大学东方语学院教师，毕业于法国高等社会科学学院（EHESS）。他现任布鲁塞尔自由大学文献学研究实验室的助理研究员、巴黎四大地中海和东方（拜占庭）研究所（索邦大学法兰西学院所属）副研究员、法国国家考古发掘协会（巴黎）考古研究负责人、《第一次十字军东征编年史》编者、马达加斯加共和国安塔那那利佛大学艺术与考古系助理教授。他曾经担任法国国防部（战争与防务研究方向）兼职研究员、叙利亚大马士革阿拉伯研究所客座研究员、法属波利尼西亚Association du Hereaia协会政治顾问。

My Shanghai Paradise Lost and Regained

Peter Andrew Christianson (U.S.A.)

Proofread by George Fleming

Often, novelists and movie producers conjure up unique settings of beauty, atmosphere, nostalgia, or intrigue to charm their audiences. Sometimes they borrow from magical realism and create places that beguile their readers or viewers while sometimes leaving them puzzled and unable to suspend disbelief enough to enjoy the story, because the spot appears entirely out of place, an ad hoc concoction to create the desired flavor for the audience. Whenever a writer resorts to this tactic, the work typically gets shredded to smithereens in the readers' reviews on amazon.com and similar sites. So many readers want a time and place that seems believable and is congruent with reality, not a seeming fairyland that was concocted to enthrall and enchant.

Living in modern Shanghai, it's important for many of us to find oases of mysticism and beauty. We dwell in a concrete jungle with high rises, cinder block apartments, shopping malls, and skyscrapers that stretch as far as the eye can see — which isn't very far, given how these massive structures block our view. Many of us pine for places that connect us with nature or with the beauty and simplicity of the less mechanized world of the past. Yet the steel and cement sprawl on relentlessly for mile after mile, leaving few redoubts of Eden for romantics and mystics.

Nor does it help that Shanghai is as flat as an unrolled calligraphy scroll. I've had friends here who have moved away in large part because they missed climbing hills and mountains and could not be happy in the monotony of Shanghai's topography. Poets and song lyricists wax melodiously about how one does not truly value what one has until one has lost it. "Well, you only need the light when it's burning low, only miss the sun when it starts to snow, only know you love her when you let her go," according to one popular song. New residents of Brasilia and other planned cities miss the organic spaces found in cities that arose naturally. People recently transplanted to Alaska or St. Petersburg pine for ample sunlight to view the crystalline sheen of icicles and the glow of freshly fallen winter snow. And many of us here in Shanghai long for hills to picnic on, mountains to climb, scenic overlooks on which to admire the lovely landscape beneath, cliffs to perch on and survey the world below.

And in this world below, it can hardly be coincidental that almost all cultures and religious traditions see mountains as sacred. In Judaism, Moses is said to have received the Ten Commandments on Mount Sinai. Similarly, Christians believe that Jesus transfigured himself on Mount Tabor and preached his most important sermon on another mountain. Yet another mountain, Mount Olympus, was believed by the ancient Greeks to have been the abode of their gods, the most powerful of whom, Zeus, was supposedly born in a cave on Mount Ida. Meanwhile, modern Greek Orthodoxy reveres Mount Athos. Another country with an ancient history, China has numerous holy mountains for Buddhism and Daoism and their various sects. On the other side of the world, the Klamath tribes of present-day California believed the spirit of the above-world descended from heaven to live on Mount Shasta.

But if a movie producer created such a numinous summit smack in the middle of Shanghai's concrete jungle, a retreat of lush forests and blooming flowers as if the Garden of Eden had been recreated amidst the bustling streets, office parks, and sterile luxury apartments of our metropolis, many of us would laugh at the incongruity of it and write it off as just another attempt to captivate an audience with something implausible. For this reason, you can imagine how spellbound I was when I stumbled upon just such a place, a seeming sacred hill, almost at my back door.

After moving to SISU a few years ago, I was transporting some antiques to my new home, and my van whizzed past a lovely wooded hill ascending discordantly out of a sea of highways, office buildings, and high rises. Intrigued beyond comprehension, I quickly jotted down the nearest street corner and returned shortly after I had finished all my unpacking and rearranging. I discovered that the hill was fenced off like a low-security prison. I asked all the people I came across how to get in, and I got conflicting information, blank stares, or was told it was a military property off-limits to civilians. I finally came to this construction maze where a passerby said I could make my ingress, and it seemed very dubious; there was a long walk to a very unobtrusive entrance, and the whole time I expected some officious Chinese guard to jump out at me with "*Ni zhao shei*" ("Who are you looking for?") or "*Ni you shen me shi qing*" ("What business do you have here?"). But to my astonishment I walked unmolested into this paradise, this hill of lush forests, butterflies, birds, beautiful sounds and fragrances. It was like Dorothy trading in black-and-white Kansas for Oz in color, like finding Narnia in a wardrobe or Prester John in Avalon. There were many utterly incompatible scenes — verdant trees against a backdrop of cranes and high rises. Birds and butterflies perched on blooming shrubs only partly occluding the world of cement and glass in the foreground, like Valhalla behind William Blake's "dark, Satanic mills." Juxtaposition on steroids.

This farfetched reality, I discovered, was called Yuexiushan or Guangdong Elegant Garden. It was named after a street it bordered, and they'd imported semi-tropical trees and shrubs in honor of its name. After searching for it on Google, Yahoo, and Baidu and finding nothing relevant, I wondered if it was all a figment of my overactive imagination. Asia has, after all, many sacred places that are mere allegories, like Agartha, Shangri-La, and Shambhala. Even the Daoist heaven-grottos are sometimes literal physical locations and other times are portrayed as metaphors.

Metaphor or reality, I wasted no time in telling all my friends about it. No one I told about it had been even vaguely aware that Shanghai had such a hidden gem. Several friends clamored for me to take them so that they could see with their own eyes that Shanghai did indeed have such a bewitchingly wondrous place. So when I set out the second time with a friend, it was with a bit of trepidation, lest we arrive and discover that no such location existed in the real world. But, to my relief, everything was just as it had been a week and a half before. The hill was neither a parable nor a dream; it existed in this dimension, its physical reality as palpable as the asphalt and steel world that encompassed it.

My friend and I enjoyed one of the most idyllic afternoons in our lifetimes hiking through this arcadian retreat from our daily lives. We walked through bucolic forests. We sat in picturesque pavilions and admired the site and fragrance of the flowers that surrounded us. We climbed to the top and stood transfixed by the sight of the city of Shanghai down below us in another world.

Obviously I was overjoyed to have finally found my "rural" escape within the city. I was convinced that this place would be my hideaway to recharge the battery of my soul as long as I lived in Shanghai. I plotted out picnics, hikes, gatherings with friends, plans to watch the sun rise and set from the top of the hill. It felt too good to be true. And, finally, in a sense, it was. You can easily imagine my chagrin when I brought another friend to my secret garden and saw that the gate that had been my entry was now locked up. Perseveringly, I brought him around to the other side, and we scaled the wall, and I was back in paradise. But this taste of paradise was very short-lived. Two guards soon approached us and reprimanded us for climbing the wall. They told us that the hill had been bought by the military and was no longer open to the public. Commanding us never to return, they escorted us out of the hill and soundly latched the gate behind us.

Understandably, I mourned the loss of my little paradise. But, as the saying goes, when one door to happiness closes, another opens. Shortly after my door to happiness at Yuexiushan was bolted shut, I moved to a new home in the far north of Shanghai. It wasn't long before I discovered the Wusong Wetlands Park, a delightful tract of marshes, ponds, grassy lawns, flowers, streams, woods, river banks, and, yes … a little hill overlooking it all. So now I have a new land of bliss to escape to, and like my old paradise, my new one is just as incongruous and just as much a product of magical realism in this city we call home.

About the Author:

Peter Andrew Christianson, American, studied Chinese and international relations for his undergraduate degree at the University of Minnesota, while his two Master's degrees from the University of London were in history. He taught at several other universities in China before coming to SISU where he currently teaches at the School of English Studies.

失而复得的上海天堂

Peter Andrew Christianson（美国）

张宏雨　译

梁晓雪　审校

通常，小说家和电影制片人会营造出一些或优美、或煽情、或怀旧、或奇异的场景来吸引读者或观众。有时，他们借用魔幻现实主义使观众着迷；有时，为了迎合观众的口味，他们刻意设计出的场景太过离奇，导致读者或观众感到困惑不解，难以置信，无法完全投入到故事中。每当作家运用这种手法时，亚马逊或其他类似网站上的评论都会将其作品批得体无完肤。那么多的读者都希望自己读到的时代和地点有真实感，与现实相符，而不是为了取悦读者而营造出的虚假仙境。

在现代化的上海生活，寻觅美和神秘之所在十分重要。我们生活在水泥森林之中，高楼、公寓、商场及摩天大厦远无边际——其实并不远，因为这些庞然大物几乎完全阻挡了我们的视线。很多人都向往能与大自然亲密接触的地方，或者怀念过去那个简单、机械化程度低的美好年代。然而，在这无尽蔓延的钢筋水泥中，伊甸园的浪漫和神秘已所剩无几。

更别提上海的地貌就像一张铺开的书法卷轴，平坦无比。我有一些朋友已经离开了，主要是因为他们想念爬山的乐趣，而上海单调乏味的地形并不能让他们满意。诗人和歌词作者对“失去时才懂得珍惜”这种心态都有过诗意的表达，一首流行歌曲唱道：“火烧尽时你才需要火光；雪开始下时你才想念阳光；放手之后你才发现自己深爱着她。”在巴西利亚等事先规划的城市，新来的居民们都非常想念自然形成的、有机的城市空间。那些最近移居至阿拉斯加或圣彼得堡的人往往对充足的阳光充满渴求，因为他们想要看到反射着阳光的冰柱以及日光照耀下的雪花。而在上海居住的我们则渴望有山坡可供野炊，有高山可供攀爬，有观景台可供我们欣赏一览无余的美妙景色，有悬崖峭壁可供我们攀岩并领略山下的世界。

而在这山下的世界里，几乎所有的文化和宗教传统都视“山”为神圣之地，这绝非偶然。在犹太教中，摩西领受十诫的故事发生在西奈山上。同样，基督教徒认为耶稣是在他泊山上显灵，并在另一座山上进行了他最重要的一次布道。古希腊人认为奥林匹斯山是众神的栖身之所，且众神之父宙斯出生在艾达山一个洞穴里。希腊现代东正教敬畏阿索斯圣山。中国，作为一个同样拥有悠久历史的国家，有着不计其数与佛教、道教及其教派相关的圣山。在世界的另一边，历史上的美洲克拉马斯族原住民（居住在现加利福尼亚地区）认为，上神们的灵魂是从天堂降临到沙士达山上。

但是，如果一位电影制片人在上海这样一个水泥森林的中心创造出一座超自然的山脉，山上绿树如荫，鲜花盛开，就好像在熙攘的街道、办公园区以及奢华的公寓楼之中腾空而出一个伊甸园，这种不协调会让我们感到好笑，会觉得这是制片人为了吸引观众所进行的又一个荒谬尝试。正是因为这个原因，你可以想象，当我在上海偶然发现一个类似圣山的地方几乎坐落在我家后方时，我是多么地震惊！

几年前，我搬到了上海外国语大学的公寓楼。我开车将收藏的古董运到新家，面包车呼啸而过，经过一座郁郁葱葱的秀丽小山，这座山蜿蜒而上，与周围的高速公路、商务楼还有高层建筑格格不入。这般景象让我大为不解，于是我匆匆记下附近的街道名称，在把古董放进新家整理好后，我很快就回到了这个地方。我发现，这座山被栅栏隔起来了，像是一座处于低警戒状态的监狱。我向每一个过路人询问如何进去，可是，他们要么给出前后矛盾的回答，要么就是一脸茫然，还有人告诉我那是军事基地，普通人不得进入。终于，在这座迷宫某处，一位路人告诉我可从这里进入，我将信将疑，走了很久才看到一个毫不起眼的入口。一路上，我一直在等着某个警卫突然跳出来问我："你找谁？你有什么事情？"然而，让我惊讶的是，我一路无阻地走进这个天堂，山上绿树葱茏、鸟语花香、蝴蝶翩翩起飞——就像桃乐茜在奥兹国历险，像在衣柜中发现纳尼亚王国，或在阿瓦隆发现祭司王约翰。这里的美景与周围背景形成鲜明对比——青葱的大树掩映在起重机和高楼之中，鸟儿与蝴蝶嬉戏于鲜花盛开的灌木丛中，灌木丛只能部分遮住后面的水泥玻璃建筑，就像在威廉·布莱克所描述的“黑色的、撒旦的工厂”后面发现瓦尔哈拉殿堂[1]，真是巨大的反差。

我发现这个远离现实的地方名为粤秀山，又名粤秀花园，是根据它邻近的一条街命名的，为了使它名副其实，人们运来亚热带的树木和灌木种植于此。我在谷歌、雅虎、百度上查询此地，一无所获。于是我想，这会不会只是我想得太多而产生的幻觉。毕竟在亚洲，有很多神圣的地方都只是出现在传说中，例如阿加尔塔[2]、香格里拉、香巴拉王国。甚至道教传说中的石窟也是亦真亦幻，一会儿真实存在，一会儿又杳无踪迹。

不管是真实还是虚幻，我都迫不及待地将这一发现告诉了我所有的朋友。所有人都表示，他们还从未听说过上海还有这样一块不为人知的宝地。有几个人吵着让我带他们去亲眼见识一下，以确认上海确实有这样一个神奇的地方。当我和我的一位朋友再一次前往此地时，我感到些许恐惧，担心当我们到达时，会发现它并不存在。不过，当看到一切照旧时，我顿时如释重负。这座小山实实在在地矗立在此，就像它周围的柏油马路与钢筋世界一样，不是幻觉，也不是梦境。

田园般的山间令人忘却俗世，我和我的朋友在这里度过了人生中最惬意的一个下午。我们坐在如画般的亭子里歇息，欣赏美景，沉迷于花香之中。我们爬到山顶，俯瞰城市风光，又被山脚下的另一番景象深深震撼。

显而易见，我终于在这座城市里找到了能让我远离喧嚣的“桃源”，我为此欢欣不已。我相信，只要我在上海，这个地方便是我的灵魂休憩之地。我开始计划在此野炊、徒步、和友人相聚，在山顶看日落日出。一切简直美好得不像是真的！果真，从某种意义上

1 北欧神话中主神兼死亡之神奥丁接待英灵的殿堂。
2 传说中居住在地心的文明。

说，这份美好幻灭了。有一天，我带另一位朋友来到我的秘密花园，却发现它的入口被锁了起来，我内心的失望与难过溢于言表。我不死心，带他到另一侧，我们发现有堵围墙，于是翻了过去，终于又重新回到这个天堂。然而好景不长，很快就有两名保安向我们走来，斥责我们的翻墙行为，他们告诫说，这片地方已被军队买下，不对公众开放，让我们不要再来。他们把我们送出园区，之后就重重地锁上了我们身后的大门。

你可以想见我的万分惋惜之情。不过，古话说："当上帝为你关上一道通往幸福的门时，会为你打开另一扇窗。"在我失去我的快乐之地粤秀山后不久，我搬到了上海北边的新家。很快，我便发现了吴淞湿地公园，那里有宜人的沼泽、池塘、草坪、鲜花、溪流、绿树、河岸以及……一座小山，能俯览园内一切景色。现在，我又有一片可以逃离喧嚣的世外桃源了，正如同我之前的人间天堂一样，它矗立在一片繁华与喧闹之中，与周围的景象形成鲜明的对比；我们以上海为家，而吴淞湿地公园就是这座城市里一个魔幻般的现实存在。

作者简介：

Peter Andrew Christianson，美国籍，本科在明尼苏达大学就读汉语和国际关系专业，后来获得英国伦敦大学文化史和历史学双硕士学位，目前在上海外国语大学英语学院担任教师。

Happiness Trail

Romain Vuattoux (France)

Proofread by George Fleming

Happiness Trail, Linfen, Jing'an, Shanghai

Jing'an recently grew bigger by merging Zhabei District and the former Jing'an District. What is to discover in the newly acquired parts of Jing'an? Off the beaten path of downtown Jing'an, Linfen Sub-district is located in the north of the district (former Zhabei District). Linfen is not directly accessible by metro, but is well serviced by buses, and can conveniently be reached with the new "Mobike" bike sharing systems. Linfen's Happiness Trail is not a famous tourist scenic walk that is publicized to foreign tourists (or even to the Chinese ones), but the trail offers several wonders for those curious to visit the authentic neighborhoods of Shanghai, and can be a great learning place for all interested in urban planning or simply for those who wish to learn about the "real" Shanghai.

The Happiness Trail will let you walk through the life of ordinary neighborhoods of Shanghai. However, these ordinary neighborhoods are perhaps not so ordinary as they appear. They are in fact a great example of how the local government works to improve the daily life of the residents. From children to elderly, no one is left behind in the neighborhood planning. For all civil servants and urban planners who are looking at innovative ways to improve their towns or cities, Linfen may be a place of interest. In fact, Linfen is considered a model sub-district, and has a great reputation in Shanghai.

If you live in Shanghai, it can be a great place to learn how your neighborhood works and what kind of life is offered to ordinary Shanghai residents. Linfen's local government and its volunteers have been working tirelessly for years before, since and after the Shanghai Expo, to give meaning to the "Better City, Better Life" motto of the Expo. During the Expo, the neighborhood hosted several delegations and offered home-stays for tourists, and it still does today.

I started at 353 Linfen Road, which is at the center of the trail, and then was taken on a guided tour. The trail takes you through the neighborhood, where you can use your phone to scan QR codes that will give you information about your surroundings.

Aijian Neighborhood

A few things can be learnt here about community management. Members of the neighborhood committee are in every compound in Shanghai, and they are the people that make sure that everything runs smoothly in a neighborhood. In Linfen the team has 5 elected members and dozens of volunteers that can address issues seven days a week during working hours. These neighborhood committee members have 6 particular tasks to accomplish (such as visiting residents when they have a serious illness or if any unexpected problem occurs in their family). In the neighborhood, one of the building's ground floors offers a multi-function room, available (free of charge) to all residents, and easily accessible (handrails have been set up along the hallway for those who have trouble walking). The communal room is a place where residents can come and meet each other for tea, to play cards, or organize activities such as reading discussion groups or calligraphy. The room is air-conditioned for the hot days of summer, or cool days of winter, and is also used once a month to celebrate all the birthdays of the elderly people in the neighborhood. A psychologist and a retired volunteer medical doctor come once a week to answer questions and check on residents.

The neighborhood is kept clean and maintained with the help of the local authorities. When I visited the trail, communal parts (staircases) of the residential buildings were being renovated (cleaned and repainted), at a very small cost to the residents, thanks to the sponsorship of the government. The government paid 28,000 RMB on top of the 2,000 RMB given by the residents (100 RMB per family).

Shanghai Expo Family and Charity Shop

The trail continued with a visit to Chen Shuchu's apartment. Mr Chen is one of the home-stay families that have continued to host people from all over the world since the Shanghai Expo. He will welcome you in his comfortable home, host you with a traditional Chinese warm welcome for "guests from afar" and share his memories while vaunting the merits of his beloved Shanghai.

The neighborhood is also experimenting with a charity shop. The idea behind the shop is to have people donate certain items that are then sold to collect money for the poor and needy of the neighborhood. I was told that improvements were sought. This is an experiment and as is often the case with the local governments in China, improvements are found through trial and error.

Harmonious Neighborhood

The next neighborhood is the "Harmonious Neighbourhood" where you can find another communal room that is used for dancing and other activities by different groups each day. There again, the residents have decided to decorate the hallways of their buildings. The cables that often hang loose in the hallways in Shanghai's old buildings have all been placed in pipes, and new handrails and plants have been installed in the hallways. The upgrades were very affordable to the residents, providing them with simple solutions that improve their living environment and quality of life. Unlike many of the "upgrades" that happen in other places around Shanghai, these do not require the complete destruction of the neighborhood and displacement of its residents. The neighborhood, as most others in Shanghai, is also equipped with bulletin boards where information about activities' schedules can be shared and newspapers are replaced daily, so that residents who do not use the Internet can remain informed.

Community Service Center

The newly renovated community service center centralizes all the services that residents of the sub-district need. From housing registrations to social security, unemployment registration, medical expense reimbursement… staff are able to answer most of the questions in one location, instead of going to several offices as was previously the case.

Youth Center Library

Next stop on the trail we have the Youth Center Library, which is a part of a network of libraries that include the big Shanghai Library. Residents can enjoy the very bright and comfortable library, tucked inside a comfortable corner of one of the neighborhoods, surrounded by greenery. The kids' playing room is super clean and full of fun, and makes you want to return to your childhood to enjoy it. The library offers multimedia rooms and reading rooms. All sorts of cultural activities are organized (free of charge again). The list is long, but some of the most popular ones are: blogging, presentations about traditional tea culture or traditional fashion, cooking classes, reading groups and performances organized by local groups… A café is planned to be set up outside of the small youth center, and will definitely make this space one of the most wonderful libraries of Shanghai.

Community Recreation Center

Mr Li is a passionate and dedicated director of the center; he will proudly provide all the information that makes his center a top-rated facility. All sorts of activities are offered (free or at below market rates). Mr Li is rightfully proud to show the awards he has received for the management and transparency of the center. As he disapprovingly picked up a cigarette butt left on the floor by a user of the center, he explained that popular activities are monitored, and unpopular ones are replaced with new ones. An "innovation room" for kids and teenagers offers activities where the young can experience building all sorts of fascinating toys, practice their basic engineering skills with all sorts of safe equipment, learn how to cook, or even print in 3D. There is of course a ping pong room, a gym and another library. Some rooms cater to various activities (dance hall and theater), and there is even a movie theater which shows movies for only 2 yuan daily (twice a day during the summer). Some cartoons are played for kids in the morning while the parents can go and do some sport. A summer camp is organized and supervised by university volunteers and the nursery is so popular that Mr Li is trying to find new ways to satisfy the long list of parents who wish to join. It seems that Mr Li is limited only by the space he has available to him, but his creativity reaches beyond these walls.

Community Renewal

The last part of the trail takes you into the most recently upgraded neighborhood. There, buildings have not been torn down to start from scratch, but the path and green spaces have been redesigned to improve access, and the sidewalks have been equipped with a soft walking path for more pleasant roaming around.

Linfen is a lively neighborhood, and much like any living organism it is constantly changing. Although Linfen would appear to be an ordinary neighborhood to a passer-by, it is far from a boring neighborhood for its residents and neighbors. It is a dynamic area that is full of life and filled with activities for its residents and district neighbors. The trail will help you gain a sense of the efforts made by dedicated and passionate staff and volunteers of the local government to make their place comfortable for all.

Information Center: 2nd floor, 353 Linfen Road

Where to start the trail: 1915 Changzhong Road

Directions: Metro Line 1, Pengpu Xincun Station or bus stop at Gonghexin Road & Wenxi Road

Nearest bus stops: 206, 850, 118, 597, 745, 749, 812, 850, 912

Contacts: for a guided tour, contact Stella, 13816983328

Special Note: *Thanks to Yang Chao and all the kind people at the "Happiness Trail" for answering my many questions and taking the time to show me around.*

About the author:

Romain Vuattoux, French, studied International Relations for his Bachelor Degree in Canada, then worked in China from 2007 to 2011 (2010–11 at SISU). He then studied Sustainable Urban Management at Malmo University in Sweden for his graduate degree before returning to SISU in 2013. He has a deep-rooted interest in urban sustainability.

幸福之路——社区体验之旅

Romain Vuattoux（法国）

梁晓雪　译

上海静安区临汾社区的“幸福之路”

自从上海的闸北区和静安区合并后，新静安的面积变大了很多。在这片新并入的地域，我们能发现什么呢？沿着静安区中心街道前行，就来到了坐落在北部的临汾社区（位于原闸北区）。这里没有直达的地铁，却有发达的公交系统，你也可以骑着时下流行的摩拜单车抵达这里。临汾社区的“幸福之路”并非什么著名的景点，并不被外国游客（甚至是中国游客）熟知，然而在这里，游客们可以满足他们的好奇心，近距离观察上海老百姓的日常生活；同时，对于那些对城市规划感兴趣或渴望了解“真实的”上海的人们来说，这里也是绝佳的学习场所。

“幸福之路”引领你走入上海寻常人家。然而，这些街头邻里并不像看上去那么普通——实际上，他们是当地政府提高民生的鲜明典范。社区规划考虑了老老少少在内所有人的利益。对那些有意采取创新方式以改善民生的政府官员和城市规划师来说，临汾社区是一个可资借鉴的参考。实际上，临汾社区是这方面的模范社区，在上海享有盛名。

如果你住在上海，你可以在此地更好地了解街道办事处是如何运作的，上海老百姓是如何生活的。自举办上海世博会以来，临汾路街道办事处及其志愿者们就在不懈努力实现世博会的口号“城市，让生活更美好”。世博会期间，临汾社区接待了许多代表团，并且常常以家庭为单位接待外国游客，这一做法延续至今。

跟随着导游，我从幸福之路的中心——临汾路353号——开启了这次旅程。沿着幸福之路可以穿过整个社区，沿途还可用手机扫描二维码，获取周边信息。

爱建新家园

在爱建新家园，你可以了解到不少关于社区管理的情况。上海各地都有居委会，他们的工作就是确保社区内的一切井然有序。临汾居委会有五位当选委员以及数十位志愿者，他们周一到周日工作，处理社区的大小事务，其中包括六项具体的任务（如探访病重居民或家中有突发状况的居民）。社区居民楼的一楼有个多功能室，对所有居民免费开放，进出十分方便（过道安装了扶手，以帮助行走不便的人）。在公共活动室里，居民可以喝茶、打牌或组织活动，如读书小组和书法小组。屋内设有空调，冬暖夏凉，每个月还会为社区内所有过生日的老人举办庆祝活动。此外，还有心理咨询师及已退休的医生志愿者每周来一次，为居民进行检查和答疑。

社区环境非常干净，这与当地政府的勤于维护是分不开的。我参观时，正值居民楼的公共楼道进行整修（包括清洁和维修）。政府对此类工程予以补贴，资助了28000元，而全体居民总共只需支付2000元（平均每户才100元）。

世博人家和幸福超市

我们参观的下一站是陈叔楚（音译）的家。陈先生的家温馨舒适，自上海世博会起就一直接待外国游客。陈先生会用传统的待客之道迎接远道而来的朋友，分享他的回忆，并和客人们介绍他所热爱的上海。

社区还有一个正在试运营的“幸福超市”，这里会义卖人们捐赠的物品，义卖所得将捐赠给社区里经济上有需要的人。他们告诉我，这一举措将在未来进一步完善。中国的地方政府还有许多类似的创新举措，他们在不断摸索中逐步完善提高。

美丽楼组

我们参观的下一站是“美丽楼组”，小区里有一个公共活动室，每天有不同的社团在此组织活动，包括舞蹈社。这里的楼道也被整修过，上海老公房过道中常见的松垂下来的电线被统一收纳到了管道里，此外还安装了新的扶手，放置了绿植。整修费用对居民来说并不昂贵，但居民的居住环境及生活质量却通过以上这些简单举措得以改善。和周边地区的“整修”不同，这里的整修并不需要大兴土木或劳师动众。和上海其他地方一样，这里的社区也有公告栏，告知社区活动的日程安排。这里还会更新每天的报纸，这样一来，不怎么用互联网的人也可以及时了解时事要闻。

社区事务受理服务中心

装饰一新的社区事务受理服务中心集中提供所有居民需要的服务，从房屋登记到社保、失业登记、医疗费报销……在这里，居民可以得到几乎所有问题的解答，而不需要为办一件事而跑好几个地方。

青春社区和少儿图书馆

接下来我们参观了青春社区和少儿图书馆。这里的图书馆坐落在绿树成荫的社区一隅，与上海图书馆联网，居民们可以在明亮、舒适的图书馆里阅读。孩子们的游戏室非常干净，充满欢乐，令人禁不住渴望重回孩提时代。图书馆提供多媒体室和阅览室，还举办各种各样的文化活动（仍然是免费的）。这里的文化活动种类繁多，最受欢迎的包括：写博客、传统茶文化/服饰展示、烹饪班、阅读小组以及当地团组的表演。青春社区外面还将设一个咖啡馆，这必将使这里成为上海最棒的图书馆之一。

社区文化活动中心

李先生是社区文化活动中心的主任，他充满热情，兢兢业业，可以自豪地列举出这里作为上海最佳活动中心之一的种种理由。这里定期举办丰富多彩的文化活动（仍然是免费的，或者远低于市场价）。李先生完全有理由为他们过去所获得的各种奖项自豪，因为这里管理有方、机制透明。他有些不悦地捡起地上一截丢弃的烟头，解释道，所有受大众欢迎的活动都被组织得井井有条，不那么受欢迎的活动很快就会被新的活动取代。专门针对青少年开设的“创新教室”提供了有趣的玩具和安全的器械，帮助孩子们锻炼手工技能、学习烹饪，甚至进行3D打印。当然，这里还有乒乓室、健身房以及图书馆。有些房间作为多功能厅，可以举行多种活动（如舞蹈厅和剧院）。这里甚至还有个影院，每天放映一部电影，门票只要两元（夏天每天放映两部电影）。早上，孩子们可以来看动画片，这期间家长可以去运动健身。中心还提供夏令营活动，主要由大学生志愿者组织。亲子园也十分火爆，李先生说他正在想办法让更多尚在排队报名的家庭加入。看起来，尽管场地有限，但李先生的创新力是无限的。

美丽家园

最后，我们来到了新整修过的居民区。这里的楼并没有被拆掉重建，但道路和绿化带都被重新设计了一下，以便行人通行。道路两边增加了步道，人们可以在天气好的时候散步。

临汾是个充满活力的社区，就像很多生活区一样，它也在不断变化。尽管对于普通路人来说，这里并不显眼，但是对住在这里和周边的居民来说，它充满意趣。“幸福之路”一行让游客充分体会到当地政府的工作人员和志愿者为改善民生而付出的诸多努力。

信息中心：临汾路353号二楼

游览起点：场中路1915号

交通指南：地铁一号线彭浦新村站或共和新路闻喜路公交站

附近公交：206、850、118、597、745、749、812、850、912路

联系方式：向导Stella，13816983328

特别鸣谢：感谢杨超（音译）以及所有耐心回答我问题、花时间带领我游览“幸福之路”的人。

作者简介：

Romain Vuattoux，法国籍，在加拿大获得国际关系本科学位，2007年至2011年在中国工作（其中2010年至2011年在上海外国语大学工作）。之后他在瑞典马尔默大学攻读硕士（城市可持续管理），随后于2013年返回上海外国语大学工作至今。他对于城市可持续发展有浓厚的兴趣。

The Hungarian Architect Who Escaped to Shanghai

Anna Pikó (Hungary)

Proofread by George Fleming

When I go to a new city, I like to capture its spirit through its arts including music, paintings, photos, movies, literature, watching the behavior of people, their gestures, how they spend their free time, the communications between them, the food, and the beauty of its old and new architecture. I have seen so many old houses and new buildings in this city. I especially like to wander from Yan'an Road W. to Nanjing Road W.

In my eyes, Shanghai is a magical place with its brilliant hues and enthusiastic people. I feel something unspeakable, amazing, and I feel it is very familiar to me. If I had to name the building that I like the most, or that most resonates with me, it might be the Hubertus Court (today the Metropolo, Jinjiang Hotels) on Yan'an Road W. (918-928), designed by a Hungarian, completed in 1937. The Hubertus Court was built as an investment by Hubertus Properties, of which the architect Laszlo Hudec was director. The Hudec family occupied the ground floor apartment from 1937 until their departure from Shanghai in 1947. Many features of this striking modern building were lost during its conversion to the Metropolo Hotel, including the original entrance and large garden.

Courtesy of Anna Pikó

Hudec's work — living at the crossroads between China and Europe, spanning nearly 30 years of Shanghai's economic and cultural "glory days" — includes the first skyscraper in Asia. His life story gives an extraordinary inside look at the first rush of Europeans to China, of its first modernization and of the turmoil of the 20th century. At the beginning of the last century Shanghai was a melting pot of different cultures with at least 20 non-Chinese nationalities and architectural styles. Hudec was proficient in all kinds of architectural styles such as Gothic, Eclectic, Neo-Classical, Modern Art Deco, Tudor, American Colonial, etc. His projects included schools, colleges, universities, churches, chapels, halls, hotels, private homes, apartment buildings, row-houses, residences, garages, banks, clubs, office buildings, commercial buildings, hospitals, theatres and weekend houses. Several of his plans and designs were award winners. That was the most interesting period of his architectural work in Shanghai. He designed the tallest building in the Far East, the 22-storey Park Hotel (1931–34) on Shanghai's marshy ground with a high-speed elevator, air-conditioning system and ball room. He was also charged with designing and constructing the city's largest theater, the 2,500-seat Grand Theater (1931–33).

Hugyecz László Ede (1893–1958, later L. E. Hudec) was born in the town of Besztercebanya in Zolyom County of the Austro-Hungarian Empire (now in Slovakia) on the 3rd of January in 1893. His nationalities were Hungarian and Slovak. In his early years he worked with his father, a famous master builder. He studied architecture at the Royal Joseph Technical University in Budapest between 1910 and 1914. Hudec's Beaux-Arts training at the university equipped him with the fundamentals of Classical Architecture, the style and knowledge of European building design and construction becoming the foundation of his lifelong work.

In 1914, at the beginning of WWI, he was enlisted in the Royal Hungarian Army. He was captured by Cossacks on the Russian battlefront, then lived as prisoner of war in a Siberian camp in Habarovsk, then in Krasnaya Rechka. In 1918, after an adventurous trip he escaped, making his way through Harbin to Shanghai.

Initially in Shanghai his intention was to earn money to get back home. Here his name became *Hudec* after the spelling of his original name *Hugyecz*'s pronunciation, rewriting from Cyrillic to Latin letter by letter.

Hudec joined the American architectural firm of Rowland A. Curry. He arrived in Shanghai at the beginning of his career, coinciding with the city entering its most dynamic decades. At this time Shanghai was undergoing its first development boom and their office became the busiest in the city.

In 1920, after WWI, when the Treaty of Versailles was signed, the Austro-Hungarian Empire was dismembered, and Hudec's hometown Besztercebanya became part of the new Czechoslovakia. Given the dire economic situation in Hungary and his comfortable life in Shanghai, he decided to remain on a permanent basis since he was becoming a well-known architect. Following the collapse of the Austro-Hungarian Monarchy, he had no consular protection and was completely at a loss as to how to maintain his citizenship status. In the 1920s a lot of Hungarians lived in Shanghai. Most of them had the same problem.

Courtesy of Anna Pikó

In 1925, Hudec founded an architectural firm and opened his own practice in Shanghai. His work was extremely wide-ranging. His clients included the members of the international expatriate community (Americans, Germans, Hungarians, Britons, etc.) and lots of Chinese customers. Following a trip to the United States in 1927–28, Hudec turned whole-heartedly towards Art Deco and Modernism, designing some of Shanghai's most memorable buildings of the period. He went on to become one of the most celebrated and prolific architects in Shanghai, where between 1918 and 1947, he designed over 70 major buildings. In addition to these projects, he designed several hundred buildings and supervised their construction. Most of them are still standing today.

After the Munich Agreement in 1938, Hungary reoccupied former territories before WWII, then Hudec received Hungarian citizenship and was issued a permanent passport. Between 1942 and 1945, Hudec used his position as honorary consul in Shanghai to save many Central European Jews from the Shanghai ghetto as he disapproved of their persecution. Despite great pressure from the German Nazis and the Japanese as well, he always maintained his independence in this regard. He protected the Jews and Central Europeans including Hungarians in Shanghai without reference to religious difference despite the risk to his own safety.

He lived in Shanghai with his German wife, Gisela Meyer, and their three children in houses designed by himself at 17 Lucerne Road and 57 Columbia Road before moving to an apartment in the Hubertus Court in 1937. Hudec left Shanghai in 1947 with his family for the United States.

Here is a list of Hudec's most memorable works:

1) American Club, 1925 — 209 Fuzhou Road

2) Avenue Apartments, 1930 — 1383 Beijing Road W.

3) Beudin House, 1920 — 150 Fenyang Road

4) Columbia Circle, 1920s — Lane 329 Xinhua Road
5) Country Hospital, 1926 — Yan'an Road W.
6) Estrella Apartments, 1927 — Corner of Ruijin Road and Huaihai Road M.
7) Grand Theatre, 1933 — 216 Nanjing Road W.
8) Houses on Rue Ratard, 1920 — 852-892 Julu Road
9) Hubertus Court, 1937 — 918 Yan'an Road W.
10) Hudec House, 1933 — 127 Panyu Road
11) Chen House, 1924 — 675 Julu Road
12) China Baptist Publication Building (CBPB), 1932 — 209 Yuanmingyuan Road
13) Christian Literature Building (CLB), 1930 — 128 Huqiu Road
14) Joint Savings Society (JSS) Building, 1927 — 261 Sichuan Road M.
15) Katz House, 1918 — 457 Shaanxi Road N.
16) Liberty Apartments, 1934 — 258 Wuyuan Road
17) Madier House, 1922 — 79 Fenyang Road
18) Moore Memorial Church, 1931 — 316 Xizang Road M.
19) Park Hotel, 1934 — 170 Nanjing Road W.
20) Sun Ke House, 1920s — 22 Panyu Road
21) The Normandie, 1924 — 1858 Huaihai Road M.
22) Wu House, 1938 — 333 Tongren Road

About the author:

Anna Pikó, Hungarian, studied Chinese Language and Literature at Beijing University and Hungarian Language and Literature, Sinology and Linguistics at Eötvös Loránd University in Budapest. She taught Hungarian Language and Culture at SISU from February 2017 to June 2019.

逃亡至上海的匈牙利建筑师

Anna Pikó（匈牙利）
梁晓雪　译

每当我到达一个新城市，我都会通过以下方式了解这座城市的底蕴：音乐、绘画、照片、电影、书籍、当地人的行为举止、消遣方式、沟通交流、食物以及新老建筑。我在上海见到了很多新老建筑，我尤其喜欢从延安西路漫步到南京西路。

在我眼中，上海是一个神奇的地方，有着灿烂的色彩和热情的人民。其令人惊叹之处，无法用言辞表达，也让我感觉似曾相识。如果说哪座建筑我最喜欢、最能触动我的内心，那应该是延安西路918–928号的达华公寓（现锦江都城达华酒店）。它是由匈牙利人邬达克设计的，于1937年竣工。这座建筑是达华地产投资的，这是邬达克自己的地产公司。自1937年开始，邬达克家族就在达华公寓底层居住，直到1947年离开上海。这座极具现代风格的建筑后来被改造成为达华酒店，改造期间抹去了很多早先的建筑特色，包括极具创意的入口以及大花园。

邬达克的作品融合了中欧两地建筑的特点，横跨上海近30年经济文化的光辉岁月，邬达克还缔造了亚洲第一座摩天大厦。他的人生经历让我们得以了解欧洲人来中国的第一波热潮、上海迈向现代化的步伐以及20世纪的动荡时局。20世纪初，上海是不同文化的大熔炉，至少汇集了20个国家的建筑风格，而邬达克在不同风格之间切换，游刃有余：哥特式、折中主义、新古典主义、现代装饰主义、都铎式、北美殖民地风格等。他承接的项目包括小学、学院、大学、教堂、小教堂、礼堂、酒店、私人住宅、公寓楼、排屋、民居、车库、银行、俱乐部、办公楼、商业楼、医院、剧场及度假村。他的不少设计方案和作品收获了奖项。这个时期也是他建筑生涯的黄金时期。他在上海的泥沼地面上设计建造了当时远东最高的建筑：22层高的国际饭店（1931–1934），里面装有高速电梯、空调系统及舞厅。他还负责设计重建这座城市最大的剧院——能容纳2 500人的大光明电影院（1931–1933）。

1893年1月3日，拉斯洛·埃德·胡杰茨（1893–1958，后改名为拉斯洛·邬达克）出生于奥匈帝国泽尔伊欧姆省的拜斯特尔采巴尼亚（现位于斯洛伐克共和国境内），曾先后拥有匈牙利和斯洛伐克两种国籍。早年的他跟随建筑师父亲工作，1910至1914年间，他在布达佩斯的皇家约瑟夫理工大学学习建筑。通过大学期间的学院派训练，他培养了深厚的古典建筑学基础，掌握了欧洲建筑设计风格及知识，这为他一生的职业奠定了基础。

1914年正值一战爆发，他加入了匈牙利皇家军队。在俄国前线，他被俄国哥萨克骑兵俘虏，先是被送到西伯利亚的哈巴罗夫斯克战俘营，后又被送至红列奇卡。1918年，在一次转移途中，他冒险出逃，取道哈尔滨来到上海。

起初，他打算在上海赚够回家的路费就离开。他按照“胡杰茨”的发音，将名字中的西里尔字母改为拉丁字母，给自己取了个新名字：邬达克。

邬达克进入美国建筑师罗兰·A. 克利开设的克利洋行工作。他职业生涯之初恰逢上海的经济腾飞阶段，他所在的公司也因此成为当时业务最繁忙的事务所之一。

1920年，一战结束了。奥匈帝国由于《凡尔赛条约》的签署而分崩离析，邬达克的家乡成为新成立的捷克斯洛伐克的一部分。相比匈牙利的经济不景气，上海的生活舒适且惬意。邬达克决定，既然自己已经小有名气，还不如在上海安定下来。伴随着奥匈帝国的瓦解，他失去了领馆的保护，也不知如何维持自己的公民身份。那期间，上海住着很多匈牙利人，他们大多面临着同样的问题。

1925年，邬达克成立并开张了自己的建筑设计事务所。他的业务范围极为广泛，客户不仅包括在中国的外国侨民群体（美国人、德国人、匈牙利人、英国人等），也包括很多中国人。1927年至1928年他去了趟美国，之后他就全心全意地爱上了装饰主义和现代主义艺术，带来了一系列令人瞩目的建筑作品。接下来，他成为上海最著名、最多产的建筑师之一。从1918年至1947年，他共设计了70多座主要建筑，还设计并监工了几百座建筑，其中大多数屹立至今。

1938年《慕尼黑协定》的签订使匈牙利重新夺回二战前的领土，邬达克正式获得匈牙利国籍并得到永久护照。1942年至1945年期间，邬达克作为匈牙利驻上海领事馆的荣誉领事，从上海的犹太人居住区中挽救了许多来自中欧的犹太人。他反对对犹太人的迫害，尽管面临来自德国、日本纳粹的巨大压力，但在这一问题上始终坚持自己的立场。他不顾自身安危，向犹太人、中欧难民（包括在上海的匈牙利人）伸出援手，不管他们有何种宗教信仰。

他和他的德国妻子吉塞拉·迈耶及三个孩子生活在他自己设计的房子内。他们曾数次搬家，居所包括吕西纳路17号及哥伦比亚路57号，最后在1937年住进达华公寓底层，直至1947年携家人离沪赴美。

邬达克最重要的建筑作品包括：

1) 美国总会，1925年，福州路209号
2) 爱文义公寓，1930年，北京西路1383号
3) 盘滕住宅，1920年，汾阳路150号
4) 外国弄堂，20世纪20年代，新华路329弄
5) 宏恩医院，1926年，延安西路
6) 爱司公寓，1927年，瑞金一路和中淮海路路口
7) 大光明电影院，1933年，南京西路216号
8) 巨籁达路住宅，1920年，巨鹿路852–892号

9) 达华公寓，1937年，延安西路918号
10) 邬达克故居，1933年，番禺路127号
11) 爱神花园，1924年，巨鹿路675号
12) 浸信会大楼，1932年，圆明园路209号
13) 广学会大楼，1930年，虎丘路128号
14) 四行储蓄会大楼，1927年，四川中路261号
15) 何东公馆，1918年，陕西北路457号
16) 自由公寓，1934年，五原路258号
17) 法租界公董局总董官邸，1922年，汾阳路79号
18) 沐恩堂，1931年，西藏中路316号
19) 国际饭店，1934年，南京西路170号
20) 孙科住宅，20世纪20年代，番禺路22号
21) 诺曼底公寓，1924年，淮海中路1858号
22) 吴宅，1938年，铜仁路333号

作者简介：

Anna Pikó，匈牙利籍，曾在北京大学就读本科，取得汉语言文学学位，之后在位于布达佩斯的罗兰大学取得匈牙利语教学硕士学位和语言学博士学位，2017年2月至2019年6月在上海外国语大学担任匈牙利语专业教师。

International Bonding Zone — SISU International Faculty Trip to Yangshan Port

George Fleming (UK)

On 27th May 2016 there was a special outing to the Shanghai Free Trade Zone for Shanghai International Studies University's international faculty. We packed onto the bus in the rain at 7:40 in the morning, and set off.

I learned after discussion with several of my fellow faculty that none of us had visited the FTZ — or even the surrounding part of southeast Shanghai — before. Our first port of call was the administrative building of the Shanghai Free Trade Zone United Development Co. Ltd., cutting an imposing but lonely figure against the dreary morning skyline. After a short break to stretch our legs, we piled back on board and continued to

Yangshan Free Trade Port Area. This involved another long journey across the thirty-kilometre Donghai Bridge, straight from the Shanghai mainland southwards to the Yangshan Islands. Travelling along the bridge, we wondered how the lorries hurtling along beside us (and the bridge) would fare on a windy(ier) day. Looking out from the bus windows, we could see some of the fifty wind turbines of the Donghai Bridge Offshore Wind Power Demonstration Project.

As we got out, our phones told us we were in Zhejiang Province — the islands of Yangshan being in Hangzhou Bay, and administered as part of Shengsi County in Hangzhou. The international faculty were also surprised to discover an overlooked section of the Great Wall, which we dutifully “climbed”.

From our vantage point, we looked down at the busy Yangshan Port as Rita Wang from United Development shared some impressive facts and figures about the port, including its fifteen-metre deep-water harbour that allows the latest New Panamax container vessels to moor up, and its connection to over fifty ports in 36 countries via more than eighty shipping routes.

Next on the itinerary was a return to United Development headquarters to learn about the evolution and general policies governing the Free Trade Zone. Rita gave us a presentation called *Succeed in China*, which illustrated the improvements and opening up of the FTZ while offering a candid portrait of the issues that have hampered foreign investment in the past. Previously, businesses came up against restrictions in investment, trade, finance, the role of government, and general red tape. In particular, there was a clear contrast between the slow development pre-2013 and afterwards with the approval of Wholly Foreign-Owned Enterprises, which piqued interest among several international faculty members, and the role of the FTZ as a testing ground for new ideas that can then be rolled out nationwide. *Succeed in China* certainly generated much interest among us, to the extent that there were not enough copies of the accompanying leaflet to go around.

With our minds full of questions, it was time to fill our bellies — and we were not disappointed. We had lunch within charming surroundings at *Shuyuan Renjia*, with beer, red-braised pork, and iceplant with sesame sauce. Some of the translations around the restaurant gave us more food for thought, however…

The last part of the trip was a short stop at Dishui Lake, at the south-easternmost point of Shanghai, before heading back to the city.

Thanks to Romain and Karen for the photographs and to Christine and Grace for organising. It was a great opportunity for us all to get to know each other a bit better and strengthen our international ties.

<u>About the author:</u>

George Fleming studied Chinese language and history at Cambridge University for his undergraduate degree before moving to Shanghai to pursue a postgraduate degree in interpretation and translation at SISU. He then became a full-time translator for three years, before (re)joining the translation department at the Graduate Institute of Interpretation and Translation, SISU from March 2015 to June 2018, to teach Chinese-English translation.

上海自贸区——洋山港之旅

费祖志（英国） 译
梁晓雪 审校

2016年5月27日，上海外国语大学的外国专家组团参观了上海自贸区。早上7点40分我们坐上大巴启程。

通过交谈，我了解到此行的外国专家们此前没有人参观过自贸区，甚至没有人来过上海东南部的周边地区。我们参观的首站是上海自贸区联合发展有限公司的行政办公楼，大楼孤零零地伫立在乌云密布的天际线下，显得格外壮观。短暂的休息活动后，我们踏上了去往洋山深水港的旅程，期间我们途经东海大桥。大桥全长30公里，从上海朝南延伸至小洋山岛。行驶在大桥上，我们不禁好奇身边一辆辆飞驰而过的大货车在大风天气中是如何行驶的。从车窗向外看，我们能够看到东海大桥风电示范项目的约50台海上巨型风车高高矗立着。

下车后，手机提示我们已经来到了浙江省——洋山港位于杭州湾，隶属杭州市嵊泗县管辖。我们惊奇地发现一个造型类似长城烽火台的高台[1]，顿时觉得一定要爬上去看看。

我们从这一制高点俯瞰洋山港，同时来自上海自贸区联合发展有限公司的王融融向我们介绍了洋山港，相关的数据令人印象深刻。洋山港有15米深，可容纳最新的巴拿马型集装箱船停泊卸货，该港口与36个国家的50 多个港口有货物往来，覆盖80多条航线。

接下来我们又回到了上海自贸区联合发展有限公司总部，以了解自贸区的演变和相关政策。王融融为我们做了题为“在中国取得

1 即洋山深水港的观景平台。

成功”的PPT展示，向我们介绍了自贸区的开发及成就，同时也介绍了以前外商投资所遇到的困难。之前，外企在投资、贸易、金融、政府角色和行政审批方面常会遇到重重关卡，不过，2013年自贸区获准设立外商独资公司后，自贸区飞速发展，与之前的缓慢进展形成了鲜明对比。此外，自贸区现在已经成为新设想的试验场，合适的项目有望之后在全国推行。这一前景让外国专家们十分兴奋。“在中国取得成功”的介绍会引起了外国专家们的极大兴趣，连自贸区的宣传册都被一抢而空。

带着满脑子的问题，我们乘车去吃午餐。午餐一点都没有让我们失望。我们在“书院人家”餐厅喝啤酒，吃红烧肉和芝麻沙拉酱冰草。不过，餐厅周围一些公示语的翻译让我们浮想联翩……

滴水湖是我们此行的最后一站，它位于上海东南部。之后我们顺利返校。

在这里，我要感谢Romain和Karen帮我们摄影，感谢张赟和梁晓雪组织这次活动，本次活动是一次机会，让我们增进对彼此的了解，加深我们的友谊。

作者简介：

George Fleming（费祖志）在剑桥大学获汉学学士学位，毕业后来上海外国语大学攻读口译专业研究生。在做了三年全职翻译后，于2015年3月至2018年6月期间担任上海外国语大学高级翻译学院笔译系汉英笔译教师。

Breathtaking Natural Places in China

José Carlos Redondo Martínez (Spain)

Proofread by George Fleming

China is, after Russia and Canada, the third largest country in the world, as far as total area is concerned. When I first came to China, I went to a small bookshop and laid my eyes on a map of China and that made me realize how big this country was. Even though I had arrived to work as a Spanish language teacher, from the very beginning of my stay in the province of Hunan, I had the urge and desire to discover and experience the natural wonders of this vast country. When my tight university schedule allowed me, I used to go to the train ticket booth across the Xiangtan University campus and buy a train ticket to see new places.

Zhangjiajie, Hunan Province

On my first journey, however, I did not take the train. My Chinese friends and I drove by car for more than 5 hours from Xiangtan city until we reached the northwestern part of Hunan Province. We arrived at sunset and the orange colour of the setting sun contrasted with the dark green colour of the dense forest which covered the tall, yellowish quartzite peaks. A beautiful scenery to be drawn and painted, I thought to myself. The following morning, we woke up early and entered the famous Zhangjiajie National Forest Park. A World Heritage Site since 1992, Zhangjiajie was recognized as the first National Forest Park in China in 1982 and later as a Global Geopark by UNESCO in 2004. As a Geopark, the city maintains a geological heritage of world relevance; its objectives are to explore, to develop and to improve the relationship between this geological heritage and the other cultural and natural elements of the area.

The most relevant geographical features of this wonderful Geopark are its landforms of quartz-sandstone pillars surrounded by marvellous green forests harmonically set among the foggy clouds. These particular rocky towers have endured in a better way the physical erosive process that has removed the rest of the geological structure. The world-wide famous James Cameron's film *Avatar* was inspired by these quartzite pillars and their foggy surroundings.

In Zhangjiajie the natural elements such as quartz-sandstone rocks, untouchable natural forests and the everlasting sea of clouds make this place an unforgettable reverie that has been expressed in wonderful images portrayed by the famous photographer Zhou Mingfa.

The first things you see on entering the park are a cable car and a small train that take you to the different areas inside the park. It was a bit rainy so we decided to take the cable car and it was a fascinating sensation since you have the feeling of being immersed in a sea of fog. You are just literally floating on the clouds. While the cable car was going up I saw the big quartz-sandstone pinnacles as natural skyscrapers all surrounded by a vast green forest. When I reached the top, I got off the cable car and I started to walk up the millions of stairs that run along the park. The scenery was absolutely breath-taking. A blast of pure fresh air with the scent of conifers filled my nostrils and my brain. Up there, there was only the sound of the tree branches moving slightly in the wind.

Walking up and down the rocky stairs was not an easy task, but it was really worth it to come across some Tujia girls and have a chat with them about their ethnicity and cultural traditions. The Tujia are one of the minorities who live, together with the Miao Minority, in this remote area of Hunan province.

They told me many things about the way they live (always in contact with nature and respecting the environment), the way they dress (beautifully colourful, embroidered dresses with silver hats and bracelets) and their gastronomy (the tasty *sanxiaguo* 三下锅: a mix of broth, walnut seeds and smoked meat with a spicy touch of pepper). It was very satisfying and very enriching to have talked to such a nice group of people who unveiled for me the traditions of a small minority who really identify themselves with nature and the environment. They are an example to pass onto future generations.

Courtesy of José Carlos Redondo Martínez

Walking down the pillars was not easy and my knees started to hurt, so I sat down on a big rock next to a thin water stream that run down the hill. I took out a small bag of potato crisps from my backpack and as soon as I opened it, a couple of monkeys approached me. To be honest, even though they were not very big, they had sharp canines and that scared me a bit. I threw some crisps to the ground: the monkeys grabbed them very fast and stuffed them into their mouths. They seemed to be satisfied so they did not follow me downstairs.

Once I reached the bottom of the park, my friends and I decided to go to the well-known Huanglong Cave, which is magnificently spacious. It has an underground navigable river and hundreds of stalagmites that reminded me of the Cave of Valporquero in León province (northwestern Spain). But Huanglong Cave was much bigger and wider: we covered the thirteen big halls and saw several waterfalls and pools. We even took a boat along the underground river. All the passageways and halls were lit up by colourful lights that gave the place a fairyland appearance.

After the whole day walking up and down Zhangjiajie forest and covering all the cave passageways, we withdrew to our wooden cabin in Zhangjiajie village. It was an amazing trip that made me realize how beautiful this vast country is and how many more beautiful places were there waiting for me to discover.

Jiuzhaigou Valley, Sichuan Province

The first place I visited outside Hunan was Sichuan Province. I took a 19-hour train from Changsha to Chengdu, the capital of Sichuan Province. During the train ride I could start to practice my Chinese with the help of a small Chinese language phrasebook. I began to realise that what was written in the books and what the people speak is sometimes totally different. In that train carriage, there were passengers from different places and most of them spoke their regional dialects which were completely unintelligible for a humble Spanish teacher with only a beginner's level of Chinese. The road wound around Hunan rice fields and the clear streams, rocky hills and vast open green prairies of Guizhou Province. The scenery was absolutely amazing, similar to those you can find in the typical postcards in a tourist shop. After many hours, the train finally arrived in Chengdu. Once there, I took the opportunity to go and see the Giant Panda Reserve. The panda bear is a unique species and Sichuan is the only place in the world you can see it wild and free. It is really worth it to see the giant animals playing around and furiously chewing on bamboo shoots.

Courtesy of José Carlos Redondo Martínez

The following morning, after being unpleasantly surprised by the highly polluted air in Chengdu, I took a bus northward to the famous mountains of Jiuzhaigou Valley. Along the way I dozed off for a while and, suddenly, I woke up to the sounds of a flock of sheep which were blocking the road. I opened my eyes and gazed out of the window: deep green valleys with rocky summits and long rivers told me that the smog and the traffic jams of the big cities were very far away. This was a new land. Once I arrived at Jiuzhaigou village I stayed in a youth hostel run by a young Tibetan couple who talked to me about the Tibetan past and present influences of this area. I slept like a log that night and woke up very early in the morning to enter the Jiuzhaigou National Park the first. Once I stepped into this Natural World Heritage recognised by UNESCO since 1992, I felt I had entered a totally different world; it was just me and nature. The park is located at the foot of the Minshan mountain range and it covers a vast area of 72,000 ha (UNESCO, 2017).

I started hiking up the hills towards the Virgin Forest on the east side of the area. Along my way up I could contemplate wonders such as the

Mirror Lake, the Five-Coloured Pool and the Swan Lake. The water was so clear you could see your own reflection in it. In the crystal-clear waters, I saw a shoal of fish swimming freely around some tree branches and leaves that had fallen off and become part of a calcareous tufa rock. Absolutely beautiful. The huge variety of trees with their multi-coloured leaves decorated the landscape as if it were a famous painting. On the tree branches many birds chirped with joy. One had the feeling of being in a fairyland. Amongst the tall pine trees were scattered some small waterfalls whose waters run free down the hilly forest. I also found some local Tibetan people who were very happy when I greeted them "*tashi delek*". Everybody I found within that valley was happy and peaceful, as if they mingled with the awesomely beautiful landscape which provided you with everlasting tranquillity. A total harmony between human beings and nature. For the first time in a long while, I felt at ease in a peaceful place, far from the pollution, the traffic jams and the noise of the big cities. I was discovering a new China, a China that is not written about in the books but which nevertheless exists.

I walked my way down to the centre of the valley and, while I drew out a piece of yak meat to stave off my hunger pangs, I sat down on a rock in front of the magnificent Nourilang Waterfall. The power of the water plunging and splashing around together with its great sound almost drowned out the voices of some Chinese tourists. Once I had taken a break admiring the waterfall, I continued my way towards the western part of the valley, towards the famous, 3,101m-altitude glacier lake, Long Lake.

On my way up, I was astonished at the beauty of this typical alpine landscape where the horizontal bottoms of the valley are occupied by pristine lakes that contrast with the vertical snow-capped mountains full of rock glaciers. This reminded me of the alpine Cantabrian Mountains in northern León in Spain. However, Jiuzhaigou Valley is far larger, and wilder. The Long Lake greeted me with its marvellous light blue waters that contrasted with the dark green pine trees in the surrounding area. Up there I realised that I had reached a milestone: for the first time in my life, I was above 3,000m above sea level. South of the beautiful Jiuzhaigou Valley is the Huanglong Scenic Area: a wonderful landscape with its remarkable series of pools with turquoise waters in travertine shoals (Jiuzhaigou, Huanglong and Giant Panda Habitat, 2010). This bunch of small water mirrors scattered along the valley is formed by precipitation of calcium carbonates. Amazing view. Amazing sensations. It was really worth a trip.

Tibet

After my stay in Sichuan, I took the Qinghai-Tibet Railway, the world's highest railroad by elevation. After almost two days inside a train that twisted along the Qinghai Lake, the Tanggulashan Mountain Pass (more than 5,000m above sea level) and the Nam Tso Lake, I finally reached the capital of Tibet: the sacred city of Lhasa. The city of Lhasa lies in the centre of the Tibetan Plateau at 3,600m above sea level and is crossed by the Lhasa River with its powerful current and pristine water. The Lhasa River, also called Jiqu River ("happiness river" in Tibetan), is a tributary to one of the most famous rivers in Tibet: The Brahmaputra River (Yarlung Zangbo as the locals call it). Lhasa is surrounded by a mountain range that reaches almost 5,000m altitude, giving the air purity but also a lack of oxygen that most of us foreigners need to acclimatise to. There I could breathe pure dry air. It was the opposite of the humid and wet air of Hunan.

Once I arrived in Lhasa I got the feeling of being in a totally different world: blue skies, zero air pollution, zero traffic jams and Tibetan people carrying their goods to sell in the street, Tibetan yaks passing through the pedestrian crossings, Tibetan children speaking Tibetan language while playing football with a totally frayed ball and Tibetan pilgrims burdened with tons of jewellery and objects to pray with to Buddha. The city was bursting into life and everybody seemed to be joyful. It was very interesting to see how these people welcomed you with a broad smile just by passing by them.

I stayed for a couple of days in Lhasa and I visited the beautiful golden Jokhang Temple where hundreds of pilgrims and tourists gathered together in and outside to pray to Buddha. The Barkhor Square in front of the temple was full of stalls where the locals sold a huge variety of items from jewels and religious objects to clothes and agriculture tools. This vibrant atmosphere was very attractive to the bunch of tourists who walked around from stall to stall trying to get some Tibetan souvenirs. I sat down next to a Buddhist monk on a stone bench in the square. He was wearing the typical orange and garnet robes and a pair of brown leather sandals. In a long conversation with him I learnt a lot about Tibetan history and culture and the meaning of being a Buddhist monk. He taught me about the importance of being at ease with oneself and peaceful towards other people, the great world of meditation and the good benefits every human being can get from that. He taught me that to be happy is easier than we think and assured me that a spiritual life is more important than a materialistic one where we fill our life with useless things that only bring us stress and worries. Even though he spoke broken rusty English, his message was totally understood. It was a very deep conversation that made me feel very good.

After the Jokhang Temple and the Barkhor Square, I also visited Norbulingka Park (National Cultural Relic Site) which once served as the summer residence of the Dalai Lama. It is a beautiful temple complex with several chapels all decorated with images of the Buddha and colourful tapestries that covered the walls. Inside the park, there was also a very neat garden with a plethora of colourful flowers that gave the place a special perfumed scent.

After Norbulingka Park I walked up my way to the fabulous and magnificent Potala Palace. Its architecture and shape are very precise and its location on top of a hill dominating the city and the valley gives it a royal appearance. It is the famous image on the reverse of the 50-yuan banknote. I paid the 100-yuan ticket to get in and entered the big wooden doors with their golden handles. The impressive white, thick walls contrasted with the dark black yak wool tapestries which hung on the roofs and balconies. Inside the palace there were hundreds of little rooms and many chapels as well as many sacred halls where the monks were chanting mantras. I respectfully sat behind a group of monks who were reciting the scriptures. I closed my eyes and I set my mind free, as the reverberation of their words echoed in the walls and the sound gave the hall a mystic touch. Together with that peaceful sound, the scent of incense in the air and the colourful flags made this palace a very special place to visit. Once you are inside you have the feeling of being in a different world, a piece of Heaven placed on Earth.

After my days in Lhasa, some other foreigners and I rented a van and a Tibetan guide and headed west to see the highest peak in the world: Qomolangma or, as everybody in the West calls it, Mt Everest. On our way there we drove past several mountain passes, and crossed several rivers and lakes. We even stopped at a hill near the Yamdrok Lake, a beautiful glacial lake with extremely pure blue waters. I walked down to the shore and I put my hand into the water: it was freezing! There was a herd of yaks around the lake and a shepherdess let me jump on one.

Sitting on a yak contemplating the beauty of the pristine Yamdrok Lake waters, the blue Tibetan skies and breathing fresh air; I was in heaven.

At the west of the Yamdrok Lake there is a huge mountain range that rises abruptly over the valley (Mt Noijin Kang 7,206m). We drove up the twisty road around the lake and entered this high valley. The high altitude has favoured the persistence of an ice field from which ice tongues drop down the slopes. The most famous of these glacier tongues is the Karolha Glacier. The ice was very thick and white and it almost reached the road. It was an amazing view that made you think how small we human beings were in comparison to Mother Nature.

We kept on driving south and, after a couple of observation points guarded by the Chinese army who slowly scrutinized and meticulously checked all our visas and papers, we finally entered the Qomolangma National Park — the north face of the majestic Qomolangma Peak, the most impressive mountain in the world that rises 8,848m ASL. The road wound around some deserted valleys where the only thing that broke the silence was the mooing of far-off yaks.

It was late in the afternoon and the temperature dropped drastically. We were approaching the area of the Qomolangma Base Camp and unfortunately our car broke down in a twist in the road. Mechanical problems. Our guide went to ask for help in a nearby village and we followed him. When we arrived there, some Tibetan children greeted us with a bright smile. While the mechanic was fixing our van, I played football with the children. I could not speak Tibetan, and they could not speak a word of English, but football is a universal language and we understood each other very well. Before we resumed our itinerary, I gave the children a bunch of bread buns that I had previously bought in another village. When they received the buns, they felt extremely happy. I would have never thought a bunch of buns could make anybody so happy. That reminded me of the conversation that I had back in Lhasa with the monk: we don't need lots of fancy things to be happy; happiness can be found in simple things.

It was already dark when we passed by the Monastery of Rongbuk (the highest monastery in the world) and finally reached the Qomolangma Base Camp at 5,200m altitude. The valley that came from Qomolangma was occupied by a debris-covered glacier and many water streams and a braided river ran down from it. And at its back, the magnificent Qomolangma Peak. We slept in Tibetan tents and wrapped ourselves up with yak wool blankets to protect ourselves from the dry cold Tibetan night. The following morning, I woke up early. I walked a bit towards the river and then hiked up a little hill to have a better view of the sunrise. In a few minutes, the first rays of sun started to hit the snowy summit of Qomolangma. It was one of the most amazing views I had ever seen. Absolutely breath-taking.

Courtesy of José Carlos Redondo Martínez

After all these journeys I returned home tired but extremely happy. I realized that there is a whole new world outside the big tourist cities of China. I would like to take this opportunity to give a piece of advice to readers: China is much more than an overcrowded section of the Great Wall in Beijing and the Oriental Pearl Tower with the surrounding skyscrapers in Shanghai. China is a place of natural wonders that will take your breath away: travel and you will discover them.

About the Author:

José Carlos Redondo Martínez, Spanish, PhD Candidate (Confucian philosophy and literature) at University of León, Spain. He worked in Xiangtan, Hunan Province during 2010–2012. Affiliated with the School of European and Latin American Studies from 2014 to 2017, SISU, he taught Spanish language and literature.

迷人的中国风光

José Carlos Redondo Martínez（西班牙）

张宏雨　译

梁晓雪　审校

就陆地国土面积而言，中国是世界上第三大国家，仅次于俄罗斯和加拿大。我第一次来中国时去过一家小书店，当我无意间看到一张中国地图时，才意识到中国竟如此之大。尽管我来中国的职责是教授西班牙语，但当我来到中国湖南的那一刻，我就渴望去发现并欣赏这片广袤大地的秀美风光。平时我的教学任务比较重，工作日程安排很紧，但只要一有时间，我就会去湘潭大学对面的售票厅买上一张火车票去其他地方转转。

湖南张家界

我的第一次旅行并未搭乘火车，而是和我的中国朋友一起开车。我们驱车五个多小时，从湘潭市来到了湖南省的西北部。我们到达时已是日落时分，金黄色的余晖洒落在林间，与郁郁葱葱的树木交相辉映，这片茂密的树林长在黄色的石英岩上面，高大挺拔。多么美丽的景色啊！第二天，我们早早地起来，去了有名的张家界国家森林公园，这个景点1982年成为中国第一个国家森林公园，1992年被联合国列为世界自然遗产，并在2004年被联合国列入世界地质公园。作为一个地质公园，张家界是世界地质遗产，其目的是探索其地质景观与其他人文和自然景观的关系，并促进其发展。

张家界国家森林公园以其独特的石英砂岩峰著称，岩峰四周绿树丛生，云雾缭绕，犹如仙境。石英砂岩锋是因长期侵蚀而形成的独特的地质风貌。詹姆斯·卡梅隆导演的一部非常著名的电影《阿凡达》，其灵感就来自这些奇特的石英砂岩锋以及如梦如幻的云间仙境。

在张家界，你会欣赏到很多奇美的自然风光，比如造型奇特的石英砂岩锋、郁郁葱葱的树林、一望无际的云海，这一切使得张家界成为让人难以忘怀的人间仙境。著名摄影家周明发曾用手中的相机记录下了这美丽的景色。

一进公园，你就会看到观光缆车和小火车，它们会带着你领略园中秀丽风光。那天，天正下着小雨，于是我们决定乘坐观光缆车。一路上，我们被云海包围，简直就像在云中穿行，壮观极了。缆车沿索道慢慢上升的途中，我看到了拔地而起的石英砂岩峰，就像摩天大厦一般高耸入云，被包围在一片绿树丛荫之中。到达山顶之后，我下了缆车，走在环绕公园的石阶上，欣赏周围无比迷人的景色。山间清新的空气和阵阵松柏的清香让我顿感心旷神怡。周围一片寂静，只听见树枝在风中轻轻摇摆的声音。

沿着崎岖不平的石阶上下山真不是一件容易的事，但我沿途遇见了几个土家族女孩，并和她们一起聊起她们的民族以及传统文化，我觉得一切都值了。土家族是中国的少数民族，他们与苗族一起生活在湖南的偏远地带。她们告诉我土家族的生活方式（亲近大自然，尊重环境）、传统服饰（色彩斑斓、手工刺绣的裙子，还有银制帽子和手镯）以及特色美食（如“三下锅”：由肉汤、核桃和熏肉制作而成，加入少许辣椒和胡椒粉）。能有机会和这些土家族姑娘聊天，我感到非常开心，收获颇丰。她们让我了解了这样一个与自然和谐统一的少数民族，同时也让我感受了她们的传统文化。应该把土家族的故事讲述给我们的后代听。

下山不是件容易活，不一会儿，我的膝盖就开始疼了，于是我在一块大石头上坐了下来，旁边是一条清澈的小溪，缓缓地流向山下。我从包里掏出一袋薯片，刚一打开，就有几只猴子朝我跑来。说实话，看到它们我心里还是有些害怕的，它们虽然体型不大，可牙齿却很尖利。我朝地上扔了几个薯片，它们飞快地捡起来，送到了嘴里。它们似乎对此心满意足，便没有跟随我一起下山。

一到山脚，我和朋友就决定去著名的黄龙洞看看。洞里十分宽敞，有可通行的地下河，还有数不尽的石笋，这些神奇的石笋让我想起了西班牙西北部莱昂省的瓦尔波奎罗岩洞，不过黄龙洞更大更宽。我们走过13个主洞，沿途看到许多瀑布和水池，我们甚至还坐了船游览地下河，整个洞穴被五彩斑斓的灯点缀着，犹如仙境一般。

在张家界国家森林公园上山下山，参观完所有的钟乳洞后，我们结束了一天的行程，回到村庄的小木屋过夜。这次难忘的旅行让我意识到，中国这片广袤的土地是如此的美丽迷人，这里还有更多的风景等待着我去探索。

四川九寨沟

出了湖南省，我去的第一个地方就是四川。从长沙到成都，我一共坐了19个小时的火车。旅途中，我一边看汉语实用手册，一边练习汉语，可我发现，书本里写的语言和生活中人们说的差别很大。车厢里，乘客来自中国各地，他们说着不同地方的方言，这对于一个汉语刚刚起步的西班牙人来说，犹如听天书一般。列车一路蜿蜒向前，穿过湖南大片的稻田以及贵州清澈的溪水、岩石嶙峋的山丘和一望无垠的原野，风景美不胜收，就好像我们在纪念品商店里所看到的明信片上的景色一样。很多个小时之后，火车终于到达成都站，一出车站，我就迫不及待地去了大熊猫自然保护区。熊猫是世界稀有动物，是中国的国宝，而四川省是全世界仅有的野生大熊猫栖息地。看着这些憨态可掬的大熊猫在一起玩耍嬉闹、狼吞虎咽地吃竹子，真心觉得不虚此行。

可没想到，第二天一早，成都的空气竟高度污染。我一路向北，坐车前往著名的九寨沟。路上我一直在打盹，突然，我被一阵声音吵醒，睁开眼一看，原来是一群羊挡住了我们的去路。我朝窗外望去，只看见翠绿幽深的峡谷、岩石林立的山峰和绵延向前的河流。啊，我已远离大城市的交通拥堵和空气污染，现在展现在我面前的是一个全新的地方。到了九寨沟之后，我住进了一对年轻藏民夫妇开的青年旅社里，他们向我讲述了藏民在过去与当下对这片土地的影响。那天晚上，我满身疲惫进入了梦乡。第二天，我早早就起来，去了九寨沟国家公园。这个公园在1992年被联合国教科文组织列入世界自然遗产，一走进去，我顿时感觉自己好像进入了另一个世界，和自然合二为一了。这个公园在岷山山脉的山脚，覆盖面积达72 000公顷。

我朝山东边的原始森林走去。沿途我欣赏到许多美丽神奇的自然景观，例如镜海、五彩池、天鹅海等。池水清澈见底，向水中望去可以看到自己的倒影。我看见一群群鱼儿自由自在地在水里游来游去，快活地穿梭于落入水中的枝干间，这些枝干已变成了石灰岩，实在是美丽。池水周围是层层叠叠的树木，它们五彩斑斓的枝叶点缀着这片土地，犹如一幅绝美的画卷。树上许多鸟儿叽叽喳喳，欢快地唱着歌。所有的这一切都置人于仙境之中。高大挺拔的松树林中散布着一些小瀑布，自由地奔泻于山林间。我还遇见了一些当地的藏民，当我用“扎西德勒”问候他们时，他们显得格外开心。这里的人们个个看起来都快乐而平静，就好像和这里美丽静谧的自然风光融为了一体，它给人带来一种持久的宁静与安详。在这里，人与自然完全实现了和谐统一。这是我长期以来第一次远离大城市的污染、噪音和交通堵塞，静静地享受这份美丽与宁静。我发现了中国的另一面，如此美丽的一面，它不为书本所记载，却真实存在。

我来到山谷的中心，在诺日朗瀑布前的一块大石头上坐了下来，掏出一片牦牛肉补充体力。瀑布宏伟壮观，水流一泻而下，溅起层层浪花，轰鸣声将周围游客的吵闹声都掩盖了。我一边休息，一边欣赏瀑布，片刻之后，我便朝山谷西边走去，去寻找著名的海拔3 101米的冰池，即长海。

一路上，我被这里独特而美丽的高山景象所深深吸引，山脚下是清澈的池水，山顶上是皑皑的白雪和厚厚的岩石冰川。这让我想起了西班牙莱昂省北部的坎塔布连山脉，不过九寨沟的山更为雄伟。来到长海旁，映入眼帘的是清澈湛蓝的池水，周围环绕着郁郁葱葱的松树。在那里我意识到我到达了一座里程碑：我人生第一次有如此体验，站在海拔3 000多米的地方。九寨沟的南边就是著名的黄龙景区：美丽壮观的蓝绿色池水与石灰岩浅滩相间。这些清澈如镜的池子由碳酸钙沉淀而成。眼前这一片美丽、迷人、壮观的景色让我赞叹不已。

西藏

四川之行结束后，我搭乘世界上海拔最高的铁路——青藏铁路，开启了我的西藏之行。火车开了两天，一路蜿蜒经过青海湖、唐古拉山（海拔5 000多米）、纳木错湖，最后终于来到了西藏的首府：圣城拉萨。拉萨位于青藏高原的中心，海拔3 600多米，拉萨河流经这里，河水清澈，奔涌向前。拉萨河也叫吉曲河（藏语中意为"幸福河"），是西藏著名河流布拉马普特拉河（当地居民也叫雅鲁藏布江）的支流。拉萨周边的山脉海拔近5 000米，因此空气非常纯净，但同时也存在氧气不足的问题，所以很多像我这样的外国游客要努力适应这里的气候环境。这里的空气纯净干燥，完全不同于湖南的湿热空气。

拉萨和我以往去过的其他城市完全不同：这里的天空湛蓝如洗，空气洁净透明，没有交通堵塞，当地藏民带着他们的货物沿街叫卖，藏牦牛自由地穿梭于人行横道，孩子们一边踢着已经磨损了的足球，一边用藏语交谈着。藏族的朝圣者们背着许多珠宝和其他物品做朝拜。整座城市充满活力、生机盎然，每个人都开心快活。当你与这里的居民擦肩而过时，他们会用一个大大的微笑欢迎你的到来，这真是有趣的体验。

我在拉萨待了几天，参观了美丽壮观、金碧辉煌的大昭寺，有很多游客和朝圣者在这里朝拜。寺庙的前面是八角街市集，当地人在这里摆摊贩卖各种物品，有珠宝、宗教用品、衣服、农具等等。这热闹的景象吸引了很多游客驻足，他们一个摊位一个摊位地观赏，精挑细选，希望带一些纪念品回去。我在集市旁的一条石凳上坐了下来，旁边是一位和尚，他穿着红橘相间的袈裟和一双棕色的皮革凉鞋。我和他聊了很久，了解了西藏的历史、文化以及出家人的人生意义。他告诉我要悦纳自己，和气待人，还告诉我冥想带给人们的好处。他还说幸福其实远比我们想象的简单，精神世界要比物质世界重要得多，物质世界总是充斥着琐碎的无用之事，带给我们的只有压力和烦恼。尽管他的英语说得很不流畅，我依然能领会他的思想内涵。这次谈话让我深受启发。

参观完大昭寺和八角街集市之后，我去了罗布林卡公园（中国重点文物保护单位），它曾是历代达赖喇嘛的避暑胜地。这里是一片寺庙群，其中一些小寺庙的墙上挂有释迦摩尼的画像和五颜六色的挂毯。公园里有一片干净整洁的花园，里面开满了五彩斑斓的花朵，散发出阵阵清香。

结束了罗布林卡公园之行，我去了宏伟壮观的布达拉宫。布达拉宫位于山顶之上，俯视全城和山谷，整个建筑风格高大雄伟，给人一种庄严巍峨之感。伍拾元人民币背面的图像正是以此风景为原型的。我花了一百元人民币，买了门票，跨过镶着金色把手的大木门，来到了宫殿内部。只见四周是白色的厚墙，屋顶和阳台上挂着黑色的牦牛毛毯，黑白分明，让人印象深刻。宫殿里有数以百计的小房间、许多小礼拜堂和圣堂，僧人们在这里做祷告。怀着满满的敬意，我在几位诵读佛经的和尚背后坐了下来。我闭上眼睛，放空自己，让思绪随意飘飞；阵阵祷告声回荡在大厅里，为整个宫殿增添了几分神秘。除此之外，空气里弥漫的淡淡香薰和五颜六色的经旗都使我觉得这个地方别具一格，好像另一个世界，胜却人间天堂。

在拉萨游玩了几天之后，我和几位外国游客一起租了一辆小型客车，并请了一位藏族导游，向西去参观世界的最高峰——珠穆朗玛峰。一路上，我们经过了几座高山，穿过了河流和湖水，我们还停在一座小山脚下，山旁有一片冰川湖，名叫羊卓雍措湖，湖水清澈湛蓝。我走到湖边，将手伸进水里：真是凉彻心底啊！周围，一群牦牛悠闲地走来走去，一位牧羊女让我坐在牦牛背上，静静地欣赏眼前美丽的景色：透明的湖水，碧蓝的天空，清新的空气，简直如同天堂。

在羊卓雍措湖西边的一个山谷中，矗立着一座高大的山峰，即海拔7 206米的宁金抗沙峰。我们一路蜿蜒向前，绕过湖水，来到了这片山谷。由于海拔很高，山峰长期被冰雪覆盖，并在斜坡处形成冰舌，其中最有名的就是卡若拉冰川。冰层晶莹剔透、厚重坚实，从山顶一直延伸到山脚下。这般壮观的景象让人不禁感叹，在大自然面前，人类是多么的渺小。

我们继续向南行驶，经过了几个检查站点，几位中国士兵对我们的签证、护照等进行了仔细检查，然后我们终于来到了位于喜马拉雅山北面的珠穆朗玛峰国家公园。珠穆朗玛峰是世界最高峰，海拔8 848米。一路上，道路蜿蜒曲折，环绕着几座荒凉的山谷，整个园区空无一人、万籁俱静，只听到牦牛发出的阵阵哞哞声。

已近黄昏，气温急剧下降。我们即将到达珠穆朗玛峰基地营，可不幸的是，我们的车子在道路的一个转弯处出了机械故障。于是，我们的导游去附近的一个村庄寻求帮助，我们也随之前往。当我们到达那里，迎接我们的是当地孩子们灿烂的笑容。修车师傅在修理汽车的时候，我和孩子们一起踢足球，我不懂藏语，他们不懂英语，是足球这个“世界通用语”让我们彼此理解。车子修好后，我们要重新启程了，临走前，我给了孩子们一些我在其他村庄买的圆面包，他们接过面包，无比开心。我从未想过圆面包可以让人那么开心。这使我想起了在拉萨时，那位僧人对我说过的话：幸福没有那么遥不可及，快乐其实很简单。

我们经过绒布寺时，天色已黑。绒布寺是世界上海拔最高的寺庙，过了绒布寺，我们就到了位于海拔5 200米的珠穆朗玛峰基地营。周围的山谷被冰川覆盖，许多溪流以及交织的河流从山间流下，在我们的后方就是壮观的珠穆朗玛峰了。我们睡在藏族式的帐篷里，盖着牦牛毛毯子来抵御夜晚的寒冷干燥。第二天，我一大早就起来了。我四处转了转，走到河水边，为了找到一个更好的视角来观赏日出，又往山上爬了一小段。不多一会儿，太阳便露出脸来，将它的第一缕光辉洒落在珠穆朗玛峰的雪峰上，这番壮丽的景象令人叹为观止，真是美得令人窒息！

结束了所有的旅程后，我回到了家，劳累之余更多的是开心快乐。我发现，中国除了许多旅游城市之外，还别有洞天。我愿借此机会，告诉广大的读者：在中国，除了北京拥挤的长城和上海被摩天大厦环绕的东方明珠之外，还有许许多多迷人的自然景观会让你惊叹不已。开启你的旅程，去探索发现这些神奇美丽的自然风光吧！

作者简介：

José Carlos Redondo Martínez，西班牙籍，莱昂大学博士在读（儒学及儒家经典专业）。2010年至2012年在湖南湘潭任教，2014年至2017年在上海外国语大学西方语系任教，教授西班牙语语言文学相关课程。

30 Years Ago!

Pierre Brunet (Canada)

Proofread by George Fleming

The first time I came to China was in 1985. I was Sales and Marketing Manager for a division of Alcan (Canadian multinational). The division manufactured heat exchangers used in refrigerators. As a Japanese company was trying to take our customers in North America, which was a market we dominated, I took the marketing "war" to Asia.

China was our prime target as the country was restructuring. It began to reopen to the rest of the world looking for technology and funds to grow its economy.

In parallel, the restructuring of the economy allowed the Chinese people to save, as their revenues were progressively exceeding the basic living costs. Families were able to buy a few basic luxury items, including a refrigerator. And this is where I came in.

The technical requirements for a refrigerator are quite advanced. At that time, no company in China had the capability to manufacture the key components. While the compressor was sourced from South Korea, the heat exchanger came from the Japanese company that had become our competitor. We decided to go after their Chinese customers with the assistance of an agent in Hong Kong.

The manufacturers of refrigerators were located in the larger cities near the coast: Guangzhou, Shanghai, Suzhou and Beijing. All were state-owned enterprises. Over the course of three years (1985–1987), I visited these cities at intervals of 6 months.

I recall the plants were dark, antiquated and overstaffed. The streets in the cities were full of bicycles and buses, with few private cars. People were dressed in Mao suits, or grey or dark-blue outfits. There were few stores, no modern skyscrapers and definitely no subways. In Shanghai, Pudong was primarily fields that were tended by farmers. No one spoke English. Signs were only in Chinese. The currency was dual; one for locals, one for visitors, and we could not use the local currency. I remember a taxi driver refusing to be paid in local currency. I simply could not pay with the local currency another taxi driver had given me as change.

The process of applying to visit China was cumbersome. We had to provide the details on the purpose of our visit, where we were going, the number of days in each city and the travel arrangements. We stayed in hotels that were quite antiquated. One time in Shanghai we stayed in a residence that had been built by foreigners in the 1930s. The infrastructure for tourism had not kept up with the rapidly increasing demand for rooms.

Now as I walk in Shanghai, I see modern office and residential towers everywhere. The city has expanded way beyond anyone would have dreamt of in the mid-80's. The subway criss-crosses the city, reaching far into the suburbs. Manufacturing facilities are modern and supply the world, using up-to-date technologies.

So many changes in the last 30 years. Where will China be 30 years from now?

About the author:

Pierre Brunet, Canadian, completed undergraduate and postgraduate studies in engineering in Canada and postgraduate studies in business in France. He worked for more than 32 years in the corporate world before joining Conestoga College near Toronto, in 2007. Pierre specializes in international business, with a focus on business strategy. He taught business courses in English at SISU from September 2016 to June 2017.

三十年前的中国

Pierre Brunet（加拿大）
张宏雨　译
梁晓雪　审校

我第一次来中国是在1985年，那时候我在一家跨国企业——加拿大铝业公司——担任市场和销售部经理。这家公司生产并销售冰箱热交换器。那时，有一家日本公司试图抢占我们主导的北美市场，于是，我来到亚洲，以期开拓这里的市场。

中国是我们的首要目标，因为这个国家当时正在经历改革和重组，它加快了改革开放的步伐，开始向世界敞开大门，努力寻求资金和技术，促进经济的增长。

与此同时，经济结构的调整也使得中国人民的收入逐渐超过基本的生活开支，他们开始有了积蓄，因而，很多家庭也开始有能力购买一些较为基本的奢侈物件，例如冰箱。这正是我来中国的原因。

制造冰箱的技术要求是很高的，在那时，中国还没有一家公司能制造冰箱的核心部件。冰箱的压缩机由韩国供应，而热交换器则来自一家日本公司，也就是我们的竞争对手。我们决定在一家香港代理公司的帮助下，抢占中国的市场。

冰箱生产制造工厂都在沿海的一些大城市：广州、上海、苏州和北京。这些公司全部都是国有企业。从1985至1987这三年间，我每隔六个月就会去这几个城市转一转。

在我的印象中，这些城市的工厂都昏暗老旧、拥挤不堪，街道上满是自行车和公交车，几乎看不到私家车。人们穿的都是中山装或者灰色、深蓝色的套装。商店非常之少，更不用说摩天大楼和地铁了。在上海的浦东，几乎到处都是田地，农民们种地为生。没有一个人会说英语，所有的标志牌也都是汉语的。有两个独立的货币体系，一个供当地人使用，另一个则供外国人使用，二者的货币不可混用。记得有一次乘出租车，我将之前坐出租车得到的找零付给司机，他却坚决不肯收。

来访中国的申请手续十分繁琐，我们需要提供所有的细节，包括来访目的、去往何处、在各地的停留天数以及行程安排。我们居住的旅店简陋破旧。有一次，我们在上海居住的楼房是由外国人在20世纪30年代建造的。那时候，中国旅游业的相关基础设施还远远跟不上日益增长的旅客需求。

而现如今，当我走在上海的街头，举目所及都是现代化的办公大楼和居民小区。这座城市的发展远远超出20世纪80年代中期人们的想象。纵横交错的地铁一直延伸到城市的边缘。生产设施十分现代化，使用的都是当今最先进的科技，产品正在销往世界各地。

在这30年间，中国发生了翻天覆地的变化，那么，下一个30年，中国又会变成什么样呢？

作者简介：

Pierre Brunet，加拿大籍。在加拿大取得工程学的本科和硕士学位后，他又在法国获得商务硕士学位。从商32年后，他于2007年进入多伦多附近的康尼斯托加学院任教，主要教授国际商务和商业策略。他于2016年9月至2017年6月间在上海外国语大学教授商务课程。

My Impressions from China

Vasyl Ivashkiv (Ukraine)

Proofread by George Fleming

My knowledge about China was pretty commonplace for people who have never been to this country. I knew that this is the nation with a history of several thousand years, interesting philosophy, great culture, vast territory and the biggest number of inhabitants. Naturally, I was well aware of the specificity of Confucianism, Taoism and Buddhism. Besides that, quite recently I have taken great pleasure reading *The Art of War*, a famous work by the outstanding Chinese philosopher Sun Tzu.

As a literary critic, I was more or less interested in Chinese literature, but unfortunately high-quality Ukrainian translations from Chinese writers seemed scarce. That was why only the works by Lu Xun were familiar to me. My respect for this writer was great because he also translated a chapter on Ukrainian literature from the book by Gustav Karpeles, *Overall History of World Literature*, as well as the immortal *Testament* by the Ukrainian national genius Taras Shevchenko. To my great surprise, these facts were overlooked during the organization of an exhibition of this author by a very interesting literary and memorial museum in Shanghai. Moreover, among hundreds of translations of his works into various languages, I did not manage to find a translation into Ukrainian, though there were at least five translations of other works.

My interest in China grew even bigger when the Chinese writer Mo Yan (Guan Moye) was awarded the Nobel Prize in Literature in 2012. However, I had to wait rather long to have a chance to read his works — there simply were no translations into Ukrainian, except for his Nobel lecture. This lecture proved that Mo Yan is a writer with deep national roots, and his ideas originate from the depths of folk memory. Eventually, not a very successful Ukrainian translation of Mo Yan's early novel *Red Sorghum Clan* was published, and I devoured it quite quickly. In the novel itself I could trace elements of Gabriel García Márquez and his outstanding novel *One Hundred Years of Solitude*. Interesting enough, Mo Yan's novel seems to me somewhat chaotic and not so coherent as Márquez's work, though it contains original artistic solutions. In particular, I would mention the scene with the fight against the Japanese and the main character's grandmother's funeral.

Thus, I made up my mind to accept the invitation of Shanghai International Studies University to come to China for one academic year. My task was to promote cooperation between Lviv and Shanghai universities as well as to help develop Ukrainian studies in Shanghai and China in general. Actually, our agreement presupposed writing a concise course of Ukrainian literature for Chinese students who did Ukrainian studies as a major. It proved both easy and difficult to take this decision. I realized that China was an interesting but faraway country with a totally different culture which I still wanted to get to know.

In September my wife and I arrived in Shanghai. My wife Halyna has a PhD in art criticism, is the author of numerous scholarly publications on folk ceramics, and has been given many prestigious awards. So, we had this entirely different world to be discovered by us together.

Our first impression after landing at Pudong International Airport was that Shanghai was a huge city with millions of inhabitants. At the same time, it is a modern, clean and very tidy megapolis with European or rather American architecture. However, beside skyscrapers we could often see houses with tiles on the roofs which were so wonderfully depicted in Mo Yan's novel.

Impressions of a country are very often influenced by the people you see along your way. We have always felt friendliness everywhere — on the underground, and in the streets. When we wanted to know the direction to the street we needed, young people who spoke English always approached us and offered their help.

What we were really pleased with was the genuine interest the Chinese displayed towards everything Ukrainian. We could visibly feel that at the opening ceremony of the Ukrainian research centre at Shanghai International Studies University on October 15, 2015. There an initiative was raised to hold a conference on Ukraine in spring 2016. The spirit of our motherland was extremely vivid in the museum of Ukraine (a part of the Research Centre for Ukraine) at Zhejiang Pedagogical University in Jinhua. The university was established by the Chinese teacher Li Jihua, who wrote a number of researches on Vasyl Sukhomlynskyi (a famous Ukrainian educator).

On October 24, 2015, Zhejiang Pedagogic University in Jinhua organized a meeting of Chinese students who graduated from Kyiv Aviation University in Ukraine 20 years ago. Together with their supervisor Li Jihua and other teachers they shared memories of their student years. Not only the museum of Ukraine and its exhibits reminded me of Ukraine, there also was the ceremonial bread (*korovai*) as one of the main symbols of Ukrainian hospitality. In line with Ukrainian tradition, the girls in national Ukrainian costumes greeted the guests carrying *korovai* on an embroidered towel. The bread was lavishly decorated with relief flowers made of sweet dough. Former students of Kyiv Aviation University eagerly took pictures of each other in the museum interior, in particular with mannequins in traditional folk costumes or with the Hutsul furnace made of painted ceramic tiles.

In Jinhua we had the opportunity to see China from another perspective, i.e. to learn something about its agriculture and hard-working people who reminded us of the Ukrainians. We were particularly impressed by a peasant who came to the city to sell his home-grown fruits and vegetables at the market Luojiatang in the centre of Jinhua. The peasant wore plain but tidy clothes, and had a very serious and thoughtful look, vivid features of the face and kind hard-working hands. He resembled an old man from Mo Yan's novel. We will also have in our memory trailers full of juicy mandarins (some of them had fresh leaves!), as well as delicate fruits with romantic names — like "dragon fruit" or "Buddha's eye". Another fruit we cannot help mentioning is "Buddha's hand" which is famous for its unique shape (it resembles a hand and can have up to 20 short and long "fingers"), bright yellow colour, brilliant healing properties and a flavour similar to lemon.

We spent the majority of our time in Shanghai enjoying its architecture, parks and museums. It immediately caught our eyes that the city functioned as a well-oiled machine. It means that the streets were clean, the roads ideal and there were no traffic jams at all! Perhaps, only narrow pavements which were quite often used by cyclists and motorcyclists caused some inconvenience. I have to admit that Chinese people are extremely hard-working (their working day seems to begin at 5 a.m.!), but they also are capable of having a good rest. We could very often see them gather in the park at the weekend to sing or dance together. Many people also actively train on free fitness machines, play badminton or simply go jogging. We have never seen people drinking alcohol there.

As we have noticed, Chinese women are rather indifferent to jewellery and wear quite casual clothes. Instead, they pay lots of attention to food, and I would even say that there is a cult of food in China. Step by step we got used to Chinese cuisine and liked practically all the dishes. The only things we really longed for were real Ukrainian borsch (beetroot soup) and strong coffee.

In October we went to the Shanghai Museum and were rather surprised to see a big queue. It reminded us of the long lines in Louvre Museum in Paris, Dresden Picture Gallery, and the Pergamon Museum in Berlin. It was nice to see so many young people in the museum carefully studying the exhibits and taking pictures. Interesting enough, there were quite a lot of lively five- or six-year-old children in the queue, and they reminded us of our little grandson.

Love of flowers seems to us one of the most essential features of the Chinese. The richness of flower-beds in city parks and in the streets fascinated us. We saw this art in all its perfection at the magnificent Pudong Century Park.

Shanghai parks are one of its main tourist attractions. One immediately notices sophisticated designs with park roads and paths, waterfalls, amazing abstract compositions with stones, various types of trees (namely, maple trees, magnolias, pine trees, fir trees and larch trees), neatly-cut bushes, flower-beds of different shapes, flower clocks, hieroglyphs made of flowers, and sports playgrounds. We were surprised that marigolds, which are very popular in Ukraine, were so common in Shanghai. Looking at them we immediately remembered the lyrics from a Ukrainian song by Mykola Synhayivskyi, called *Marigolds*:

Marigolds were planted by my mom
In my morning native land
And she taught me how to sing spring songs
About my flowering hope.
When I look at those marigolds
I see my aging mother
I see your hands, mommy,
Your kind words I hear, my dear!

There are many flowers that are grown in Ukraine, and we were delighted to see them in Shanghai as well, namely calendulas, zinnias, garden violets and many others.

I would also like to mention how tolerant the Chinese are to foreigners and people of different religions. We had a chance to feel this while attending masses in famous Catholic churches in the city, namely Xujiahui

Cathedral and the Basilica of Virgin Mary, the journey to which was really unforgettable. This Roman Catholic Basilica is considered to be the center of Christian pilgrimage in China and is situated on the "snake hill". After almost an hour in the underground we walked for about two hours from the metro station Sheshan to the Basilica. On our way we saw beautiful parks, interesting attractions, a clear beautiful lake and the alley with metal sculptures of contemporary Chinese artists. The Basilica appeared in front of us somewhat unexpectedly, as the whole complex of buildings is situated up the hill, which is surrounded by a huge park. The church impressed us by its grandeur as it is an enormously high red-brick building that can house up to three thousand people. A magnificent figure of Virgin Mary with Jesus in her arms immediately attracts attention and creates an atmosphere of exquisite solemnity.

The Neo-Gothic Xujiahui Cathedral struck us by its perfect architecture, i.e. through the contrast with modern constructions its composition makes the image of a megapolis even brighter. All this is achieved not only through the church's unique architecture but also by the fact that it is built with red bricks, while all the other buildings around it are white and grey.

The cathedral is complemented with light sculptures of Jesus Christ and the apostles which adorn its façade. The upper part of the neighboring building was built in the pagoda style. This turns out to be a peculiar Chinese accent in the architecture of one of the most beautiful districts of this wonderful city.

We were rather surprised to learn that about 12,000 people attend this cathedral at Christmas. Fir trees and other greenery, as well as colorful flower-beds, serve as a frame for the cathedral. Besides, all this makes a small square in front of it one of the most favorite places for inhabitants of Shanghai and tourists. To us this cathedral has reminded the Neo-Gothic

St. Elizabeth Cathedral in Lviv, Ukraine, which dates back to 1903.

We have noticed that Shanghai architecture represents a harmonious combination of the past and present, traditional and international features. Buddhist temples, Muslim mosques and Christian churches peacefully coexist with skyscrapers. This point is exemplified by the Longhua Temple, the Jade Buddha Temple, and other religious buildings. Due to the lack of time we have not "explored" the magnificent Yuyuan Garden yet.

We have seen only a part of Shanghai, and this wonderful city cannot provide exhaustive information about China on the whole. That is why in spring 2016 we hope to see many other places of this still mysterious country for us, in particular Beijing, Nanjing, Guangzhou, the Great Wall of China, and the famous Terracotta Army of Qin Shi Huang. I do believe we will have unforgettable impressions!

About the author:

Vasyl Ivashkiv is a Doctor of Philology, Full Professor, and Chair of the Philareth Kolessa Department of Folklore Studies at Lviv Ivan Franko National University (Ukraine). He is now teaching at the School of Russian and Eurasian Studies at SISU. He was born in 1958, graduated from Lviv Ivan Franko State University, and completed his post-graduate studies at Taras Shevchenko Literature Institute at the Academy of Sciences of Ukraine. He is the author of three scholarly monographs, namely *Ukrainian Romantic Drama of the 1830s–1880s* (Kyiv, 1990), *Artistic, Literary-Critical and Folkloristic Paradigm of Early Works by Panteleymon Kulish* (Lviv, 2009), and *Ivan Tobilevych (Karpenko-Karyi), His Life and Works* (Ternopil, 2011). Vasyl Ivashkiv is editor of nearly a dozen educational publications of works by Ukrainian writers and over a hundred scholarly papers in Ukrainian and international journals. He supervised ten post-graduate and doctorate students who successfully defended their theses.

His scholarly interests embrace Ukrainian literature of Romanticism and Realism (the 19th century), namely drama, works by Taras Shevchenko, Panteleymon Kulish, Mykola Kostomarov, Lesia Ukrainka, Ivan Franko, Ivan Tobilevych, Marko Kropyvnytskyi, as well as Ukrainian folklore and folklore studies.

我的中国印象

Vasyl Ivashkiv（乌克兰）

梁晓雪　译

和很多从未来过中国的人一样，我对中国的了解只有皮毛。我知道这个国家有数千年的历史、深邃的哲学思想、伟大的文明、辽阔的国土及全世界最多的人口。当然，我对儒学、道家、佛教思想也有一定了解。最近，我在阅读中国伟大哲学家孙武的名著《孙子兵法》，获得很多乐趣。

作为文学评论家，我多少对中国文学有些兴趣，但遗憾的是，中国作家的作品鲜少有质量上乘的乌克兰语译本。这就是为什么我只熟悉鲁迅先生的作品。我十分敬仰鲁迅，因为他曾将古斯塔夫·卡珀利斯《世界文学简史》中介绍乌克兰文学的章节以及乌克兰国宝级天才塔拉斯·舍甫琴科的不朽著作《圣约》译成了中文。我吃惊地发现，上海有一家很有趣的文学纪念馆（鲁迅纪念馆），曾经举办过鲁迅的展览，但是忽略了如此重要的史料记录。另外，鲁迅的作品有不同语言的数百种译文版本，但我没有找到任何作品的乌克兰语译本，尽管很多作品有至少5种语言的译本。

自从莫言（本名管谟业）获得2012年诺贝尔文学奖后，我对中国的兴趣更加浓厚。然而，除了他被翻成乌克兰语的诺贝尔获奖感言之外，我还需要等很久才能读到他的作品。他的致辞表明，他是一名本土作家，他的灵感来自深厚的民间土壤。当莫言的早期小说《红高粱》终于有了一个质量欠佳的乌克兰语译本后，我很快就读完了。我在字里行间寻到了加夫列尔·加西亚·马尔克斯及其伟大作品《百年孤独》的影子。有趣的是，尽管莫言的小说具有原创的艺术风格，但作品结构对我来说有些零散，不像马尔克斯的那么连贯，特别是书中描绘抗日战争以及主角奶奶葬礼的部分。

于是，我决定接受上海外国语大学为期一年的教职。我的任务包括促进乌克兰利沃夫国立弗朗克大学和上海各大学间的合作，同时协助发展上海乃至中国的乌克兰研究。事实上，两校协议中预先规划了乌克兰文学作品简读课程的设计，供乌克兰语专业的中国学生学习。对我来讲，赴中国任教的决定说起来容易，做起来难。中国虽然充满生趣，但也遥远而陌生，我想进一步了解它。

9月，我和我的夫人抵达上海。我夫人哈丽娜是艺术批评博士，出版了多部关于民间陶瓷的学术作品，也获得过很多重要奖项。我们将共同探索这个迥然不同的世界。

抵达浦东国际机场后，我们的第一印象就是上海是个人口众多的大城市，同时，它也是一个现代、洁净、整齐的大都市，有很多欧式或美式风格的建筑。然而，除了摩天大楼，也时常可以看到瓦片屋顶的民居——正如莫言小说中所形象描绘的那样。

我们对中国的印象往往来自碰到的路人。不论是在地铁里还是在大街小巷中，我们遇到的人都十分友好。每当我们需要问路时，会讲英语的年轻人总是会主动走近并提供帮助。

最让我们高兴的是中国人对乌克兰的一切都兴趣盎然。这一点尤其体现在2015年10月15日在上海外国语大学召开的乌克兰研究中心揭幕仪式上。此次活动决定在2016年春季举办一个关于乌克兰的国际会议。此外，位于金华的浙江师范大学乌克兰博物馆（是乌克兰研究中心的一部分）生动地展示了我们国家的精髓。浙江师大是由李姬花老师创立的，她曾写过关于著名乌克兰教育家瓦西里·苏霍姆林斯基的教育思想的研究文章。

2015年10月24日，浙江师范大学在金华组织了留乌20周年同学会，这些校友20年前毕业于乌克兰基辅国际民航大学。众校友和当时的带队老师李姬花等人欢聚一堂，共同回忆往昔时光。除了乌克兰博物馆的众多展品，传统的乌克兰面包也让我想起了乌克兰，我们在节庆时吃这种面包，它代表了乌克兰的热情好客。和乌克兰的传统一样，身着乌克兰民族服饰的女孩们捧着放在刺绣巾上的面包欢迎宾客，面包上装饰着用甜面团做成的浮雕花。校友们在博物馆内合影留念，与身穿乌克兰民族服饰的模特一起拍照，或在贴着彩绘瓷砖的胡塞尔炉前留下倩影。

在金华，我们有幸看到中国的另一面，比如了解到中国的农业和辛勤耕作的农民，他们让我们想起了乌克兰人。在金华市中心一个菜场，我们遇到一位卖自家水果蔬菜的农民，他给我们留下了深刻的印象。他衣着朴素干净，有一种严肃的、若有所思的表情，五官轮廓分明，拥有一双劳动人民的手。这位农民神似莫言小说中的老人形象。我们印象很深的还有一车车新鲜多汁的柑橘（有些还带着新鲜的叶子），也记住了一些有着动听名字的美味水果，如火龙果、龙眼。有个我必须要提到的水果叫“佛手（瓜）”，以其独特的形状闻名（形似一只有多达20根长长短短“手指”的手），色泽明黄，有显著的疗效，口味类似柠檬。

我们大多数时间生活在上海，欣赏这里的建筑、公园以及博物馆。我们很快就发现，这座城市像一座润滑良好的机器在不停运作：街道干净整洁，很少堵车。当然，有些人行道比较狭窄，有很多自行车和摩托车行驶，可能会发生拥堵。不得不说，中国人工作特别努力（工作日的一天似乎从清晨五点就开始了！），不过他们也有很多休闲娱乐的方式。周末，我们经常看见人们聚集在公园里唱歌、跳舞，也有很多人在公共健身器材上锻炼身体、打羽毛球或慢跑。我们从未见到有人在公共场所喝酒。

我们也注意到，中国女性对于珠宝首饰不太在意，衣着也比较随意，但是她们对于“吃”很讲究。我甚至觉得中国人有饮食崇拜。我们也逐渐适应并喜欢上了几乎所有的中国菜。我们唯一想念的就是正宗的乌克兰红菜汤[1]以及浓咖啡。

10月，我们去了上海博物馆，我们惊奇地发现博物馆前排起了长队。这不禁让我联想到巴黎的卢浮宫、德累斯顿画廊及柏林佩加蒙博物馆前的人头攒动。我很高兴看到有如此多的年轻人在博物馆内专心致志地观看展品并拍照。有趣的是，有很多活泼好动的五六岁孩子也在队列中，不禁让我想起了我们的小外孙。

在我们看来，中国人的一大特点是热爱鲜花。街心花园和街道两侧都有鲜花盛开。浦东世纪公园的花展更是达到了美的巅峰。

上海的公园一向是游客聚集地。你可以立即注意到精心设计过的花园小径、喷泉，抽象的艺术石雕及种类繁多的树木（包括枫树、玉兰树、松树、杉树以及落叶松），修剪齐整的灌木，形状各异的花坛、花钟，花卉组成的象形字以及运动场。我们吃惊地发现，在乌克兰广为种植的金盏花在上海也同样很受欢迎。看到它们，我们立刻联想到乌克兰歌词作者米可拉·辛哈衣夫斯基写的《金盏花》：

金盏花是我母亲种的

在我清晨的故乡

她教我唱春天的歌

---

1 红菜汤来源于乌克兰，是一种以红菜为主要材料，保留红菜基本色彩和口感的汤，在东欧有不同的做法和菜式。除了在俄罗斯、乌克兰和白俄罗斯外，红菜汤也在罗马尼亚、斯洛伐克、摩尔多瓦等其他东欧国家广受欢迎。中国所谓的“罗宋汤”或者“红菜汤”用的是西红柿、卷心菜等，系该菜式在中国的本土化产品，口味与正宗红菜汤大有不同，但可能更适合中国人的口味。

关于我盛开的梦想
当我看着那些金盏花
我看到我年迈的母亲
我看见您的手，妈妈
我听到您亲切的话语，亲爱的妈妈！

我们很高兴能在上海看到许多在乌克兰也很常见的花卉，包括金盏草、百日草、紫罗兰等。

中国人对于外国人以及不同宗教的信徒非常宽容。我们在参加徐家汇天主堂和佘山圣母大殿的弥撒时深刻体会到这一点。那是一次令人难忘的经历。坐落在佘山上的圣母大殿是中国天主教著名的朝圣地。在搭乘近一个小时的地铁抵达佘山地铁站后，我们又步行两个小时到达教堂。沿途有风景怡人的公园、有趣的景点、清澈的湖水以及中国当代艺术家的金属雕像作品长廊。由于教堂的整座建筑都伫立在山顶，坐落在公园之中，所以当它突然映入眼帘时，我们有点意外。高大宏伟的教堂由红砖砌成，可容纳多达三千人，给我们留下了深刻的印象。怀抱耶酥的圣母玛丽雕像引人注目，精巧绝伦，给人以神圣肃穆的感觉。

新哥特式风格的徐家汇天主堂以其完美的建筑结构令人惊叹，它建筑风格独特，红砖外表与周围的灰白色现代建筑形成鲜明对比，反而更彰显出国际大都市的魅力。

大教堂外部有耶稣和圣徒的小型雕塑。周围建筑的屋顶是宝塔风格，使这里成为这座美丽城市中最具中国建筑特色的地方。

我们惊讶地得知，圣诞节时会有一万两千人在这里参加活动。杉树等其他绿植以及五颜六色的花坛点缀了整个教堂。前方的小广场是上海居民及游客最喜欢的地方之一。此地让我们联想到始建于1903年的乌克兰利沃夫的新哥特式圣伊丽莎白天主教堂。

我们注意到，上海的建筑风格融合了古典与现代、传统与国际化。佛教寺庙、穆斯林清真寺、基督教堂与摩天大楼相得益彰，龙华寺、玉佛寺等宗教建筑就是这方面的例子。由于时间有限，我们还没来得及探访美丽的豫园。

我们只窥见了上海的一角，当然，这座伟大的城市并不足以展示中国的全貌。因此，我们希望在2016年春季游览更多的地方，比如北京、南京、广州，去看长城、大名鼎鼎的秦始皇兵马俑等，以进一步了解这个对于我们来说仍然神秘的国度。我相信，我们将拥有难忘的记忆。

作者简介：

Vasyl Ivashkivis，哲学博士、教授，乌克兰利沃夫国立弗朗克大学民俗学系主任，目前在上海外国语大学俄罗斯东欧中亚学院任教。他出生于1958年，硕士毕业于乌克兰利沃夫国立弗朗克大学，随后在乌克兰科学院的塔拉斯·舍甫琴科文学研究所获得博士学位。他出版了三本学术专著：《1830–1880年间的乌克兰浪漫主义戏剧》（基辅，1990年）、《潘特利蒙·库里史早期作品的艺术、文学、民俗范式》（基辅，2009年）和《伊万·托比里维奇（卡朋克–卡伊）——其人其书》（捷尔诺波尔，2011年），主编了数十本教育性的乌克兰作家文章合集，在乌克兰和国际刊物上发表了100多篇论文。他指导的10名研究生都顺利完成了论文答辩。他的主要学术方向是19世纪的乌克兰浪漫主义和现实主义文学，如戏剧，塔拉斯·舍甫琴科、潘特利蒙·库里史、米考拉·科斯托马罗夫、蕾西亚·乌克兰卡、伊万·托比里维奇、马尔科·克罗皮尼斯基等人的作品，以及乌克兰民俗和民俗学研究。

Cross-cultural Bridge　文化桥梁

On the Road of Life: "I Cried Because I Had No Shoes…"[1]

Curtis Evans (U.S.A.)

Proofread by George Fleming

Prologue

His workmanlike calligraphy, though not exceptionally artistic,
had a stark beauty and grace born of simplicity — and suffering.

There must be as many tragic stories about beggars as there are beggars. Many of us have a story about a beggar that we have run into — or who

1 "…until I met a man who had no feet." — an old aphorism.

has run into us.[1] Who are these anonymous beings that haunt the streets, that seem to live in an inaccessible, parallel netherworld? As I came to find out, at least some of them manage to find purpose and dignity even in their straitened existence.

The Screever

In the spring of 2015, I began to take notice of a screever, one of those sidewalk artists who in China solicit money by writing characters on pavements (instead of drawing pictures, as does the typical Western screever or sidewalk artist, as he is sometimes known).[2]

His hands had been amputated just below the wrists.

He set up shop three or four times a week in the afternoons and early evenings on a sidewalk by the side of a five-star hotel around the corner from my apartment. Kneeling down and facing the sidewalk, his baseball cap hiding his face as it protected him from the sun, he intently, slowly, and carefully scratched out a long and complex composition on the dark-gray bricks with a piece of white chalk held between his two nubs.

He was of slight build but strong, standing about 160 cm. He invariably dressed neatly in a clean cotton shirt and denim blue jeans, and always carried a large, black backpack.

Although I thought I was inured to vicissitudes and misfortunes, to life's rude mistreatment of our fellow man, the first time I saw his visage I

---

1 I was once in a fast food outlet in the Hangzhou East Railway Station quietly eating a sandwich and in deep thought. Suddenly I felt someone jabbing me vigorously in the back. I turned around to see an old, white-bearded mendicant, in tattered, dirty clothes and with extraordinarily long, bushy Taoist-like eyebrows. It was he who in a most un-Taoist manner had prodded me with the pointy end of his walking stick, hoping that I would bestir myself to offer up a few coins. I do not know how he came up with such a rude form of impetration, but it was not effective.

2 The mendicant screever should not to be confused with the calligraphers that frequent public parks in China. These hobbyists show off their skills by writing on flagstones with large brushes (or sometimes sponges on the end of a stick), using water instead of ink. Their objective is not pecuniary but artistic — their reward is the approbation of people who gather round to admire their work before the water on the pavement evaporates.

was shocked. When I first bent down to give him a coin I saw that he not only lacked hands, but his face had been horribly burned — at first glance, it looked like a puddle of melted burgundy wax and formed whorls of flesh, like multilayered, partially scraped palimpsests, leaving only undecipherable traces on the raw, red parchment of his face. Nonetheless, the underlying, deep lineaments were not harsh and attested a warmth and gentleness of mien. He looked out of two kindly eyes; only one of them seemed to be fully normal. Fortunately, it seems that a kind surgeon somewhere along the way had tinkered with the place where his nose ought to be; a slight bridge showed signs of having been built up with a small strip of skin and there were signs of other reconstruction. This must have greatly improved his visage; he now had a recognizable face, but from my layman's vantage, he appeared to have had little or no other reconstructive or cosmetic surgery.

He showed up several times a week on the same section of sidewalk; it was obviously his territory.

He invariably wrote the same two essays. They were intriguingly entitled *Shenghuo zhi lu* (*The Road of Life*) and *Zhi zhangbei fumu* (*Ode to Elderly Parents*), though I could not read much more than that when walking past at my usual gait.

The finished work was composed of 211 characters. Each character was written on half of a 12cm × 24cm pavement brick. When completed, the two essays were almost a meter wide and stretched some four meters down the sidewalk.

He wrote using simplified regular-style (*kaishu*) characters, with no punctuation marks to break up the long stream of characters in his essay — Chinese language has managed for thousands of years without such marks. When read aloud line by line, they had a pleasing cadence and rhyme, with natural breath stops, making punctuation superfluous.

To complete the whole work took him about five or six hours, depending on whether he took rest breaks.

It would not be easy for someone with two normal hands to write. He wrote inverted characters and in reverse order, from right to left. The piece must be read from the bottom to the top, like this:

Courtesy of Curtis Evans

Line 3: *When I was only two and a half years old*

Line 2: *I wish all good people a life of peace.*

Line 1: *The Road of Life*

Ignore for a moment the mental gymnastics involved in writing upside down; this can be learned with practice and, in any event, it is not as complicated as mirror writing. However, from a physical standpoint, writing upside down is more difficult than it sounds.

From the perception of the reader standing on the sidewalk looking down facing someone who is writing upside down characters, the stroke order is the same as when normally writing Chinese characters. But to the writer of upside-down characters, everything is reversed. Now instead of the easy, natural, downward strokes of the brush towards the writer, as in normal calligraphy, they were laborious upward-pushing strokes of the chalk in a direction away from the writer.[1] Instead of a fluid and natural top-to-bottom, upper-left-to-lower-right sequence of strokes, one must arduously push the chalk away from oneself in an awkward bottom-to-top, lower-right-to-upper-left sequence.

He later told me why he persisted in writing the characters upside down: it is to respect his readers. By writing upside down and backing away from the lines as he works, he shows his respect by constantly facing them, not forcing them to pore over his shoulder. Each character is written with extreme deliberation, sincerity, and consideration for the reader.

When weather was good, he was there almost every day, starting about three o'clock. (Where did he go when it rained?) He spent almost six hours on his knees, hunched over his work with chalk firmly held between his stubs. He completed his masterpiece around eight or nine o'clock and ended by washing down the sidewalk with a couple of liters of water that he carried in his backpack. When he headed home for the evening, all that was left of the canvas of a day's struggle was a slightly damp sidewalk.

I was surprised that his two stumps were so extremely sensitive. He was able to reach into his backpack to get out his cell phone to make and receive calls. He wrote text messages with ease, using only the tip of his right nub.

He became part of the neighborhood; I saw him three or four times a week and began to admire his perseverance. After several months of

---

1 The exceptions are horizontal strokes; these are written from right to left instead of left to right.

occasionally dropping some loose change into his bucket, I decided to try to get to know more about this mysterious, determined person. I struck up a conversation with him one day as I knelt beside him to admire his calligraphy.

His name is Mr. Lu Zeping. In addition to his native topolect (which I found almost unintelligible), he speaks a standard flavor of Mandarin, so we had no problems communicating. It was obvious that he was highly intelligent, but I was relieved to find that he was also pleasant to talk with and seemed kind and gentle.

The Road of Life and Ode to Elderly Parents

I was intently curious about his chalk opus. It more than just told his story; through it, one could glimpse a worldview that was infused with Confucian thought and Chinese culture.

At first, I did not understand most of the two essays. He readily provided assistance to help me figure out a few locutions. Finally, I asked him for permission to take a picture of his work in order to study it more deeply and translate it at my leisure. Again, he readily assented. I took out my camera that I usually carry and took a couple of shots.

Here are my translations:

The Road of Life

I wish all good people a life of peace.

When I was only two and a half years old,

Unfortunately, a room in our house caught on fire.

This cruelly roasted my hands to a crisp and left me with a life of bitterness.

Without hands, everything I do is always hard.

In my heart, the bitter tears of despair have already dried.

In order to survive, I write characters upside down using [the stumps of] my two hands.

[The nubs of] my two hands hold the chalk as I beseech good people.

Even a single stroke is accomplished only with difficulty.

It is not that I do not make great efforts;

I have been doing my utmost to write these characters in order to survive.

Our fate is not in our hands.

When I was a two-year-old baby, I was cruelly burned by fire.

Flood and fire show no mercy, but people do have feelings.

In taking great pains to write upside-down characters, I beseech good people.

Our fate is not up to us.

When I was two years old, I had the misfortune to be maimed by fire.

I greatly appreciate passersby who have taken pity on me.

The offering of the widow's mite shows true feeling.

My gratitude is beyond expression.

I wish all good people much peace.

Ode to Elderly Parents

Of all life's myriad rules and regulations that govern morality, we should respect filial piety the most.[1]

The words of the ancients are still able to warn obstinate people.

Even if one is only ninety percent benevolent and courteous, that is still as deep as the ocean.

---

1 *The original baiju qiangui* 百距千规 is the phrase that I saw a passing scholar politely dispute with Mr. Lu during our photo shoot. It only makes sense to me if *ju* 距 (originally, some sort of male bird) is changed to *ju* 矩 (a carpenter's square) to match *gui* 规 (a carpenter's compass).

Even a mere three inches of loyalty and filial piety are more precious than gold.

Even young crows and sparrows know to repay their mothers by feeding their mothers when they get old.[1]

And even the lamb does not forget to kneel and give thanks as it suckles.

In the same way, children and grandchildren now need to fully show their filial piety.

To avoid suffering frequent regrets in the future, do not wait until old age to do this.

In the years that he has been writing on the sidewalks, he must have written this same script hundreds of times (I ran into him on twenty or more separate occasions as he was writing it). Each time takes hours of strenuous, concentrated effort and care.

His chalk-on-pavement supplication seems to be an endless orison, a ceaseless incantation to the cosmos. At the same time, it is also an example of sapiential literature, an admonition to return to morality, and an exhortation to filial piety. It shows a willingness to accept fate, but rather than being merely a cry for help, I find it much more a cry of courage.

To thank him for his help and his inspirational message, and because I was curious about him, I asked him to lunch not long afterwards. We lunched together several times in local restaurants in the months that followed; after the meal, he would leave, kneel on the sidewalk, and start writing.

I wanted to try to help him in a more concrete way, so because of my interest in photography (which was sparked by my best friend who calls

---

1 This comes from an ancient belief that crows and other birds repay their mothers by feeding them when they get old, as expressed in the saying, *wuya fanbu* 乌鸦反哺.

it "painting with light"), I suggested to Mr. Lu that we do a photo shoot. Perhaps getting his story some publicity might help him or others like him.

The Photo Shoot

The weather at the end of June was warm and comfortable. The light was perfect — the overcast day had that wonderful Shanghai mixture of cloud cover and smog that results in a beautiful diffusion of soft light and an absence of harsh shadows.

He had invited me to his home for lunch before the shoot. His lived in a single small room. A kitchen and bathroom were shared with people who lived in five or six other rooms on the same fourth-floor walkup located somewhere in the low-rent suburbs far out in western Shanghai.

We went together to a supermarket where he bought food for the meal. Just as at the restaurants where we had eaten together, no one batted an eye, looked askance, nor seemed the least bit perturbed by the sight of him or me, a foreigner.

Back at his home, I was amazed to see him quickly chop a few vegetables, a bit of pork, and some ginger and then skillfully combine them with soy sauce, cooking oil, a smidgen of sugar, and a few drops of sesame oil. Within forty-five minutes, he had put together a delicious meal of rice, three dishes, and a soup.

After lunch we headed into the city by subway, arriving about three o'clock at his regular venue by the hotel. Without a word, he immediately set to work with his usual intense concentration and determination.

I took picture after picture, straight through from three o'clock until eight o'clock. I knew that only a handful would be any good, but hoped for one or two exceptional ones. As it started to get dark, I switched to faster and faster lenses in order to capture images with available light and avoid need for flash.

I settled down to work, my two cameras hanging from my neck and a half-dozen lens in my pockets. I concentrated on capturing four of the five types of shots required of every Photojournalism 101 photo essay project: Establishing shots (for example, wide-angle shots of Mr. Lu as he unlimbers his backpack, takes out his chalk, and starts to work, with the sidewalk and buildings in the background), easy-peasy. Mid-range shots (e.g., passersby glancing down at what Mr. Lu is doing), no problem. Detail shots (close-ups of an individual character being written on a paving brick), check. Various action shots (passersby generously dropping alms into the plastic container, someone pausing to take a picture of the sidewalk opus, Mr. Lu washing down the sidewalk at the end of the day, or as he heads home in the evening), okay. And then the finale: Portrait shots. This meant taking close-ups of his face. This was hardest to make myself do, so I waited until near the end of the shoot to get in close and try to capture his spirit by focusing on his eyes.

For a photo editor, the most important shot is the "ambush shot": catching the subject off-guard and surprising and delighting the viewers. But there was no ambushing Mr. Lu, who was the quintessence of concentration, with every move deliberate and with no wasted motion.

How my presence may have affected passersby is hard to say. I saw one foreign lady from the hotel who, seeing me taking pictures, took out her cellphone and also snapped some pictures. She said that she was going to have her tour guide translate the writing for her. She was one of the many people that day who gave generously.

While most people gave no more than a sideward glance (many of them no doubt preoccupied or having seen him many times before), some lingered to read his message. Some even stopped to admire his calligraphy and his gumption. One man earnestly discussed with him a slight textual mistake or ambiguity in the script, but it was the polite deputation of two exegetical scholars exchanging learned opinions. I never saw anyone disrespectful to him. Only once or twice did I even see anyone step on his sidewalk compositions, vulnerable though they were to the hoards of pedestrian feet.

All the passersby and myself seemed to know that without our good fortune in life it might be we, mutatis mutandis, who were kneeling instead of walking on the sidewalk.

The Backstory

A photo essay can tell a story without any words, visually answering the questions of who, what, when, where, and how. But these are only visual answers to superficial questions. There is no answer to the transcendent question of why.

Why did he exhaust himself with scrivenings on the sidewalks? Why was he on the street in the first place? What were the details of his life? What kind of a person is Mr. Lu? What kept him going, day after day? And, what had he learned from his years of kneeling on sidewalks? Slowly, I was able to piece together much of his story.

He was born in a mountain district in Hefeng County in Hubei Province on the 30th of January, 1977.[1]

The next winter, a lady was given responsibility for his care while his parents were in the fields.

---

1 Mr. Lu has an older sister in Hefeng County and a younger brother who is a migrant laborer. They are members of the Tujia ethnic minority.
Hefeng County is administered by the Enshi Tujia and Miao Autonomous Prefecture, in southwestern Hubei Province. It is a secluded and poor mountainous region, though an expressway when completed in the next two years should lessen its isolation and stimulate its economy.
Mr. Lu was born at the tail end of the Year of the Dragon, according to the traditional Chinese calendrical system.

"Suddenly a disastrous fire broke out in our home that seared my face. Because I was an infant, my instinctive reaction was to claw wildly. This led to my tender hands being charred to the bone. By the time my father and mother hurried to my rescue, I was burned beyond recognition and the fingers on my hands were cinders. At that time in the mountain district where we lived, there was no hospital nor clinic — my parents had to depend on some local doctor's herbal preparations to apply to my burns."

So this was the formational tragedy of his life. How does one cope after such an inauspicious start in life? What future lies ahead for such a one?

"When I was six years old, my parents tried to send me to school but none accepted me. My parents did not give up and finally sweet-talked the teacher of a small village school into allowing me to enter. I finished primary school without incident and at sixteen years old I was graduated from junior high school."

Then, as is all too frequent with farm children, he had to leave school. His parents could not afford the high school tuition.

He was unable to be of much help to his parents on their farm. No business wanted to employ him.

"Nonetheless, I refused to sit idly at home all day. Although my body is crippled, my spirit is not; it is strong. In my heart, I was always thinking about what I needed to do. I started picking up trash in my village as a way to earn spare change."

Two years passed, and by his eighteenth birthday the great outward migration of farmers moving to the cities in pursuit of work was in full swing. He decided to join the exodus and seek his fortune. Not telling his parents, he left with no idea of where he would wind up.

He bought a bus ticket and struck out for Wuhan, the provincial capital. Wandering aimlessly among its tall buildings, he was without a single friend or relative. The money he earned from recycling was quickly gone, but he had no desire to return home.

One day while walking in front of the railway station, he suddenly decided to jump on a train, destination unknown. He slept under the seats to avoid the conductor. The next day he ended up in Hangzhou, a city of six million. He was dazed and bedazzled by the skyscrapers and streams of people and vehicles. He had no money, so he stood outside of restaurants hoping for handouts, which kind owners sometimes provided. He slept in parks or on benches in railway stations.

"Several days passed this way, but this kind of life was not what I wanted. I joined others in picking up trash and bottles to recycle. Afterwards, I bought vegetables and sold them on the street."

After a year and a half in Hangzhou, he met a girl from his same village who had come to Hangzhou to work. What happened next he expressed simply as:

"She saw that I was dependable, sincere, and strong. We fell in love and married."

At age twenty-one he returned to his hometown, where they had their first daughter. His wife took care of their daughter and he did some small business in order to support the family. He did this until 2002, when he was twenty-five and they had their second daughter.

"In 2005, finding conditions favorable, I started raising pigs. I fed them by gathering corn stalks for fodder in the mountainous areas of my hometown. By the end of 2005, I started building a proper pig farm. In July 2006, I received a formal award for being the first handicapped person to create a business, which was called the Hefeng County Self-Strengthening Ranch Development Company, Ltd. At that time, the Hefeng County Newspaper and the Enshi Prefecture Report both carried articles

about it. You can read them online.

"But dreams and reality are different. Raising livestock at that time required a large investment. Over a number of years, I was able to scrape together enough money to build basic pigpens and simple fodder facilities.

"I had over a hundred large and small pigs in my pigsties that required a large amount of feed each day. I lacked sufficient capital, so borrowed money from neighbors in order to purchase corn stalks and other fodder. Altogether, in various ways I owed them almost 200,000 RMB [US $29,000]. By the greatest effort, I was able to hang on for more than six months, but then disaster struck again. Most of the pigs sickened and died. This left me utterly bankrupt."

That made it tough; what followed was tougher.

"It was during that time that my wife left us. To this day she has not come back to see our two daughters or me. I hear that she is living in Guangdong Province, has remarried, and has two children there."

What motivates a man to keep going when he seems to be dogged by dark clouds of bitter rain? Where does his inner strength come from?

"My parents are in their mid-seventies and are old and weak. Aside from a bit of farming, they have no means to support themselves in the village. Farming villages are not like cities: people there do not have retirement plans or pensions."

His daughters are in his thoughts daily. Fortunately, his aging parents were caring for them, but they rely on money that he remits.

"Here are two pictures of my daughters. The oldest is sixteen years old and is a first-year student in the county high school. My youngest is thirteen years old and is about to graduate from sixth grade in a village primary school in Hefeng County."

The pictures showed two lovely young ladies, dressed in casual clothes, smiling and striking cute poses of typical teenage girls.

Whatever money can or cannot buy or is or is not the root of, the absence of money is painful. After a series of "sub-subsistence" jobs, he decided to take up screeving on the sidewalks of Shanghai.

"Since I have no other choice, I write on sidewalks beside major boulevards and seek help from kind-hearted people. I do this in order for my parents to be able to live their final years in peace and for my daughters to finish their education. I want to return the money that I owe to my neighbors as soon as possible. Furthermore, I want to provide them with information that I have learned about animal husbandry.

"I now have debts of well over 100,000 RMB [US $14,525]. Hence, at present I have no capital to go into business. As for working for others, no company will hire me in my condition. Every month the local government provides rural people without incomes a monthly stipend of 130 RMB [US $19] in farm village welfare. Basically, there was no way with what I make that I am able to take care of my parents, raise two daughters in school, and also pay back the money I owe my farm neighbors — in fact I am at a dead end. But even less was I able to shirk my responsibilities and duties or tarnish my honor."

How much can a man make by screeving? On a good day, it could total 150 to 200 RMB (US $22 to $29), according to Mr. Lu.

That may sound like fair money, but it is not. During parts of spring and autumn and throughout the summer, with good luck he was able to bring in as much as 2,000 RMB a month. But the rest of the year was largely a loss due to cold weather. It probably worked out to less than 10,000 RMB (US $1,452) per year. Nonetheless, it is far more money than many people make in remote, mountainous areas of China, where they subsist almost solely on crops that they grow themselves. However, in a metropolis like Shanghai, that amount of money does not go far.

It would have been enough for him to pay for rent, food, cell phone, and transportation, with some money left over to send home for his daughters' tuition and upkeep. With luck, there would be a little something left for his parents and perhaps even a little money to lay by.

The amount he could make depended on several factors. First, the weather is critical; unlike many other forms of begging, one cannot screeve when it is raining or cold.

While it might seem that for a screever, the whole city is his scriptorium, this is not so. It is hard to find suitably surfaced sidewalks in just the right areas, with just the right amount of foot traffic.

The threat of being driven away from the site is also a constant worry. Police and city officials are charged with controlling begging and loitering. Usually they are understanding and lenient. But under pressure from nearby businesses that feel the presence of beggars affects their own livelihoods or as part of periodic official crackdowns on begging, they occasionally make the screever "move along" or even threaten to arrest them.

But most of all a screever's income depends on how determined he is and how much physical pain he is able to endure. Hunkering on one's knees on hard pavement for five hours of concentrated effort is exhausting. The only time I ever heard Mr. Lu complain was about his sore back. The pain was excruciating at times. He said that continuing to crouch over his work on the sidewalk was becoming too much for him. The need to recuperate after an exhausting day on the bricks limited him to no more than four days per week, even during good weather.

Conclusion

I was finally able to understand some of the how's and why's of Mr. Lu's life and what it means to be dependent on the kindness of strangers.

But questions still remained.

There are larger, metaphysical questions. In a country where "face" is so important, how does one with a mutilated face and no hands hold on to honor, pride, and dignity — a sense of self? Is it even possible? Yes. The Chinese concept of "face" is metaphorical, not literal. Strength of character, intelligence, and gumption trump good looks or physical perfection. A sense of "face" (in a word, "dignity") comes from within — if dignity is maintained, there can be no *diulian*, no "loss of face."

Was dignity then the source of Mr. Lu's strength and persistence, his courage and determination? Yes, that is partly the answer — and he proved that even in the life of a mendicant, dignity and honor can be maintained.

Yet, surely there was an even stronger force that made him persevere. I did have some inkling; he had mentioned it in passing during our conversations and it should have been obvious had I listened closely. It finally became clear when I consulted him about an appropriate working title for the photo essay project. I quickly suggested one that at the time seemed simple, direct, and logical: *A Day on Mr. Lu's Road of Life*. Mr. Lu vehemently disagreed and quite rightly explained that he did not want a life on the sidewalks to be *his* road of life. Instead, he suggested this title, one that brought his life into focus and moved me deeply with its power and meaning: *A Day on the Road of Life of a Disabled Father Who is Providing for His Daughters*.

What drives him to struggle on in life is the love for his daughters and parents and his sense of responsibility to support them. Perhaps it is not realistic for him to repay the investors who lost everything in his bankruptcy or to become an agricultural consultant. But it is imperative to support those whom he loves dearly.

Then came one of the most meaningful questions of all: After several months of occasional conversations, one day over lunch I asked him, "What have you learned from your years spent writing characters on sidewalks?" His answer still moves me — it leaves me full of hope and with a warm feeling about humanity and China in particular. He said that he had learned that the world is full of many, many kind people…

Epilogue

A few loose ends of this story remain. By the autumn of 2015, perhaps due to pressure from local merchants, Mr. Lu no longer showed up at his old venue near my apartment; whatever the case, he came to prefer other sidewalks in Shanghai. While I no longer ran into him and had thrown my energy into my teaching, we still occasionally contacted each other.

Getting off the grueling sidewalks and getting back into some kind of business had long been Mr. Lu's dream. In the late autumn of 2016, he finally did leave the pavements of Shanghai and returned to his home village in Hubei. Today he lives with and takes care of his aged parents and two children.

Since he is functionally unemployable, he has had to depend on himself, to employ himself. Using money he had slowly accumulated from his years of back-aching screeving, Mr. Lu has started into the pig breeding business again.

In August, 2017, I was finally able to visit Mr. Lu at his family farm on the outskirts of a small village in Hefeng County, where I was warmly welcomed by him and his family and stayed with them for a few days.

Their homestead is nestled low on a mountainside in a steep, stunningly beautiful valley with a large swirling stream in front of the house. The soothing sound of water rilling down incessantly from springs on the hillsides above can be heard day and night. After the hectic pace of life in Shanghai, as I drank in the beauty of the scene what came to mind was the

Chinese saying, *shiwai taoyuan* 世外桃源 ("otherworldly garden of the Peach Blossoms of Immortality") — a Chinese Elysium.

Their concrete house was built a few years previously by the elder Mr. Lu; it had taken him four years to finish. Mr. Lu Zeping and his siblings grew up in an old, traditional Tujia-style house, made of wooden planks framed on timber pilings and with a tile roof, that now lies in disrepair on the mountainside a few hundred feet away.

Corn and potatoes are the most important crops in Hefeng County. Corn is used almost exclusively to feed hogs; potatoes are a human staple, with fried potatoes being the most famous specialty dish in Enshi Prefecture. Beautiful Japanese banana trees (*bajiao*) dot the roadsides and give the region a subtropical feel; they are planted so that their broad, dark-green leaves can be chopped up as fodder to feed hogs.

Everything is planted, cultivated, and harvested using simple hand tools; the small plots of land on steep, terraced hillsides preclude mechanization, and I saw little evidence of animals used for draft or to pull plows. Tricycle-geared, flatbed utility vehicles (lightweight, with motorcycle engines) are used to haul materials to and from the market along narrow, steep, and windy roads.

Ostensibly, the purpose of my visit was to learn something about Chinese farm life; in the spring and summer of 2017, I translated a book on Chinese agriculture[1] and so I had a particular interest in observing Chinese farming up close. However, the primary reason to call on him was to pay silent tribute to a friend's bravery and perseverance in overcoming many obstacles and finally returning to his old homestead.

---

1 *Dudong Zhongguo nongye* 读懂中国农业, 2015, by Zhang Yunhua 张云华, translated as *Insights into Chinese Agriculture*, publication date to be announced.

I found that Mr. Lu and his father are running a modest hog operation of some fifty head. The clean and well-watered pigsties are attached to one end of their house, both for convenience and because flat land for building is at a premium. Traditional Tujia houses have their pigsties on the ground-level beneath the upstairs living quarters.[1] Like all agricultural ventures, this operation is fraught with risks, from avoiding pestilence to steering clear of bankruptcy by keeping feed costs as low as possible while hoping for a seller's market. He expects to send his first pigs to market in November.

Mr. Lu does most of the heavy work of raising feed corn, feeding the animals, and generally running the piggery, while his father puts in long days performing the many small job that require manual dexterity. His mother stays busy with housework, gardening, and cooking delicious meals of homegrown vegetables and pork.

As the sun set behind the towering pine-covered mountains of the narrow valley, our scrumptious evening meals were cooked over a charcoal brazier in the courtyard during the cool of the long, late-summer twilight. The meals consisted of sliced potatoes, a plethora of other chopped fresh garden vegetables, and lean, fresh pork and ham, all fried piecemeal in a large, shallow skillet of rapeseed oil. We gathered around the sizzling skillet and chatted happily as we noshed. The Lu family had grown or raised virtually everything that we ate, including the oilseeds used to make the cooking oil (though they had been taken to be pressed

1 This form of porcine-human symbiosis dates from ancient times in China, as attested by the modern Mandarin Chinese word for "house" or "home" (*jia* 家), which abstractly depicts a pig (*shi* 豕) under the roof of a house (*mian* 宀). This character is found in Shang dynasty oracle bone inscriptions (archaic glyphs that were the precursors of modern written Chinese) that date from more than three thousand years ago. Some Zhou and Han dynasty funerary objects sculpted in clay also depict pigs and other farm animals living under the houses of farmers.

commercially).

In an attempt to repay their hospitality and to learn more, I tried to stay busy with farm chores, mainly by helping feed hogs (twice a day) and hand shelling and winnowing some of last year's corn. I also observed the gelding of a half-dozen young boars and neutering of three or four gilts. Had I been there a week or two later, I could have helped bring in the new corn that was almost ready to be harvested; I since have learned that due to the spell of rainy weather that followed my visit, much of their corn crop that they had planned on feeding their hogs was ruined. Their simple and largely self-sufficient life living close to the land reminded me that they, like hundreds of millions of China's small farmers, work long and hard for exiguous recompense.

Mr. Lu's two daughters are even more lovely in person than in their photographs. The youngest daughter is in junior high school. His oldest just took the college entrance examination and is about to enter university. She hopes to graduate and find a good job one day. With hard work, scholarships, and luck, she may yet realize her dream.

The trip afforded a fascinating window into the life of Mr. Lu, including into the mystery of Mr. Lu's plastic surgery (that I had noticed the first time I saw his face). On my way back from Hefeng during our breakfast stop, the driver of the bus mentioned to me a story about Mr. Lu (the driver did not know his name, but, like everyone I met in the village, knew of Mr. Lu). According to his somewhat hazy (and as it turned out, faulty) recollection, it seems a number of years ago a foreign doctor who was traveling through Hefeng met Mr. Lu and took him to Shanghai to perform reconstructive surgery. I was curious about the nationality of the doctor and particularly how he happened to be wandering in the hinterlands of Hubei

Province and met Mr. Lu; back in Shanghai, in my thank-you letter, I asked Mr. Lu if he would mind telling me the story. He wrote back:

The people who provided me with reconstructive surgery were Germans. I met them in 1997, when I was eighteen years old. I had started vending on the sidewalk [in Shanghai]. I rented a room in a house in the Panjiawan area near the Shanghai Railway Station that was originally an old dwelling but that has since had its occupants moved out and been razed. As it happened, the landlord's child was a student at Tongji University. The Germans were teachers at Tongji, but were not doctors. When they came to visit their student, we met and they were curious when they saw that I cooked for myself. They were Christians. After meeting and talking with me a few times, we gradually became friends. They took an interest in helping me, and after about a year they visited me at my family home [in Hefeng] to see where I lived. Afterwards, they put me in touch with plastic surgeons at Shanghai Changhai Hospital [and provided for my reconstructive facial surgery]. When I was twenty years old, I wed and my oldest daughter was born; they again also paid for everything. Now they have retired and returned to Germany, so we are rarely in contact. It has been about two years since last we corresponded, since I do not have their phone number nor WeChat information...

I did not question Mr. Lu further about who these kind people were, other than to ascertain that they were a group of about six colleagues. One of the precepts of Christian charity is anonymity; the emphasis is on the charitable act itself, not on drawing attention to the agent of the act. Suffice to say that the world is a much richer and more pleasant place because of such Good Samaritans who help others in need.

Mr. Lu's present felicitous situation is partly due to the money he scraped together during his bitter years of screeving, born of his bulldog-determination to support the education of his daughters and to take care of them and his parents. Throughout his life, he has shown talent, intelligence, and many practical abilities in overcoming hardships and handicaps. However, as I saw during my visit, his genuine good fortune actually stems from the love and support of his parents, his two daughters, siblings, relatives, friends, and neighbors. Perhaps only with such love and support does anyone have a chance to find true happiness.

What will his future bring? Will his new venture bring him a modicum of financial success? Will he be able to pay for his children's education, help his elderly parents, and still be able to keep his own head above water, just by raising a few pigs and tilling a few tiny plots of land? I do not know. But it is clear that he has already done something of transcendent import: he has managed to maintain purpose and dignity in his life. He has already succeeded as a man.

About the author:

Curtis Evans, American, has been teaching at SISU since the spring of 2016 and now teaches writing, translation, and cinema courses. He is interested in traditional Chinese history, philosophy, and culture, and in his free time enjoys travel, studying languages, and translating.

生活之路——“我因没有鞋而哭泣……”[1]

Curtis Evans（美国）

张宏雨　译

梁晓雪　审校

前言

他的书法精美而娴熟，尽管不是堪称一绝的艺术品，但其背后蕴藏着朴实的美丽与简洁的优雅，以及他多舛的命运……

乞丐有很多，他们的悲惨故事也不胜枚举。大多数人都会有碰见乞丐的经历，或者更确切地说，是他们撞见我们。[2]这些毫不起眼的无名氏游荡在街头，似乎生活在一个常人无法接近的悲惨世界，他们到底是谁？我渐渐发现，尽管处境如此的窘迫，有些乞丐仍然找到了生活的意义和尊严。

街头写字行乞者

2015年的春天，我开始注意到一位街头行乞者，他和中国其他的街头“艺术家”一样，通过自己的艺术表演来获得路人的行赏。不过他的表演不是在西方常见的画画，而是写字。[3]

他的双手从手腕处被截掉。

他在一家五星级酒店旁的人行道上行乞，就在我所住公寓的转角处。他每周来这里三四次，从下午待到傍晚。他双腿跪地，脸朝地面，头上戴着一顶棒球帽遮挡阳光。他用手腕夹住一只白色粉

1　这是一个谚语，全句是：“我因为没有鞋而哭泣，直到我遇到一个没有脚的人。”

2　有一次我在杭州东站的一家快餐店里边吃三明治边思考人生，突然间感觉到有人重重地戳我的背。我转头一看，是一个白发苍苍、衣服破旧不堪的乞丐。他有着道教徒那种长而密的眉毛，可是他的举动却十分有悖道教的作为方式——他用他的拐杖尖端戳我，以期我能施舍点零钱。我不明白他为什么请求得这么粗鲁，这种请求显然是没有效果的。

3　这位街头的行乞者和在中国的公园中常见的书法爱好者是不同的。后者主要展现他们用巨大的笔刷（有时是绑在棒子末端的海绵）蘸水在石板上书写的才能。他们展示艺术，不求敛财。在水写书法作品蒸发前，围观群众的关注是对他们最好的鼓励。

笔，在深灰色的砖块上认认真真、一笔一画地写着复杂的汉字。

他不太高但强壮，身高大约1米6，总穿着干净整洁的棉T恤和蓝色牛仔裤，背着一个大大的黑色双肩包。

尽管我对人们的坎坷与不幸都早已司空见惯，但是当我第一眼见到他的面容时，我震惊了。我弯下腰给他硬币时，发现他不仅没有手，脸也被烧得面目全非：乍看之下，就像一滩融化了的蜡坑或搅拌过的血肉，或是部分被刮去重写的多层抄本，在他羊皮纸般的脸上留下不可破译的字迹。尽管如此，他面部的轮廓线却并不粗糙，而是展现了一种温和的风度。他两只眼睛都能看见，目光和善，但只有一只眼睛是完好的。他的鼻子可能被某个好心的医生简单地处理了一下，用一块皮肤架起了一个不太明显的鼻梁，也能看出其他修复的痕迹。这很大程度上修正了他的面部，至少看起来还像张脸。但是除此之外，他看起来没有接受过任何别的治疗或整容手术。

他每周都会来这里几次。很明显，这儿成了他行乞的固定场所。

他总会写同样的两篇散文，一篇叫《生活之路》，另一篇叫《致长辈父母》，不过每次经过的时候，我都只能扫上一眼，看不了太多。

两篇文章加起来一共211个汉字，他在每块12×24厘米大小的路面砖上写两个字，这样完成之后，便形成了一个大约宽1米、长4米的长方形。

他用的是简体楷书，整篇文章没有一个标点符号——曾有几千年，汉语都是如此。一行一行地读下去时，你就会发现，即使没有标点，也能感受到其轻快的节奏和韵律，且意群明显。

完成这两篇文章大概需要花费他五六个小时的时间，这需要看他中途有没有休息。

这项工作对于有双手的人来说都不简单。他的字是反着写的，并且整篇的书写顺序是从下到上，从右到左。读整篇时要从下往上读，就像这样：

第3行：小时只有两岁半

第2行：好人一生平安

第1行：生活之路

不说颠倒顺序来写字所需的脑力负荷（这可能可以通过练习实现，并且不像镜像书写那么复杂），但体力上，颠倒顺序的书写也远比想象中困难。

对于路人来说，他们看到的汉字是按正常顺序书写的，但对于坐在对面的书写者来说，所有的字都是反过来的。这就意味着，在书写汉字的时候，书写者不能按照正常的、简单的笔画顺序来书写，而是按照相反的、更难的笔画顺序来书写。[1]也就是说，他不是按照从上到下、从左到右的顺序自然、流畅地书写，而是努力地往远离身体的方向使劲，按照从下到上、从右到左的顺序艰难地书写。

后来，这位行乞者告诉我他坚持这样写字的原因：尊重读者。通过这样书写，他就可以一直面向读者，而不是迫使读者从他背后来阅读，从而表达对读者的尊重。每个字都体现他的认真和诚意，饱含他对读者的体贴。

天气好的时候，他几乎每天都来，从三点开始，一直跪在地上，弯着腰，用手腕夹着粉笔卖力地写字，持续大概六个小时。（下雨的时候他会去哪呢？）等他的作品完成已经是晚上八九点了，接着他会用自己带的几瓶水将地面冲洗干净，当他回家时，忙碌一天的痕迹便消失不见，只剩微湿的人行道。

他的两只手腕十分灵活，这让我非常惊讶：他能够用两只手腕从背包中拿出手机接电话和打电话，他甚至可以毫不费劲地用他手腕的末端发短信。

渐渐地，他似乎成了社区的一部分，每周我都会见到他三四

1 特例是写“横竖撇捺”的“横”这一画时，他从右往左写，而不是从左往右。

次，我开始佩服他的坚韧不拔。开始几个月，我路过他的时候偶尔会给他一些零钱，但这之后，我想更了解这位神秘而又意志坚定的人。有一天，当我蹲在他旁边欣赏他的书法时，我们聊起了天。

他叫卢泽平，除了会说我根本不能理解的家乡方言，他还会讲一口标准的普通话，所以我们沟通起来也没什么困难。显而易见，他很有智慧，不过除此之外，他也善于言谈，并且十分友好，这让我倍感欣慰。

《生活之路》和《致长辈父母》

我对于他的书法作品充满着好奇：这不仅仅是在讲述他自己的人生故事，其中更蕴含着儒家思想和中国文化。

起初，他写下的大部分内容我都不太明白，但是，在他的积极帮助下，我弄懂了一些汉语的惯用语。而后，我询问他是否可以将他的作品照下来，以便我在闲暇之余仔细研读并翻译出来，他欣然答应。于是，我拿出随身携带的相机，拍了几张照片。

原文如下：

生活之路

好人一生平安
小时只有两岁半
家中不幸房起火
烧残双手苦一生
无手做事时时难
心中痛苦泪已干
双手倒写求生存
两手拿笔求好人
一笔一画苦写成
不是有力不去使
为了生存苦写字
命运波折不由人

自幼两岁火烧残
水火无情人有情
苦写倒字求好人
一生命运不由己
两岁不幸火烧残
感谢行人可怜我
一分一文是真情
感激之情难以诉
但愿好人多平安

致长辈父母

百距千规孝为尊[1]
古言尚可警顽人
九成仁礼深如海
三寸忠孝贵比金
鸦雀素知回哺意[2]
羔羊不忘跪至忱
今朝需尽儿孙孝
莫待老来忏悔频

这些年来，他一直在街道上写这两首诗，一定写了好几百次。我曾撞见他几十次，他都在写这两首诗。每次，他都要花费好几个小时，艰难、认真、专注地写着。

他用粉笔写就的求告好似永无休止的祷告和永不停歇的圣歌。同时，这又是充满智慧的文字，唤醒人们内心深处的道德，劝诫人

1 我拍照的时候，看到一个路过的学者和卢先生讨论“百距千规”这个词。我个人认为如果把“距”（本义是一种公鸟）换成“矩”（本义是木匠用的直角尺），搭配“规”（本义是木匠用的圆规）更合适。

2 这源自一个中国的传统信念：乌鸦和其他的鸟类会通过喂养其年老的母亲来回报养育之恩，俗称“乌鸦反哺”。

们坚守孝道。作品表现了他对命运的坦然接受，他不是一味地向人们索取帮助，而是向人们展示自己的勇气。

随后，我邀请他和我一起吃饭，一是为了感谢他对我的帮助以及带给我的灵感，二是为了更多地了解他，满足我对他的好奇心。于是，在接下来的几个月里，我和他一起在附近的餐厅吃了几顿饭。他吃完就继续跪在人行道上写字。

我希望能用更具体的方式，给他实实在在的帮助。因为我对摄像很感兴趣（灵感源自我的一位朋友，他将摄像比作“用光绘画”），所以我建议给卢先生拍摄一组照片。或许用这样的方式，能让更多的人知道他的故事，从而帮助到他和像他一样的人。

拍摄照片

六月底的天气温暖而舒适，光线也非常适宜——上海多云的天气夹杂着淡淡的雾，光线十分柔和，又不会产生严重的阴影。

在拍摄照片前，他曾邀请我去他家吃午饭。他住在上海西边远郊的廉租房里，那里没有电梯，他住在四楼的一个小单间内，同一层里还有五六个单间住着人，他们共用厨房和卫生间。

我们一起去超市买做饭所需的食材。和在我们一起吃过饭的餐厅里一样，周围的人并没有向我们投来诧异或者怀疑的目光，也没有因他的外表或因我是个外国人而显露出一丝的惊讶。

回到家中他开始做饭，非常熟练地切菜、剁肉，准备生姜等一些调料，一切就绪之后，便开始炒菜，他将食材放入锅内，倒入一些酱油、食用油，加了少量的糖和几滴芝麻油，不到45分钟，一顿丰盛可口的午餐就准备好了，一共三菜一汤加上米饭。

午饭之后，我们乘坐地铁赶往市中心，到达他行乞的老地方时，已将近下午三点。他二话不说，放下包裹，开始写字，依然是那么的专注和坚定。

我拿出相机，不停地为他拍照，从下午三点一直到晚上八点。我知道，可能只有那么一小部分照片拍得还算不错，但我还是希望能有一两张拍得特别好的照片。夜幕降临，天色渐晚，为了更好地采光，同时避免使用闪光灯，我采用了快镜。

我脖子上挂着两台照相机，兜里装着六七个镜头，开始为他继续拍摄。为了达到基础摄影报道课对照片项目的要求，我努力去捕捉四五个不同类型的镜头。比如定场镜头：我使用广角镜头来拍摄正在工作的卢先生——他打开背包，掏出粉笔，开始写字，他的背后是熙熙攘攘的街道和高大的建筑。这对我来说小菜一碟。中景拍摄：以路人俯视的视角拍摄卢先生。这对我来说也没什么大问题。细节镜头：对人行道砖上的每个汉字进行近距离拍摄，给它们特写。这个我也还算擅长。动作镜头：包括拍摄行人对卢先生的施舍，行人驻足拍摄人行道上的作品，卢先生在晚上洗刷人行道，以及他在夜幕中踏上归途等场景，这些对我来说也还可以。最后是人像镜头：主要是对卢先生脸部的特写，这对我来说是最难的。于是，我把这一部分放在整组拍摄的最后，找机会靠近他，试图通过聚焦于他的眼神来捕捉他的精神世界。

对于一位摄影编辑来说，最重要的是捕捉一些主角不经意间的举动，用这些出其不意的镜头给观者带来新鲜感和愉悦感。但是，这次的拍摄却很难实现这一点，因为卢先生自始至终都非常专注，除了一笔一画地写字，他没有什么多余的动作。

我并不清楚我的这一行为是否对过路行人产生了影响。我注意到有一位外国女士从宾馆出来，看见我在拍照，也掏出自己的手机拍了几张。她告诉我，她会让导游将照片里的字翻译给她听。那一天，慷慨解囊的人很多，她是其中一位。

路人当中尽管有很多只是瞥了他一眼（很明显，他们当中很多人都心事重重，或是见过卢先生好多次了），但是还是有些人会停下来阅读他的作品，甚至有人会驻足欣赏他的书法，赞叹他的毅力。有一位路人还热心地与他讨论起了文章的内容，指出了文章中的一点小错误或读起来模棱两可的地方，不过，他们的讨论是礼貌客气的，是一次知识的交流。我从来没见到过有人对他表现出一丝的不尊重。只有一两次，我见到有人踩在了卢先生的作品上，不过，在熙熙攘攘的人群中，写在石砖上的汉字的确显得不那么起眼。

所有的路人包括我似乎都意识到，若不是运气好，也许跪在地上的就是我们。

背后的故事

照片无言，却可道尽人物、事件、时间、地点、状态。但这些都只是表面上的内容，背后的原因难有解释。

他为什么要煞费苦心地在人行道上写字呢？他又是怎样来到露天的街道上的呢？他的生活到底是怎样的呢？他又是一个怎样的人呢？是什么驱使他每天都来到这里呢？他年复一年地跪在街道边写字，又收获了什么呢？渐渐地，我拼凑出了他背后的故事。

1977年1月30号，他出生于湖北省鹤峰县的一个山区。第二年冬天开始，当他的父母在田间耕作的时候，有个女人会负责照顾他。[1]

“突然，家里爆发一场大火，我的脸被烧焦。因为那时候我还是个婴儿，我的本能反应就是疯狂地乱抓，这使得我娇嫩的双手严重烧伤，骨头都裸露出来，我父母赶来救我之前，我已被烧得面目全非，手指也全都烧成灰烬。那时候，在我们住的山区里，没有一家医院或诊所，我的父母只能寻求当地医生的帮助，用一些中草药医治我的伤口。”

他的人生由此构筑在这个悲剧之上。一个人，在人生的起点，就遭遇如此大的劫难，接下来他要怎么做呢？他随后的人生命运又会如何呢？

---

1 卢先生在鹤峰县有个姐姐，还有个弟弟是个农民工。他们是土家族人。鹤峰县隶属于恩施土家族苗族自治州，在湖北省的西南部，是一个与世隔绝的贫穷山区，不过两年后通车的高速公路会增加此地与外界的联系并促进经济的发展。根据中国农历系统，他的出生时间是龙年的末尾。

“我六岁的时候，父母想尽办法让我去学校念书，但是没有一所学校愿意接受我。我的父母没有放弃，终于，他们说服了一所乡村小学的老师接纳我。就这样，我顺利地读完了小学，并且在16岁的时候初中毕业。”

不过，接下来，和大多数农民家的孩子一样，他因为父母担负不起高中学费而辍学。

但是他不能帮父母干农活，也不能打工，因为没有一个老板愿意雇佣他。

“然而，我不愿意整日坐在家中无所事事。虽然我的身体残废了，但我的精神还是健全的。我一直在默默地思考我可以做些什么。我开始在村子里拾垃圾，挣一些零花钱。”

两年后，也就是在他18岁的时候，掀起了一股农民工进城务工的热潮。于是，他也加入了进城大军，决定去碰碰运气。没有告诉自己的父母，也不知道自己会去哪里，他就这样离开了自己的村庄，踏上了进城之路。

他买了一张开往省城武汉的车票。到达武汉后，他便开始毫无目的地闲逛，穿梭在高楼大厦之间。在那里，他一个朋友或亲人都没有，通过捡垃圾赚的钱也很快花光了，但是，他没有一丝回家的念头。

一天，他在火车站前闲逛，突然萌生了一个念头：随意跳上一列火车，让火车带他前往未知的远方。上火车之后，他躺在了座位下面，以防列车员查票。第二天，车抵达了终点，即拥有600万人口的杭州。面对熙熙攘攘的人群、川流不息的车辆和一排排的摩天大楼，他顿时觉得头晕目眩、眼花缭乱。此时此刻，他身无分文，于是，他站在一家饭店门口，希望有人能施舍他一些零钱，有时一些有同情心的老板会这么做。晚上，他通常在公园或是火车站里的长椅上度过漫漫长夜。

“我就这样过了几天，但这并不是我想要的生活。我还和其他人一起捡过垃圾废品，之后还在街上卖过菜。”

在杭州待了一年半后，他遇到了一位同乡的姑娘，她是来杭州打工的。对于接下来发生的故事，他只是轻描淡写道：

“她觉得我靠得住，很真诚，也很强壮。我们相爱了，于是就结了婚。”

21岁的时候，他回到自己的家乡，他们的第一个女儿在那里出生。他的妻子负责照顾女儿，而他做一些小生意养家糊口。2002年他25岁时，他们的二女儿出生。

“2005年的状况还不错，于是我开始养猪。我在山区里收集玉米秆作为饲料喂猪。2005年年末的时候，我开始搭建一个不大不小的养猪场。2006年7月，我收获了第一份事业上的成功，我建立了鹤峰县自强牧业发展有限公司，成为第一个自主创业的残疾人。那时，鹤峰县报和恩施州报对此事都进行了报道，你在网上可以看到。

“可是，梦想和现实是有差距的。饲养牲畜需要大量的投资，几年之后，我终于筹集了足够的钱，建造了简易猪舍，还做了一些简单的饲养工具。

“我一共养了一百多头大小不等的猪，这意味着每天都需要大量的饲料。然而，我手头上的资金却不足，于是我从邻居那里东拼西凑了一些钱来购买玉米秆和其他饲料。就这样，我差不多欠了他们20万人民币。我努力让猪舍又维持了6个多月，然而，灾难再次发生，养的猪大部分都生病死掉了，这下我彻底破产了。”

之后发生的事情更是雪上加霜。

“就是在这个时候，我的妻子舍我们而去，直到今天，她都没有回来看我或者我们的女儿一次。我听说她现在在广东，已经结婚了，并且有两个孩子。”

是什么让这位饱受苦难折磨的人继续前行呢？支撑他的力量又源于何处？

“我的父母也已经七十多岁了，年迈体衰。除了种庄稼获得的一点微薄收入，他们没有其他经济来源。农民不像城里的居民，他们老的时候既没有退休金也没有养老金。”

每天他都会想着自己的女儿，还好，年迈的父母可以帮忙照看，但是需要他不断地向家中汇钱。

“这里有两张我女儿的照片。大女儿16岁了，在县里读高一。小女儿13岁，在鹤峰县念小学，马上就要毕业了。”

照片上是两位年轻可爱的小姑娘，她们穿着休闲装，脸上露出灿烂的笑容，举止动作和同龄人一样可爱。

不管钱是不是万能的，没有钱的确很可怜。陆续打了些零工后，他决定来上海街头写字赚钱。

“因为我别无选择，只能在大马路两边的人行道上写字，努力寻求一些好心人的帮助。我这么做，是为了让我的父母能安享晚年，让我的两个女儿能完成她们的学业，我还想尽快还清邻居们借给我的钱。此外，我还想分享我学到的一些有关家畜养殖的知识。

“现在，我还剩10万元的欠债，所以，目前我还没有资金去创业。至于说打工，没有一家工作单位会雇佣我。每月，当地政府会向没有收入的农村人口发放130元的补贴作为农村福利。事实上，我根本没有能力照看父母，抚养女儿，偿还欠债——说白了，我已走投无路。但是，尽管这样，我依然不能逃避责任，也不能贬低自己的尊严。”

在街头写字能挣多少钱呢？卢先生说，运气好的话，一天总共可以挣到150到200元。

听起来似乎不错，可是事实却并非如此。春季和秋季的部分时候以及整个夏天，运气好的话，他一个月可以有2000元的收入，但是，剩下的日子，由于天气的原因，他都会入不敷出。一年大概有不到1万元的收入。不过，与偏远山区的居民相比，他的年收入已非常可观了。在那些地区，人们的经济来源主要依靠种植的庄稼。当然，在上海这样的大都市，这点收入是远远不够的。

他的收入足够支付房租、伙食费、电话费和交通费，同时还能结余一些寄到家中，支付女儿的学费以及生活费。运气够好的话，还可能剩一点留给父母，甚至存一点备用。

他收入的多少由几个因素决定。首先是天气，这很关键，不像其他的行乞者，每当下雨或寒冷时，他便不能在街头写字行乞。

我们似乎会觉得，对于一个街头写字的行乞者来说，整个城市的每个角落都可以成为他写字的地方，然而事实并非如此。很难在一片合适的区域找到一条地面适合写字且人流量适中的街道。

此外，他还整日担心自己会被赶走。警察和城管会对行乞者和流浪汉进行管理，他们一般很体谅，也很宽容。但是，附近的一些商铺觉得行乞者会影响生意，便会对他们施加压力。此外，警察和城管也会接到官方的任务对行乞者进行周期性监管。因此，他们偶尔会要求行乞者“离开此地”，甚至威胁说要逮捕他们。

不过，对于行乞者来说，收入多少主要取决于个人的耐力和意志。跪在坚硬的人行道上五个小时，一动不动、专心致志地写字是一件让人筋疲力尽的事儿。唯一一次听到卢先生抱怨，是他说背疼，有时会疼痛难忍。他告诉我，长期蹲伏在这里写字，他的身体已经有些难以负荷。在人行砖上跪一下午，他不免透支体力，需要好好休息才能恢复。所以，即使天气很好，他一周最多也只能工作四天。

结语

我终于大致明白了卢先生的生活，他为什么要在这里写字，他如何生存，以及路人的慷慨施舍对他的意义。但是，我仍然还有很多疑惑。

还有很多深层次的问题。在一个如此看重“脸面”的国家，一个被烧得面目全非的人如何维护自己的荣誉、自尊和尊严？甚至有没有可能维护？答案是肯定的。汉语的“脸面”通常取的是其比喻意义，而非表面意义。毅力、智慧以及进取心这些内在的东西要远胜美丽的外表。“脸面”（即“尊严”）来自内在——如果捍卫了尊严，就无所谓“丢脸”。

那么，卢先生的毅力、坚持、勇气和决心是源于内心的尊严吗？是的，但这只是部分原因——他证明了，即使是一个乞丐，也依然可以捍卫自己的尊严和荣誉。

当然，还有一个更强大的力量一直支撑着他坚持下去。一开始我不是太明白，他在我们的对话中提到过，我听得很认真，但是他讲得比较隐晦。当我和他商量摄影报道的标题时，我才终于弄清楚。我提出了一个比较简单、直接、符合逻辑的标题：《卢先生的人生之路：一日缩影》。他强烈反对，解释说他并不希望他的人生之路就是在人行道上。他说出了一个题目：《守护女儿的残疾父亲的人生之路：一日缩影》。这个题目说出了他人生的重点，也让我感动不已。

他坚持的动力就是对女儿和父母的爱，还有强烈的责任感。也许，对他这样一个身无分文的人来说，还清贷款或者做一个农业咨询师是遥不可及的，但是，供养那些他深爱的人还是义不容辞的。

我们就这样相处了几个月，一天，吃午饭的时候我问了他一个问题，或许是所有问题当中最重要的一个。“这么多年来你一直在街边写字，你有何收获呢？”他的回答依旧让我万分感动：“我明白了世界上有很多很多的好人……”这句话犹如一股暖流在我心间涌动，让我感受到了满满的希望，尤其是让我感到中国浓厚的人情味。

后记

故事到此并未结束。到了2015年秋天，也许由于沿街店家带来的压力，卢先生不再出现在我住所附近的老地方，他转移到了其他的人行道上。虽然我不再碰见他，平常把精力都投入到教学中，我们仍然保持着联系。

卢先生一直抱有梦想，就是离开辛苦写字乞讨的人行道，回老家做点小生意。终于在2016年的晚秋，他离开上海回到湖北老家。

目前他和家人住在一起，照顾年长的父母和两个孩子。

他因身体条件而不宜受雇，所以他只能依赖自己。他用多年辛苦慢慢积攒下来的钱，重启自己的养猪事业。

2017年8月，我终于找到机会拜访卢先生位于鹤峰县郊外一个小村庄的老家，并受到了他全家热情的接待。我在那里住了几天。

他们的家坐落在山谷中，位于一个地形陡峭、美得令人窒息的村庄，房子前面还有一条弯曲的河流。从早到晚都可以听到连绵不绝的从山腰泉水传来的美妙流水声。由于长期生活在节奏紧张的上海，面对此情此景，我不禁联想起中国古人所说的“世外桃源”。

他们家的混凝土房子是由卢先生的父亲在几年前建造的，花了大概四年时间。卢泽平先生及其姐弟生长于传统的土家楼中。这是一种在木质地基上搭建木板和瓦片屋顶的建筑。此楼在几百英尺以外的山脚下，已经废弃了。

鹤峰县最重要的作物是玉米和土豆。玉米主要用来喂猪，土豆则是给人吃的。恩施自治州的特色菜就是炸土豆。芭蕉树点缀着道路两边，仿佛进入了亚热带地区。种植这些作物的主要原因是其宽大的深绿色叶子可以剁碎作为猪饲料。

所有作物的播种、养殖和收割都使用简单的手工农具：梯田地形妨碍了机械化种植，当地也很少用动物来劳作或拉犁。在这种又窄又陡的蜿蜒地形中，人们用机动三轮车在市场来回搬运货物。

我的拜访基于几个原因。其中之一就是了解一下中国农村生活。2017年上半年，我翻译了一本有关中国农业的书，[1]一直想要亲自去看看农村的情况。不过，最重要的原因是去拜访这位让我敬佩的朋友。他的坚毅和忍耐使他克服了人生的很多障碍。我发现卢先生和他的父亲养了约50头猪。干净且水分充足的猪舍连接着他们房子的一端，一方面是因为这样比较方便，另一方面平地比较适合搭

---

1 《读懂中国农业》，2015，作者张云华，英文版出版日期待定。

建建筑。传统的土家楼将他们的猪舍建于地面层，位于楼上生活区的下面。[1]养猪业和其他农业生产一样，存在一定的风险，比如虫害、价格不断攀升的饲料以及供过于求的市场。他期待着第一批猪可以在11月份上市。

卢先生负责绝大多数体力活，包括种玉米、喂猪和清理猪圈，而他的父亲花不少时间做精细的手工活。他的母亲则忙着做家务，在田里劳作，并用自己种的蔬菜和家里养的猪做可口的饭菜。当太阳落于被松树覆盖的高山山谷中，在夏末长长的黄昏中，可口的晚餐已经在庭院的炭火盆上准备就绪。做晚餐时，她把土豆片、其他切好的新鲜蔬菜以及瘦猪肉和火腿放入巨大的浅口锅里，用菜籽油翻炒。我们在滋滋作响的锅旁边吃边聊天。几乎所有吃的东西都是他们家自己种的，包括制作油的油菜籽（尽管他们需要出钱来榨油）。

为了回报他们的热情款待，以及更了解他们的生活，我尝试了各种农活，主要包括一天两次的喂猪，手剥、风选去年收割的玉米。我还观察了六只公猪和三四只母猪的阉割过程。如果我在那边再待一两周，我甚至可以帮忙参与今年玉米的收割工作。我回来之后不久得知，由于雨水过多，那些准备被用来当猪食的玉米收成不好，大都被糟蹋了。他们的生活简单且自给自足，与农地共存；就像中国数以亿计的农民一样，他们巨大的工作量只带来微薄的回报。

卢先生的两位女儿比照片上更可爱。小女儿在上初中，大女儿刚结束高考，准备上大学。她希望毕业后能够找到一份好工作。凭借勤奋、奖学金和运气，她也许能实现自己的理想。

这次访问使我更了解卢先生的生活，包括他经历过的一次整容

1 这种人猪共生的系统要追溯到中国古代了。由现代汉字“家”为证：该字为上下结构，上面的宝盖头有房子的意思，下面的“豕”便是猪的意思。这个字在三千多年前的商代甲骨文上有记载（甲骨文是古代象形文字，现代汉语的前身）。有些周朝和汉朝的陶塑陪葬品中，也描绘了猪和其他家畜居于农夫房子下面的场景。

手术（初次见面时我已注意到了）。在驾车回鹤峰的路上，我们停下来吃早餐，司机向我提到关于卢先生的一件事（司机不清楚他的名字，不过就像村里的其他人一样，也知道他这个人）。根据司机师傅的模糊记忆（后来发现他记忆有误），前几年有一位国外的医生来到鹤峰旅游偶然碰见卢先生，于是带他去上海做脸部整容。我对这位医生的国籍感到好奇，尤其是他如何在湖北的穷乡僻壤撞见卢先生的。回到上海后，我在给卢先生的感谢信里问及此事。以下是他回信的有关内容：

“帮助我整容的几个外国人来自德国。我们是在1997年认识的。那时候我只有18岁，刚（到上海）开始摆地摊。我在火车站附近的潘家湾租了一个老房子，后来那里拆迁了。房东家的小孩正好在同济大学上学。那些德国人是同济大学的外教，而不是医生。他们来学生家里玩，看见我自己做饭吃，比较好奇。他们是基督徒。在几次见面和聊天后，我们慢慢成了朋友。他们一直对我很关心，给了我很多帮助。我们认识差不多一年的时候，他们还来我老家（鹤峰）做客，了解我的家庭情况，然后给我联系了上海长海医院做整容手术（还为我承担了整容的费用）。我20岁的时候结婚和生大女儿，他们也支付了所有费用。不过他们现在已经退休回国，联系得非常少了。我们差不多有两年多时间没有联系了，因为我也没有他们的电话或者微信……”

对于这些帮助过他的善良人，我并没有过多地追问。我所知道的就是：那六个德国人是同事。在基督教里，做慈善的人往往不想他们的名字被公开，因为他们只想做善事而不是为了留名。可以这么说，这些乐善好施的人让这个世界变得更美好了。

目前卢先生的状况有所好转。他忍辱负重多年，积攒了钱照顾女儿供她们受教育，还照顾自己的父母。在他的人生中，他运用自己的才能、智慧和很多实际的能力去克服各种艰难险阻。然而，从这次拜访中，我观察到他的幸运其实来源于周围人的爱和支持，包括他的父母、孩子、兄弟姐妹、亲戚、朋友和邻居们。也许只有拥有他们的爱和支持，他才能找到真正的幸福。

卢先生的未来会是怎么样？他的小生意能让他赚到钱吗？他能不能仅靠几十头猪和几块小田地负担起孩子的学费，赡养他年长的父母，并支撑自己的生活呢？我不知道。但我知道他已经非常努力地做好了最重要的事：在生活中保有目标和尊严。作为一个人，他已经成功了。

作者简介：

Curtis Evans，美国籍，从2016年春季在上海外国语大学任教至今，教授写作、翻译及电影赏析。他对中国古代历史、哲学及文化有着浓厚的兴趣。在业余时间，他喜欢旅游、学习语言和做翻译工作。

Learning Chinese

Ourania Katavouta (Greece)
Proofread by George Fleming

As many people already know and experience, language is a journey. It is a journey to get to know the people that speak a specific language. In ancient Greek there is a saying that goes as follows: «Αρχή σοφίας ονομάτων επίσκεψις» and it means that you start to become wiser the moment that you learn the meaning of names (or words). But the meaning can be deeper or broader: you can find out the essence of a place, or the soul of a person, by knowing the language he speaks. So, this is what I think about learning Chinese.

First of all, learning a language helps to communicate with the people. Sometimes I tell my friends a joke that includes hints of truth: "I speak my best Mandarin with taxi drivers and the people at the vegetable market." And this is true. Because they are curious about this "外国人" (foreigner) and they ask questions: "你是哪国人？" (What is your home country?), "你有丈夫吗？" (Are you married?), "你在上海多长时间？" (How long have you been in Shanghai?). I heard these questions so many times that I even know the order, which question leads to the next one. They are very friendly and happy when I try to answer back with my broken Chinese and many of them call me at their stall. And then the smiling lady at the vegetable stall offers me some scallion for free. Sometimes I take it just because of the gentle offer; sometimes I refuse politely by saying that I don't need them. Sometimes they try to sell me more vegetables — the ones they suggest are the best to cook or eat at each season. If I am a bit tired or in a bad mood, it just takes a walk at the market and some words with the people there to feel better. They make jokes, and they speak to me. I answer as best I can. Still, this experience wouldn't be possible without my attempting to speak the language. And I feel a bit happy and proud when they understand some of my words. Or confused if they don't.

This is living proof of how language works. This is how you can get a bit more connected to the place where you live.

Then, it is my personal interest in learning Chinese, because it is a fascinating language. Day by day, I discover elements of it that make it more fun, more interesting. Of course, it is a very difficult language; everybody admits it, including me. Yes, you can forget it easily; yes, the pronunciation is a constant obstacle; but you can do it. It takes time and effort but nothing is impossible.

I even have my personal way of learning Chinese or, better, of remembering the words. Usually I make some combinations based on meaning. For example, the word for "young" is 年轻 that literally means: "year light", so I think a person that doesn't have the burden of many years on his shoulders is a young one. Cool. Or the word for "fear" is "怕". The left part is the radical for the heart and the right side is the color white. So, in my mind I translate: when you are afraid your face becomes white, so here it goes! In Greece we also have a similar phrase. When someone is afraid we say, "white as a sheet," so I made the connection. Or the way some adjectives are created: Do you have money? You're rich! (有钱). Do you have a name (that stands out)? Then you're famous! (有名).

I even have my favorite phrases: 慢走，都可以，慢慢来.

I like the greeting 慢走. I think it shows affection, even said by a stranger in the street or the shopkeeper. I remember when I first noticed it. It was winter and I had bought some roasted chestnuts from a stall on the street. The weather was cold; the seller was a young man who fancied a chat, so we did. When I left, he said 慢走 with a sweet expression on his face. It made me think about the meaning of it. Literally, "walk slowly," don't rush, take your time, don't be stressful. And in our modern times of hurrying this greeting seems so meaningful.

Then, there is this brilliant verb: 可以. Yes, it can happen: 可以. No, it can't: 不可以. Or both are possible: 都可以. "Do you want the red or the black?", "Shall we go today or tomorrow?" 都可以.

And last but not least, there is this wise proverb that people keep telling me about learning Chinese: 慢慢来. I hope so.

<u>**About the author:**</u>

Ourania Katavouta, Greek, graduated with a Master's degree in Modern Greek Literature from Aristotle University of Thessaloniki, Greece. She is engaged in the academic field of modern literature and teaching Greek as a foreign language. She has been teaching at the Department of Western Languages, SISU, since September 2014.

学习汉语

Ourania Katavouta（希腊）
梁晓雪　译

很多人在经历后都感悟到，学习语言的过程就像是一场旅行。在这场旅行中，你会逐渐了解说这门语言的人。古希腊有句谚语："学习语言使人睿智。"然而，语言背后的涵义更为宽广：通过学习一门语言，你可以更深入地了解一个地方的精髓，了解一个人的精神世界。这是我对汉语学习的感悟。

首先，学习语言有助于和当地人交流。我有时会给朋友讲我经历的趣事：在菜场买菜和乘出租的时候，我的中文是最好的。这是真的，因为这群人对我这个外国人非常好奇，会问我："你是哪国人？你有丈夫吗？你在上海多长时间？"这样的问题我听过太多次了，我甚至能背得出它们的先后顺序。他们非常友好，只要我试图用蹩脚的汉语回答，他们就很开心，还有很多人在摊位后跟我打招呼。有时爱笑的卖菜阿姨还会送我一些葱。有时我会欣然接受她的好意；有时我会婉拒，说我不需要。有时，他们试图让我买更多的菜，比如推荐我买某种时令蔬菜。如果我哪天感到疲惫或是心情不好，我只需要逛逛菜场，和那里的人们聊聊天，我的心情就会变好很多。他们会跟我开玩笑，和我交谈，我也尽可能回答他们。当然，交流的前提是我乐意尝试这门语言。当他们听懂我讲的话时，我感到开心和骄傲。若是他们听不懂，我会觉得挫败。

这一经历充分说明了语言的作用，语言可以让你与当地的联系更加紧密。

其次，我对汉语的学习有着极大的兴趣，因为汉语充满魅力。随着学习的深入，学习汉语的乐趣也显现出来。毋庸置疑，汉语非常之难，人人都这么认为，我也不例外。你很容易前学后忘，发音永远是绕不开的障碍，但这并不意味着你无法学会汉语。只要付出时间和汗水，一切皆有可能。

我甚至有自己学汉语、记词汇的方式。我通常会联想记忆，例如，“年轻”这个词，字对字翻译成英语的话就是“year light”，于是我就会联想到，一个人如果经历的年份很少，那就很年轻。很妙吧？再比如，“怕”这个字，左边的“忄”代表“心”，右边是“白”，于是我就联想到：当你害怕时，你的脸会发白。这样一来就记住了！希腊语也有类似的说法，当形容一个人非常害怕时，我们会说“脸吓得像张白纸”，因此我自然就联想起来了。形容词的记忆也有异曲同工之妙：“你有钱吗？”，因此“有钱”就代表富有；“你有名吗？”，因此“有名”就是形容名气大。

我甚至有我最喜欢的中文句子：慢走，都可以，慢慢来。

我非常喜欢“慢走”这句问候语，这短短的两个字饱含着深情，即便是街头的陌生人或是商店老板说出这两个字，你也会感受到浓浓的温情。我第一次注意到这个用法是在一个寒冷的冬日，我在街上买板栗，店伙计是一个年轻的小伙子，他想和我说话，于是我们就聊了一会。当我离开时，他微笑着跟我说：“慢走！”这引发了我的思考。从字面上看，“慢走”就是慢慢走，不用急，不要慌，不要有压力。在当今这个人人都行色匆匆的社会，“慢走”两个字是如此的意味深长。

其次，我还有个非常喜欢的动词：“可以”。它可用于多种场景：“可以”——是的，会发生；或者“不可以”——不行，不会发生；或者“都可以”——两种情况都有可能。如：“你想要红色的，还是黑色的？”或者“我们今天去还是明天去？”你可以回答“都可以。”

在我学习汉语的过程中，人们总是不断地用这句充满智慧的话鼓励我：“慢慢来。”我亦希望如此。

作者简介：

Ourania Katavouta，希腊籍，毕业于亚里士多德大学，获希腊现代文学硕士学位。她的学术领域为现代文学及对外希腊语教学。她自2014年9月于上海外国语大学西方语系希腊语专业任教至今。

San Mao: A Tale Hidden on Three Continents — Marking the 25th Anniversary in Telde of the Passing of Chinese Writer San Mao

Carlos de Cueto Nogueras (Spain)

Translated by Huang Yixuan (China)

Proofread by George Fleming

The Olive Tree in My Dreams

Don't ask me from whence I came,

It's far, far away.

Why have I been drifting for so long?

I drift — for the birds that soar on high,
For the creek that flows in the valley,
For the great prairies,
But above all,
For the olive tree in my dreams.

My Path to China

San Mao is one of the most famous and influential figures in Chinese culture and literature of the past hundred years. Her writings have improved understanding of Spain in China, Japan and South Korea. The romantic, nostalgic halo she gave Spain remains even today, and the country continues to attract great interest from Asia. In fact, Huang Yixuan's decision to learn the language of Cervantes came from reading San Mao:

"I grew to know Spain through her work, which gave me an impression of a people full of *joie de vivre*. It was for this reason that I decided to study Spanish, so that I might be able to retrace her steps."

The works of this towering literary figure also motivated me to immerse myself in Chinese culture and to teach at Shanghai International Studies University. It was thanks to San Mao, too, that I discovered a great country which I came to adore and of which I now feel a part, and participated in a tremendous project to translate one of San Mao's works into Spanish and thus make her known to the entire Spanish-speaking world.

By making the same journey of discovery as this exceptional author, who was truly ahead of her time, and who used her unique and sensitive style of writing to capture the hearts of her readers and transform their dreams, I had the good fortune to become acquainted with Huang Yixuan, my student, on the master's programme in Latin American studies at the University of Granada. This was the beginning of a close friendship; together, we planned this project, by which we hoped to help more people to better appreciate San Mao's wonderful contributions to improving understanding of Spanish culture in China.

San Mao: A Tale Hidden on Three Continents

For historical reasons, and because of barriers of culture and language, San Mao's life and work have not enjoyed as high a profile as they deserve. San Mao was one of the first Chinese to go abroad at a time when her country was almost entirely closed off to outside cultural influences. The result was that she made her mark on her countrymen in a way achieved by none before her. San Mao allowed the Chinese to begin to understand Spain and Ibero-American countries.

The majority of people in these countries, meanwhile, have little idea of the intimate connection between San Mao and their homelands. It is important to realise just how significant San Mao's work was in the exchange of culture between three continents: Asia, Europe, and America. Today, such cultural exchange is even more pertinent than in the author's lifetime, given today's monumental scale of movement and exchange in people and cultural products between different geographical regions. Our cultural project focused on creating a series of long-term cultural events to enshrine San Mao in popular memory, as much as in China as in the places that appear in her books, and to thereby forge more permanent bonds between these different regions.

San Mao's pilgrimage began, and ended, in her beloved China. In between, she saw half of the world and had adventures which were to make her an enthralling person. She penned novels which top the charts in China even today. San Mao has become an idolised and classic figure who has taken her female readers on a visual feast of the cultures and places in her books.

"San Mao: A Tale of Three Continents" is a cultural collaboration launched on the 25th anniversary of the writer's death. It restores San Mao's work to its rightful place, and will be based on her life and work in Telde, where she lived with the love of her life, José María.

In recent years, as China has continued to open up, international exchanges of people, whether for tourism, study, or official business, have been particularly intense. Over the same period the craze for Chinese language and culture in Ibero-American countries, and the interest in studying and understanding Spanish in China, testify to the growing and stronger relations between these two regions. Nevertheless, exchange remains preliminary, superficial and immature. Both China and Spain have realised the important role that culture plays in these exchanges.

Accelerating mutual understanding in the cultural sphere is one of the factors that will determine success of exchange activities, which is how we came to start this project aimed at commemorating San Mao in China and bringing her to public recognition in Telde, Spain. Firstly, retracing San Mao's journey could attract potential readers to come to China as tourists. Their visit would then serve to promote the image of Spain and Latin America and make them more familiar to the Chinese. Secondly, Chinese culture is embodied in San Mao and her works; it lives and breathes throughout. At the core of the cultural mosaic she portrayed in her novels is a globalist outlook tempered with the values of traditional Chinese culture and oriental philosophy. We hope that through this project, Western readers will get to know San Mao, and thereby improve their understanding of Chinese culture. Lastly, one must inevitably mention the potential economic benefits: if successful, the project will promote Spain, and especially the Canary Islands, as a cultural and tourist destination for the Asian market.

The opening-up and socio-economic development of China has boosted outbound tourism, although Chinese tourists have tended to concentrate on southeast Asian or English-speaking countries for ease of travel and communication. Given the competitive edge of the tourist destinations to which the Chinese are accustomed, it is important to work and boost activities to promote cultural exchange from other countries like Spain or Latin America by taking advantage of the strengths and attractions of figures and life experiences like those of San Mao. There is no better form of publicity than a project like this, provided through a relatively well-known Chinese public figure and a programme of events introducing her personal experiences in Spain and other Latin American countries. This programme will do much to spread knowledge about these places and excite interest among the Chinese public.

Our project had three main objectives. First, it was essential to examine San Mao's works in the context of the study of her life, and in particular, her relationship with Spain and Latin America. Second, it was important to translate San Mao's works into Spanish and publish them in Spanish-speaking countries. The third and final objective was to formulate a programme of events, some temporary and some permanent, in both China and Spain, that would commemorate San Mao and thereby forge a permanent link between these countries. In turn, this would encourage understanding and closer ties between Chinese and Hispanic cultures.

An Eastern Writer and Her Western Tales

The exhibitions in Telde and Beijing are the chief part of this project. The exhibition is divided into five themed areas. San Mao was an avid collector of used objects, and would often purchase special mementoes of her travels around the world. Also on display will be some of her manuscripts and paintings. Next to the latter, there will be a space with recordings of San Mao's monologues. San Mao recorded various monologues on different occasions, the most important of which concerned her moving encounters with José María. There will also be a recording of a famous Chinese song, *The Olive Tree*, whose lyrics are taken from San Mao's most famous poem, *The Olive Tree in My Dreams*. There will also be an exhibition detailing the different Spanish-speaking countries which San Mao visited.

Other important events include a series of lectures that aim to help the public to better understand San Mao and her story. In the future, there will be a food exhibition called "A Taste of San Mao's World" devoted to cuisine, an inseparable part of cultural identity around the globe and often mentioned in San Mao's writing. Later on, there will be the *Tour of Telde* which retraces her steps and visits her old residence as well as interesting sites around Telde.

Cinema Series: travel was central to San Mao's life, and features heavily in her writing. The Chinese and Spanish films on show will be a great opportunity for viewers to learn about these different countries, and to better popularise the histories, experiences, and character of their peoples or nations.

The *Concert Series*, meanwhile, will perform songs inspired by San Mao's life and experiences, and interweave them with musical styles from China, Spain and Latin America.

Her Story

San Mao was born on March 26, 1943 by the banks of the Yangtze River in Chongqing, China. She emigrated with her family to Taiwan in 1949. Once there, she quickly exhibited a passion for literature, and changed her name from Chen Maoping. *Chen*, from Chinese *chenshu*, means "to recount", a perfect name for a writer. Her first name, Maoping, can be translated as "splendid calm" — a beautiful name, indeed, but rather out of sync with San Mao's personality. As a resident of Taiwan and welcomed as a Taiwanese, she was far ahead of her time in every aspect of her life. It may indeed have been the latter factor that motivated her decision to write under a pseudonym. In Asia, Maoping was known as San Mao, the name under which she penned all her works. San Mao, literally, means "three strands of hair". It is a reference to a famous Chinese comic of the 1940s about a poor boy who lives in a poor quarter of Shanghai; the original writer employed the boy's innocent façade to criticize the society of her time. In this manner, the original San Mao resembled the cartoon Mafalda by Argentinian writer Quino, whose tales San Mao translated into Chinese.

From childhood, San Mao displayed a strong independent streak. She enjoyed spending her spare time alone at the cemetery, reading or thinking. She liked to collect used and discarded objects that told an interesting story and which she could transform into art. These objects were a good match for her fascination with the occult; in her own words, she believed she had extrasensory perception and the ability to communicate with people in the afterlife. Her unusual personality motivated her to aspire to freedom and all kinds of new knowledge; moreover, it precipitated greater sensitivity and curiosity in her writing.

San Mao decided very early on that she would never make compromises just because she was a woman. She was determined to breathe the liberal air of Taipei. She skirted the conventions and paths deemed acceptable by society. San Mao decided not to study at university, but she taught herself philosophy and educated herself in the best way possible: by travelling around the world. Cultured, independent and adventurous, San Mao learned to speak fluent German, English and Spanish. She travelled in search of inspiration and experiences, and in the 1960s arrived in Madrid, marking the beginning of her intense ties to Spain. San Mao's life there was full of incredible experiences and unimaginable by most of her compatriots at the time. San Mao's life inspired her art and made her literary creations much more popular.

San Mao Represents a Way, a Quest, and Life — but Above All, Freedom

In 1967, after a failed relationship, a frustrated San Mao left her city and departed for Madrid to become a student. The house where she was staying belonged to a cook who worked at the "Taiwanese representative office" in Spain and who was a friend of her parents. The surrounding area was called la Conception, which at that time was relatively poor and had few Chinese. San Mao, who was by then 24, had come to Spain via Germany and the United States and several other countries on a tour of study of philosophy, foreign languages and literature. After she arrived in Spain, San Mao quickly enchanted everyone she met. It was during her stay in the Spanish capital that she met José María Quero, a 17-year-old from Jaén in southern Spain. This muscular, dark-eyed man was convinced that San Mao was the love of his life. Despite the age gap between them, San Mao fascinated José María, who fell for her at first sight. He fell fast and deeply, and resolved to pursue her until she was his. However, at the time San Mao felt that José María was too young for her.

San Mao had other plans. Over the following years, she continued to travel, study, and teach classes at university, and began a relationship which at one point was on the verge of marriage. Her fiancé, however, died just hours before the couple were due to tie the knot. This bitter blow was perhaps a sign of the tragedies that were to come and led to San Mao's first suicidal thoughts.

Love of Her Life

After this incident, San Mao overcame her previous fragility. She began another quest for inspiration in her adventures and her love life. Part of this quest became an obsession with the desert. But she would not go there alone. She continued to travel for a period before returning to Madrid in 1973. The desire to discover the desert was still strong six years after her first visit to Spain. Having completed her studies in Germany and the United States, San Mao returned to Spain to visit a friend. It was at this point that she ran into José María once again. He had just completed his military service and was training as a diver. He had not forgotten her. His feelings for her had not changed with the years; San Mao, on her part, realised that José María was no longer the immature young man he had once been. This time, she returned his feelings.

José María took a job in the Sahara Desert, well aware of San Mao's desire to live in the desert. He sent her a postcard explaining that everything was ready for them to live together there. San Mao was overwhelmed by José María's staunch support, and soon took the most important decision of her life. In 1974, she and José María registered their marriage in Ainu, North Africa.

It was in the Sahara that San Mao began to write her diaries, published in the prestigious *Taiwan Daily News*. Later on, these were published under the title *Diaries of the Sahara.* The work was to become one of her first great successes as a writer and soon afterwards a bestseller among young people in China. *Diaries of the Sahara* continues to be one of the most widely read books in East Asia today, and has become something of a cult classic, with more than 10 million copies sold. *Diaries* is San Mao's magnum opus on her Chinese-Spanish love story. Translated into Spanish and covering her life in the desert, *Diaries of the Sahara* was a tremendous success and made San Mao an immortal idol for many young Chinese. *Diaries* recounts the couple's four very happy years in the desert, where they experienced a significant chapter in the history of their home.

In 1975, an armed uprising began in Morocco under the direction of a group named The Green March, which claimed Moroccan sovereignty over the Western Sahara. The region began a slide into war, resulting in the Spanish government deciding to evacuate its citizens to the peninsula and the Canary Islands. It appears San Mao and José María were no exception, installing themselves in Tenerife in February 1976, in Telde.

San Mao sent a postcard to her sister-in-law, giving some details of her new residence: "It's pretty, nothing large, but pretty enough. We have a very small garden, with these most awful radishes that neither José María nor I like very much. However, José María, being 'the man of the household', wants to plant only radishes. I have already planted flowers." In Telde, the couple connected with the local Chinese community, with whom they both became particularly friendly. They had regular dinners with their neighbours, who retain happy memories of the endearing couple.

The period saw San Mao continue recording the more interesting details of their life. She published several books, all of which were well received.

She greatly enjoyed life on the island, and her writing soon became prolific: every week, a new manuscript was sent to the Taiwanese publishing house, which paid her by word count. José María, meanwhile, enjoyed their carefree days with a new hobby: spearfishing.

These happy years came to an abrupt end in September 1979. San Mao's family were on holiday with the couple in Santa Cruz for the Mid-Autumn Festival. During the visit, José María went out on a fishing trip, never to return. The death of her husband was a wound from which San Mao never recovered. She departed Tenerife to escape her grief, and returned to Taiwan.

Unveiling of the plaque, Former Residence of San Mao, Telde.

The house at 3 Lope de Vega Street, in Telde Municipality, Gran Canaria, was where San Mao and José María spent the happiest years of their marriage in Spain. The period was also San Mao's most productive as a writer.

After establishing herself in Taiwan, San Mao would sometimes visit the house on the island in order to keep it in good order while she tried to pack up the couple's belongings and handle the paperwork to sell the property. These visits ensured Telde remained an important part of San Mao's life and her work. Indeed, the great romance between San Mao and José María is everywhere one goes in Telde. The municipality is the ideal place to promote her work in Spain. The house where San Mao and José María once lived, and the cemetery where José María is buried, have become important sites of pilgrimage for the many Chinese who visit the Canaries.

For many years now, many people, particularly Chinese, have approached the cemetery of Santa Cruz de La Palma. Many of those familiar with the story of the love and tragedy that befell San Mao and José María Quero have ventured here to pay their respects.

El Cabildo de La Palma, with the organization of the Ministry of Culture and Historical Heritage in La Palma, assisted by the Government of Santa Cruz de La Palma and the artist José Alberto Cabrera, will put on an exhibition called "Two Islands, Two Paradises, and One Tomb". The exhibition will be based at the municipal cemetery of Santa Cruz de La Palma in memory of José María Quero (1951–1979), husband of the popular Chinese writer San Mao (1943–1991). José María Quero tragically lost his life while spearfishing off the north coast of La Palma. His remains are interred at the capital cemetery.

In order to capture the beautiful love story and tragedy of San Mao and José María Quero, the first memorial to the couple on the island was erected at La Fajana de Barlovento.

Return to Taiwan

In the aftermath of José María's death, San Mao abandoned Spain for Taiwan. Not long after her arrival, she was hired by Taiwan's *United Daily News*, who were well aware of her reputation, and who financed a trip to Latin America. San Mao seized the opportunity as a way to heal her wounds, accepted the proposal, and travelled through a dozen countries on the continent. She published a book on her adventures, *Wanshui Qianshan Zoubian (A Journey Over Countless Mountains and Rivers)*, and on her return gave a lecture in Taiwan introducing South America to the Taiwanese. *A Journey Over Countless Mountains and Rivers* was a resounding success, particularly in China, where Ibero-America had previously been virtually unknown. Once more, leveraging her unusual experience, humanitarian spirit, tender language and compelling stories of faraway lands, San Mao opened the eyes of her readers to a new world and engraved Latin America firmly into the Chinese imagination.

During her period in Taiwan, San Mao was Professor of Literature and Philosophy at Chinese Culture University. At the same time, she continued to write poetry, novels and film scripts. San Mao's mounting fame, however, did not only bring attention and acclaim; it sometimes provoked intense criticism. She was conscientious in her work and in her dealings with students and readers, and sensitive to public opinion. Together, these burdens made her exhausted and stressed, which began to take a toll on her health.

San Mao's final years were spent pining for José María and the freedom she had felt at his side. Now, she was obliged to assume the responsibilities of a public figure and to face the pressure of the role that society had conferred on her. On several occasions, San Mao described how she had communicated with José María and other friends who had passed away. She would sometimes participate in séances.

Today, Latin America is still largely unknown by many of San Mao's countrymen, but she was one of the first Chinese to have brought the region into the line of sight of Chinese readers. In *A Journey Over Countless*

Mountains and Rivers, San Mao revealed the sense of belonging she felt in the region. She began living with an indigenous Ecuadorian family, and she quickly adapted to their lifestyle, believing that she had been a member of this people in a previous life. San Mao further believed she had the ability to communicate with the spirits at pre-Columbus archaeological sites like Copán and Machu Picchu. When she scaled las Pampas on horseback in a fling with the *gaucho* lifestyle, she found inner peace. Although it might seem that San Mao's connection with Latin America and the Canary Islands was something of a coincidence, in reality the historical, cultural and socio-economic ties between the latter two were very strong. The Canaries were an important springboard for Spanish vessels headed for South America, and so they had a profound impact on the exchange of people and trade between Spain and the Americas.

On January 4, 1991, San Mao, the most famous Chinese writer of the 20th century, took her own life in Taipei. "Echo", as she was known, had never overcome the loss of her beloved José María. San Mao has been feted as an Asian writer who "underscored, in the most tender language, her journey of love and self-discovery. She touched the hearts of countless Chinese." A new generation of female Chinese writers has made a heroine and role model of San Mao in admiration of her independence and world-view. So it was in the most tragic fashion, and aged only 47, that the Taiwanese writer and adventurer took the path of no return. With her death and disappearance from our world, her readers were left asking how her lifelong quest led her to such despair. It is surely an overlooked detail that after the death of José María, life became meaningless to San Mao. She had probably actually died long before, on that day in 1979 when her love sank beneath the waves.

Today, San Mao's works are still considered modern literary classics for the gripping way in which exotic experiences are narrated for the Chinese readers, and for the way in which San Mao drew sensitivity and passion from the observance of everyday life. Her poetry has a magic or power only perceptible to readers with sufficient sensitivity and love of life — because these traits are those of San Mao herself. Her experience of love and loss is marked by the same magic and power.

Looking back over San Mao's life, it might seem that she was not destined for this world; her story is at once too tense and moving, like a film that grips the viewer from the very first frame. But San Mao's life was as real as the Canary Islands where it unfolded. The truth is that as exciting as San Mao's works were for her readers, the life on which they were based was very cruel indeed.

San Mao's contributions to the spread of culture are irrefutable. She is like an ambassador, transcending time, space, and culture, bridging the gaps between Chinese readers and distant Spain and Latin America. Half a century ago, her work did not receive the accolade it deserved. Today, as globalisation sweeps the world, and once distant cultures become ever closer, cultural exchange has become a prerequisite for the development of relations between nations. In this context, we have sufficient resources and a sufficient need to re-appraise San Mao's contributions to cross-cultural exchange. We are confident that by doing so, we can further promote cultural exchange and understanding between the peoples of Spain, China and Latin America.

About the authors:

Carlos de Cueto Nogueras is professor of Political Science and Public Administration, University of Granada (Spain), and has been a visiting professor at the School of International Relations and Public Affairs, SISU, every Fall semester since 2015.

Huang Yixuan graduated with an MPhil in Spanish from Beijing International Studies University, specialising in Intercultural Communication. In 2016, she gained a Master's in Latin American Studies: Culture and Management from the University of Granada.

References

Cui, J. F. & Zhao, J. 崔建飞，赵君 (1995).《三毛传》*[A Biography of San Mao]*. Beijing: 文化艺术出版社 Culture & Art Publishing House.

Lu, S. Q., Yang, Y. L., & Sun, Y. C. 陆士清，杨幼力，孙永超 (1993).《三毛传》*[A Biography of San Mao]*. Taiwan: 晨星出版社 Morningstar Publishing Inc.

San Mao 三毛 (1981).《梦里花落知多少》*[Do You Know How Many Flowers Have Fallen in My Dreams?]*. Taiwan: 皇冠出版社 Crown Publishing Co.

San Mao 三毛 (1982).《万水千山走遍》*[A Journey Over Countless Mountains and Rivers]*. Taiwan: 皇冠出版社 Crown Publishing Co.

San Mao 三毛 (1976).《撒哈拉的故事》*[Diaries of the Sahara]*. Taiwan: 皇冠出版社 Crown Publishing Co.

San Mao 三毛 (1987).《我的宝贝》*[My Treasures]*. Taiwan: 皇冠出版社 Crown Publishing Co.

Shi, Y. G., Chen, W. F., Feng, Z., & Sha, L. 师永刚，陈文芬，冯昭，沙林 (2005).《三毛私家相册》*[San Mao's Private Photo Album]*. Beijing: 中信出版社 CITIC Publishing.

Xu, H. P. 眭澔平 (2011).《三毛的最后一封信》*[San Mao's Last Letter]*. Wuhan, Hubei: 长江文艺出版社 Yangtze River Art and Literature Publishing House.

三毛，三个大洲之间遗失的记忆
——中国作家三毛逝世25周年西班牙特尔德纪念活动

Carlos de Cueto Nogueras（西班牙）

黄亦璇　译

梁晓雪　审校

橄榄树

不要问我从哪里来

我的故乡在远方

为什么流浪，流浪远方？

为了天空飞翔的小鸟

为了山间清流的小溪

为了宽阔的草原

还有还有

为了梦中的橄榄树。

我的中国之路

三毛是过去百年来中国文化和文学界最著名、最具影响力的作家之一。她笔下那个散发着浪漫、忧郁气息的西班牙，让广大中日韩读者心驰神往，至今还深深地吸引着许多亚洲读者。一些人因为受到三毛作品的影响而选择学习塞万提斯的语言——西班牙语，黄亦璇就是其中一个：

“在她的书中我读到了西班牙，也了解到那里的人们对于生活极大的热情，所以后来我就决定学西语，去三毛去过的地方看看。”

于我而言，三毛的作品也鼓励着我继续学习中国文化，并作为访问学者来到上海外国语大学任教。如果不是因为三毛，我不会与一个如此令人敬佩的国家结缘，更不会在这里获得认同感和归属感。所以我参与了三毛一部作品的西语翻译工作，希望让更多西语国家的人认识她。

三毛是一位超越了其所处时代的杰出作家，她的写作风格质朴而独特，总能将读者带入一个浪漫的梦境。我在了解她的过程中，有幸认识了我的学生黄亦璇，她当时正在格拉纳达大学学习拉美研究文化管理的硕士项目。我们成了好朋友，并决定设计一个以三毛为主题的文化项目，让更多的人了解她对西班牙文化在中国的传播所作出的贡献。

三毛，三个大洲之间遗失的记忆

由于历史原因和文化语言屏障，三毛和她的作品并未得到应有的关注。三毛出国的时候，中国在文化上还处于几近封闭的时期。作为最早一批走出国门的人之一，三毛对国内读者的世界观产生了前所未有的影响：通过她的作品，中国读者才有了一扇了解西班牙和伊比利亚美洲国家的窗口。

然而很多西语国家的人并不知道，三毛与自己的祖国存在千丝万缕的联系。三毛为亚洲、欧洲和美洲之间文化交流所做出的贡献应该得到认可。今天，不同地区之间人际和文化交流极其频繁，三大洲之间的文化交流比三毛的年代更为紧密。我们的文化项目设计了一系列长期的文化活动，希望让这位作家被人们铭记，同时为中国与西语国家之间的文化交流创造深层次的机会。

三毛的旅途始于中国，也终于中国。她的足迹遍布大半个世界，她笔下天方夜谭般的旅行经历使她的形象越发令人着迷。至今，她的小说在中国依旧非常畅销。她已成为一位受人崇敬的经典作家，将她的女性读者带入自己的旅途，享受一场文化与区域的视觉盛宴。

“三毛，三个大洲之间遗失的记忆”是为纪念三毛逝世25周年而设计的跨文化交流项目，它以三毛、荷西曾生活过的西班牙小镇特尔德为中心，旨在让人们了解她为中国与西语世界的文化交流所做出的贡献。

近年来，随着中国对外开放程度日益加深，国际交流愈加频繁，留学、旅游或公务等因素使得人员向海外的流动增加。与此同时，在伊比利亚美洲国家掀起了一股学习汉语和中国文化的热潮，中国人也对西语和西班牙文化感兴趣，这也说明中国与这些国家的交往日益紧密。然而，这种交往仍然处在起步阶段，停留在表面，有待成熟，双方也逐渐意识到文化交流对于深化双边关系的重要性。

促进文化领域的互相了解是文化活动成功的决定因素。为此我们这样设计这个项目：在中国纪念三毛的同时，在西班牙特尔德构建三毛的文化形象。一方面，通过重新介绍三毛的旅程吸引西班牙和拉美国家的潜在读者游历中国，这些游客的到来也将有助于展示其国家的风采，使得中国民间对西语国家的形象不再感到陌生。另一方面，中国文化是三毛创作的内在精神，贯穿其作品的始终。尽管她的故事多为展现异国文化，反映了一种国际化视角，但其核心精神从未脱离中国传统价值观与哲学观。我们希望通过这个项目帮助西方读者了解三毛，并增进对中国文化的认识。此外，值得一提的是这个文化社会项目将产生的经济效益：西班牙，尤其是加那利群岛，将有望扩大其在亚洲市场的影响力，吸引更多亚洲游客。

虽然改革开放所带来的经济社会发展使更多中国人能到海外旅游，但由于地理屏障和语言不通，大部分人倾向于选择东南亚或英语国家作为目的地。面对这些中国人习以为常的旅行目的地的竞争，运用三毛的经历宣传西班牙和拉美国家无疑是相当重要的战略。三毛在中国知名度极高，通过介绍她曾游历过的西语国家，介绍她写过的景点，可以达到宣传、推介的效果，激发中国游客的兴趣。没有比这个项目更好的宣传方式了。

项目有三个主要目的。第一，重读三毛经典，让人们认识到西班牙、拉美国家和她的密切关系；第二，将三毛的作品译成西语，并在西语国家出版。第三，在中国和西班牙举办短期或长期的文化纪念活动，以在中国和西语国家之间建立持续稳定的文化交流关系。如此一来，便能促进中国文化和西班牙文化间的了解，构建紧密的联系。

一位东方女子和她的西方故事

该项目的主要内容包括在西班牙特尔德和北京的展览。展出设有五个分展区，分别展示三毛的收藏、录音、手稿、旅行足迹和音乐电影等艺术创作。三毛生前极爱收集旧物，每一个旅行途中带回的纪念品，背后都有一段有趣而难忘的故事。手稿展区还将展出她的字画。录音展区播放三毛生前讲述自己和荷西经历的录音片段，同时也会播放那首脍炙人口的《橄榄树》，这首歌改编自三毛最著名的诗歌《梦中的橄榄树》。此外，展览还专设一个区域介绍三毛游历过的西语国家，让参观者跟随她的脚步了解这些地方。其他重要活动有：

系列讲座：让公众进一步了解三毛和她的故事；

“舌尖上的三毛文学世界”美食展：三毛的书中提到不少各地美食，而美食恰恰也最能表现不同的文化身份；

特尔德郊游日：带领到访者参观三毛故居，同时欣赏该小镇的清新风景；

系列电影展：旅行是三毛生活不可或缺的内容，也是其作品最具吸引力的主题，通过放映几部有关中国或西语国家的电影，能够让观众最直观地领略这些国家的风土人情，了解它们的历史文化；

系列音乐展：播放灵感源自三毛人生经历的音乐，并穿插展出来自中国、西班牙、拉丁美洲不同风格的音乐。

三毛的故事

三毛于1943年3月26日出生在中国长江沿岸的重庆。三毛原名陈懋平。“陈”，来自“陈述”，意为“讲述”，与作家身份十分相配，“懋平”意为“灿烂的平静”。这是一个很美的名字，只是似乎和它主人的性格有些格格不入。1949年，她同家人一起移居台湾。三毛住在台湾，以台湾人的身份受到欢迎，她在生活的方方面面都领先于时代。可能正是后者驱使她用笔名写作。在亚洲，她以笔名“三毛”为大家所熟知，这个名字取自20世纪40年代的一部漫画《三毛流浪记》，其中的主角“三毛”是一个流浪在上海的小男孩，漫画从这个流浪儿童的视角出发，批判当时社会的黑暗。三毛的人物设置和阿根廷漫画家季诺的作品《娃娃看天下》（西班牙语原名为Mafalda）中的主角小女孩玛法达有几分相似。这部连载漫画的中文译者就是三毛。

幼年时期的三毛就已表现出不同常人的个性。在闲暇时候她爱去墓地独处、看书、思考。她喜欢收藏旧物，了解它们背后的趣事，再把它们改造成手工艺术品。她对神秘学很感兴趣，觉得自己有心灵感应、能通灵。她独特的性格决定了她对自由、知识的渴望，也使她成为一个细腻而好奇的旅行者。

青年时期的三毛就抛开了当时传统社会施加给女性的禁锢，选择了与众不同、自由自在的人生道路。她没有上大学，而是在周游世界的过程中体验生活、丰富自己、寻找灵感。知性、独立、敢于冒险的三毛能说一口流利的德语、英语和西班牙语。20世纪60年代，她开始了在马德里的留学生活，从此与西班牙结下了不解之缘。她的人生经历之丰富，对于当时大部分中国人来说是难以想象的，这些经历为她的创作提供了灵感，也使得她的作品备受欢迎。

三毛是旅途，是探索，是生命，更是自由

1967年，三毛在经历一段感情挫折之后，离开了台湾，去马德里留学。她的房东在西班牙的“台湾代表处”当厨师，是她父母的朋友。她住在拉康塞普西翁区，一个不太富裕、中国人很少见的地方。当时三毛才24岁，参加了一个游学项目，学习哲学、外语和文学，在美国和德国等地学习，后来到西班牙，并受到当地人的欢迎。在马德里留学期间，她认识了一位17岁的哈恩小伙子，荷西·马利安·葛罗。这个朝气蓬勃、双眸深邃的男孩儿当时就觉得自己找到了人生的挚爱。尽管他比三毛小几岁，但这也无法阻挡他对三毛的痴迷。他自第一眼就深深地爱上了这位中国女孩，并承诺一定要等到三毛接受他的爱。但当时在三毛眼里，他还是个小孩儿。

三毛有其他的人生计划。后来的几年中她继续游学、在大学授课，也谋划着人生大事。然而，就在她正式举办婚礼前的几小时，她的未婚夫突然离世。这突如其来的打击让她第一次产生轻生的念头，也可能是她人生悲剧的开端。

伟大的爱情

伤痛逐渐愈合后，三毛重新在旅途和爱中寻找生活的光芒。去沙漠成为三毛的梦想，但这次不只是她一个人去了。在旅行了一段日子后，她于1973年重返马德里。当年她初到西班牙便想探索沙漠，而六年后这股欲望依旧强烈。在德国和美国完成学业后，她回到马德里去看望一个朋友，并和荷西久别重逢。刚服完兵役、学会潜水的荷西没有忘记三毛且依旧爱慕她。三毛也发觉荷西再也不是六年前的那个小男孩。这一次她接受了他的爱。

荷西在撒哈拉沙漠找了一份工作，他知道这是她梦寐以求的地方。他写信告诉她，只管来沙漠，一切都已准备好。三毛被这份坚定所感动，做出了人生最重要的决定——去撒哈拉。她在1974年与荷西在北非小镇阿尤恩结成夫妻。

正是在撒哈拉，三毛开始写很多有趣的小故事，并发表在影响很大的《台湾日报》上。这些故事后来被编撰成《撒哈拉的故事》，它使三毛声名鹊起，并迅速成为畅销书，在中国吸引了无数的青年读者。该书如今在东亚仍然被广泛阅读，累计售出一千万本，是风靡已久的经典之作。它算得上一部跨越中国与西班牙的爱情经典，已被译为西班牙语。它获得的巨大成功，使三毛成为无数中国年轻人的偶像。书中提到，三毛与荷西在沙漠度过了幸福美满的四年，还经历了这个北非城市的一次历史巨变。

1975年，摩洛哥在“绿色进军”团体的指导下，开始了占领西撒哈拉的军事运动，让该地区一度陷入战争状态。西班牙被迫将其居住在该地的所有公民撤离到伊比利亚半岛和加那利群岛。三毛与荷西也于1976年二月返回西班牙，定居特内里费岛的小镇特尔德。

三毛在给家人的信中提到自己在特尔德的新家：“它非常漂亮，不大，但是特别美。我们有一个小花园，还种了小萝卜，虽然我们俩都不怎么爱吃，但我们的一家之主荷西说，他只想种小萝卜。而我已经种了花。”三毛与荷西为人特别和善，很受当地华人社群的欢迎。他们经常和邻居聚餐，有一些邻居至今仍保有美好的回忆。

这一时期三毛的创作内容也集中在讲述生活中的趣味琐事。她出了几部作品，广受欢迎。

三毛非常享受生活在特尔德的这段日子。她的创作频率非常高，几乎每周都向台湾的出版社发稿。荷西则在空闲时间去海里潜水捕鱼。

然而，生活的幸福和宁静被荷西的离世打破。1979年9月，三毛的家人来岛上的圣克鲁斯和他们一起庆祝中秋节。期间，荷西在潜水时发生意外遇难了。这个悲剧在三毛的心里留下了无法愈合的创伤，为了不再触景伤情，她离开小岛回到了台湾。

在西班牙大加那利岛特尔德市洛佩·德·维加街3号，三毛与丈夫荷西度过了婚姻生活中最美妙的时光，这段时间也是三毛创作最多产的时候。回台湾以后，三毛多次回到特尔德的家整理修缮，最终将房子卖掉。因此，特尔德对于三毛的一生以及她的文学创作都有重大意义。她与荷西的爱情故事让这座小城充满了浪漫色彩，也让它成为宣传三毛作品的最佳地点。三毛的故居和荷西的墓地是很多追随三毛脚步远道而来的中国游客的朝圣地。

这么多年来，太多中国游客被三毛与荷西的爱情悲剧打动，来到拉帕尔玛的圣克鲁斯公墓，探访荷西的长眠之地。

在拉帕尔玛文化历史遗产处的组织和西班牙艺术家何塞·阿尔韦托·卡夫雷拉的协助下，拉帕尔玛市政厅启动了“两座岛，两个天堂，一个墓碑”的展览活动，在拉帕尔玛的圣克鲁斯公墓举行，以纪念中国作家三毛（1943–1991）的丈夫荷西（1951–1979）。他在拉帕尔玛岛北部潜水捕鱼时发生意外不幸去世，遗体被安放在该市的公墓。

为了让更多人了解这段爱情悲剧，巴尔洛文托市在拉法哈那海滩（荷西遇难地）设了第一个三毛荷西夫妇纪念碑。

回到台湾

荷西去世后，三毛离开西班牙，回到台湾。当时三毛在国内已为人所熟知，回国后不久，《台湾联合报》聘用了她，并赞助她去拉丁美洲旅行。还沉浸在丧夫之痛中的三毛希望通过旅行平复心情，接受了邀请，花了半年时间走访了十几个拉美国家，出版了《万水千山走遍》，在回台后办了一场讲座介绍南美。《万水千山走遍》又是一部成功之作，尤其在对于伊比利亚美洲全然不了解的中国。三毛再次用她的独特经历、人文关怀、柔软笔触和远方的故事向读者们展现了另一个新的世界，将拉丁美洲带入了他们的想象。

回到台湾的日子，三毛在文化大学担任文哲系教师，继续创作诗歌、小说和剧本。与日俱增的名气既给她带来了广泛的关注，也为她招致了犀利的批评。她对学生和读者非常有责任感，但对公众的评论也非常敏感。在疲惫和高压下，她的健康状况每况愈下。

在人生的最后阶段，三毛一边吃力地承担着公众人物的社会压力，一边思念着丈夫荷西和在他身边的那份无拘无束。她很多次提起自己与荷西以及去世朋友通灵的经历，还参加类似的活动，希望能够再见到他们。

直到今天，拉丁美洲对于很多中国人而言还是一方未知的土地。三毛是最早向中国介绍拉丁美洲的中国人之一。在《万水千山走遍》中，她提到自己对那里的归属感：她很轻易地就融入了一个厄瓜多尔土著居民的家庭，她甚至认为自己前世就是一个印第安人；她觉得自己能和哥庞废墟、马丘比丘等前哥伦布遗址的亡灵交流；当她在潘帕斯草原策马奔腾，体验南美牧人的生活时，内心感受到前所未有的宁静。虽然三毛与拉丁美洲、加那利群岛的紧密联系更像是一个美丽的巧合，但实际上这两个地方之间本就有着深厚的历史、文化和社会经济渊源。加那利群岛曾是西班牙人通往美洲的重要桥梁，它对西班牙和美洲地区之间的人口、商贸发展产生了重要影响。

1991年1月4日，这位20世纪最著名的中国作家在台北自杀了。三毛从未走出失去挚爱的痛苦。她被称为“柔情地书写爱情与自我探索过程，感动了无数中国读者”的东方作家。中国新一代的女性作家把她当作英雄模范似的存在，学习她独立自主的世界观。然而这位年仅47岁的作家兼旅行者却选择用这种悲剧的方式为自己的生命画上句点。大概钟爱她的读者也想问，三毛寻寻觅觅了大半生，最后怎会走向那样的尽头？要知道，对于她来说，世间万物在荷西离去以后都失去了意义。三毛恐怕早在1979年9月30日那天便已离去，跟随她那潜水遇难的丈夫一起，沉入大海中了。

三毛的作品充满了异域风情和来自平常生活的细腻与激情，在今天仍被奉为中国当代文学的经典。三毛的诗歌拥有一种魔法和力量，只有那些感情充沛、热爱生活的读者才能感受得到。她自己就是一个这样的人。她所经历的爱情与失意本身就有这样的魔法和力量。

三毛的一生似乎不属于这个平凡的世界。她的故事是如此惊心动魄、扣人心弦，就像跌宕起伏的电影一般，从第一帧画面就开始牢牢锁住人心。而这一切却是在加那利岛真正发生过的，这对于读者而言有多么的精彩，对于三毛来说就有多么的残忍。

三毛对于文化传播作出了杰出的贡献。她就像一个使节，超越时空、文化的界限，让中国读者认识西班牙、拉丁美洲这样遥远的地方。半个世纪以前，她的功劳并没有得到应有的肯定。而今天，全球化发展迅猛，文化间的距离逐渐缩小，文化交流成为促进国际关系发展的必要条件。在这样的环境下，我们已经拥有足够的资源，且认为有足够的必要，来重新评价三毛作品的跨文化传播意义。我们相信，这样做必将进一步推动文化层面的交流，增进西班牙、中国和拉丁美洲国家的相互了解。

作者简介：

Carlos de Cueto Nogueras，西班牙格拉纳达大学政治学和公共管理学教授，自2015年起每个秋季学期在上海外国语大学国际关系与公共事务学院担任访问学者。

黄亦璇，北京第二外国语学院西班牙语语言文学硕士，研究方向为跨文化交流。2016年在西班牙格拉纳达大学获得拉丁美洲研究文化管理硕士学位。

The "Awful" Chinese Language

Vicki Mayfield (U.S.A.)

Proofread by George Fleming

In 1880, Mark Twain wrote an essay titled "The Awful German Language", in which he described his frustrations in learning German, decrying the language's word order, morphology of individual words, and nouns with a gender, number, and case. In that essay Twain said he heard a Californian say "that he would rather decline two drinks than decline one German adjective". Twain's complaints, however, appear to be mere bluster, designed to give him a humorous vantage point from which he could entertain others on the lecture circuit.

As an English speaker, I can agree: learning German is no picnic, but it's close enough to English in pronunciation, grammar, and vocabulary that we can manage. And, if we English speakers make mistakes in declining adjectives, so what? It turns out that native German speakers make mistakes, too. Take that, Mr. Twain!

I am a committed language learner. In high school, college, and graduate school, learning languages was my life. German, Spanish, and Catalan occupied my time. I joined a historical linguistics study group where we researched how a modern word evolved from its Latin or Old Norse or Sanskrit origins. I sat in on endless screenings of Buñuel movies, trying to make sense of the language so I could understand the plot. I read Chomsky, Pound and Auerbach to get a handle on meaning. I sought out foreign students who could educate me in their languages. I studied abroad and travelled. The first time I read *One Hundred Years of Solitude*, I read it in Italian — teaching myself as I went along — because the English and Spanish versions weren't available yet at my university. This was fun for me: it was like fitting together the pieces of some giant puzzle, enabling me to somehow comprehend the world. Or so I thought.

Armed with languages and degrees, I had to figure out a career after graduation. I initially became a translator and interpreter. I was good, but found that I wasn't satisfied. I wanted to communicate in my words, not someone else's. Then I added programming languages — not human languages — and software expertise to my repertoire of skills, and realized I had found the tools I wanted to use to communicate. And I did, in a career that took me from academia to business and back again.

Then China called. Well, actually it called my husband, not me. While researching material for a book, he had visited Malaysia, Singapore, and Indonesia, getting his first exposure to Chinese in the overseas communities. After that, he started studying Chinese on his own. When a chance to spend 3 years in Nanjing teaching international law materialized for him, we both jumped at the opportunity. We decided we would go prepared, so we spent the summer before our departure in intensive language classes. When we got to China in the fall of 2006, I enrolled in the Chinese for foreigners classes at the university.

Mark Twain couldn't decline a German adjective. I couldn't speak *putonghua*. For the first time in my life, I couldn't connect spoken words to meaning. I did well in class with high scores on every test. I hired a tutor. I practiced. I listened to tapes. I watched Dashan on CCTV. We went to Chinese movies. But I couldn't speak.

I was frustrated. I hit plateau after plateau. Although I knew I was making some progress, making more was a struggle.

For me, it wasn't the grammar. "I want to buy this book" is pretty straightforward: "我想买这本书" [I-want-buy-this-*measure word*-book]. Chinese measure words are not difficult, since we have them in English. A flock of geese, a herd of cattle or a pod of dolphins are phrases that might come up in everyday conversation. For example, I can understand what a parliament of owls might be, but I can say with absolute certainty that I've never used that term before. It's so easy in English to just say a group of something and then just throw in whatever noun you might be considering: cars, elephants, tennis rackets, and so on.

Where I fall down the rabbit hole and into the Wonderland of Chinese is the long list of homonyms: words that sound alike but mean something different. The sound "jiàn", said in isolation, leaves me guessing. Did we catch sight (见) of the warship (舰) or the arrow (箭)? Did you get trampled (践) or splashed (溅) in the ravine (涧)? Is your sweetheart cheap (贱) or strong and healthy (健)? And, if one of us should mispronounce the word and get the tone wrong, we could go down a completely different path of dialogue that would have more to do with anatomy than geography!

And it wasn't the lack of an alphabet. Just as I had memorized brush strokes of the Old Masters in art history classes years ago, I could memorize Chinese characters (*hanzi*) and distinguish one character from another. Of course, I couldn't read *hanzi* as fast as I could read English, but I could read. I even took a class in 书法. The teacher was good, and I learned to appreciate some of the finer points of calligraphy, but just as typing in English is easier than writing for me today, typing in Chinese is also easier.

As much as I am entranced by the artistic expression of the language in visual form, I learn a language by speaking and listening. When I was a student, I had many opportunities to speak other languages: my exposure was frequent and meaningful. But in China, I lived life in English. My friends and colleagues, whether foreign or Chinese, spoke English. I never got enough repetitive daily practice in Chinese to get measurably better in a short time.

A simple task like getting my hair cut became torture. I would put it off until I couldn't deal with hair falling in my eyes anymore. Then I would grit my teeth, grab my dictionary and go. At the salon, once I communicated that I just wanted a haircut, that's when the pain would begin. At every salon in the world — Chicago or Chengdu — the hairdresser always wants to chat. In those early days, even looking directly at the hairdresser, I couldn't understand what she was saying. Then as she moved to one side or behind me as she cut my hair, I found I couldn't hear very much. Without the visual cues that are a part of spoken language, I was lost. I was fortunate that most of the hairdressers took pity on me, and gave me a haircut that approximated a desirable style.

Then, somewhere along the way, I started talking to people and they responded. In 2006, foreigners in second-tier cities were still a novelty. The young women in the markets I frequented saw me enough times that they wanted to know more about me. They always had a keen interest in exploring the contents of my shopping bags. They would ask me how to cook things that foreigners ate — like asparagus — which they sold but had never tasted. Taxi drivers started talking to me about the songs on the radio or asking me what was so interesting at that new store called IKEA that all the foreigners wanted to shop there. A friend imitated a foreigner who spoke Mandarin fluently, but all in fourth tones. When I listened to that foreigner speak, I realized how accurate the imitation was. I could listen to Teresa Teng and understand some of her lyrics without looking them up. By 2009, I finally reached the point where I could navigate living in China in a town where few people spoke English and I could do it without carrying a dictionary. Yeah!

It only took me three years of struggle to get to the level of beginning-intermediate. Then we returned to the U.S. Once at home, there was no reason for me to continue studying Chinese. I didn't think I'd use it again. Even in Chicago, which has a good-sized Chinatown, most of the first- or second-generation Chinese speak Cantonese, not Mandarin. So Chinese lay dormant for me as I focused on other things.

Unexpectedly, in 2011 Singapore called and it called my husband. We went to Singapore, where Mandarin and many other Chinese languages are widely spoken, but English dominates. I started studying Chinese again, thinking I could build on the existing knowledge base. We had good materials and enthusiastic students, but one element was missing. The goal of the course was to pass an HSK test, not to learn to use the language: that was something you would do on your own, although, how, I don't know. We memorized vocabulary, practiced reading, and took tests.

There was no opportunity to speak or to engage, not in the class, and not elsewhere. For me, as a foreigner in Singapore, I was again living life in an all-English environment. I had no reason to speak Chinese in a country where everyone else spoke English. I dropped out of class. Mastery of Chinese was just not going to happen for me.

In 2015, we returned to China for a second time. This time we lived in Shanghai in a Chinese environment. However, it didn't take long to discover that in the years we were away from China, China had changed; Shanghai had changed. Many, many young people in Shanghai speak English and speak it very well. Today it's entirely possible to get a latte at KFC, pick up some fruit from the neighborhood vendor, book a dinner reservation, and attend a literary festival all in English. Of course, knowing Chinese in Shanghai makes life easier. Getting a haircut in Chinese is still not fun, but these days I don't dread it. And, I can finally explain what I want and can understand the hairdresser.

Now, as our year is up and we pack up to leave, I'm finding my Chinese has improved. Not as much as I would have liked, but enough to enable me to do things that I want to do. I search Baidu maps in Chinese, keep my mobile phone Contacts bilingually, and send WeChat messages to Chinese friends in English and Chinese. In personal encounters with Chinese speakers, I listen to learn and try to repeat. I keep adding new words to my personal flashcard list. But mostly, I stopped stressing about my performance and learned to just value every experience to speak Chinese as meaningful. Every language is different. For me, finally, I've learned that the key to learning Chinese is to enjoy living in China.

About the author:

Vicki Mayfield, MBA, American, consultant in marketing strategy, aspiring author of fiction, and sometime photographer. She is married to an Advisor and Visiting Professor in the Middle East Studies Institute at SISU (2015–2016). She is presently based in Chicago.

“可怕”的中文

Vicki Mayfield（美国）
梁晓雪　译

1880年，马克·吐温在他的《可怕的德语》一文中描述了他学习德语的艰辛过程，“痛斥”其语序、单词的变形和名词的性、数、格等变化。马克·吐温在文中提到，他曾听闻一个加利福尼亚人说“他宁愿放弃两杯酒也不愿背一个德语形容词的词尾变化”。然而，马克·吐温的吐槽仅仅是烟雾弹，供他在巡回演讲中逗观众乐子。

作为一名母语为英语的人，我同意德语确实不好啃，但是它仍然在发音、语法及词汇方面和英语非常接近。而且，就算我们在德语形容词的词尾上犯了错，又如何呢？其实，德国人自己也经常犯错。傻了吧，马克·吐温先生！

我是一名坚定的语言学习者。语言学习贯穿了我整个高中、大学及研究生生活。学习德语、西班牙语、加泰罗尼亚语占据了我的业余时间。我加入历史语言学学习小组，研究一个现代词汇是如何从拉丁语、古斯堪的那维亚语或梵语进化而来；我看了无数次布努埃尔[1]的电影放映，试图通过听懂台词来了解剧情；我阅读乔姆斯

1　路易斯·布努埃尔，西班牙国宝级电影导演，20世纪最伟大的电影大师之一，代表作有《一条安达鲁狗》《黄金年代》《欲望的隐晦目的》等。

基[1]、庞德[2]和奥尔巴赫[3]的著作来学习语义；我找外国留学生做我的语言老师；我出国留学、旅行；我第一次读《百年孤独》的时候，读的是意大利文，一边读一边学习意大利语，因为那时我们学校没有这本书的英语译本和西语译本。做这些事对我来说很有趣，就像在拼一幅巨大的拼图，帮助我逐步了解这个世界。至少当时的我是这么想的。

毕业时，凭借我的语言和学历，我开始找工作。起初，我做翻译和口译。我做得不错，但是发现自己并不满足。我想表达自己的意思，而不仅仅是转述别人的话。接下来我又学习了计算机编程语言（这次不是人类语言）以及软件专业知识来扩充我的技能库，我觉得我找到了想要用来沟通的工具。于是我的职业生涯从学术界转换到了商界，后又转回来了。

接下来中国召唤了我，事实上被召唤的不是我，而是我的丈夫。在这之前他已经去过马来西亚、新加坡和印尼进行调研，也因而首次在华人圈子里接触了中文。之后，他开始自学中文。当他收到去南京教授三年国际法课程的邀请时，我们兴奋地抓住了这个机会。我们决定有备而去，因此出发前的夏天参加了密集的语言培训。我们在2006年的秋天抵达中国之后，我加入了学校为外国人开设的中文班。

马克·吐温搞不懂德语形容词的变化，而我不会讲普通话。我人生中第一次无法将发音和语义联系起来——尽管我每次班级考试都能得高分。我刻苦练习中文，还请了一名家教，听磁带，看中央电视台主持人大山的节目，和先生一起看中国电影——但我还是不会讲普通话。

---

1 艾弗拉姆·诺姆·乔姆斯基，美国语言学家，他的《生成语法》被公认为20世纪理论语言学研究上最伟大的贡献。
2 埃兹拉·庞德，美国诗人、文学评论家，意象派诗歌运动的重要代表人物。
3 埃里希·奥尔巴赫，德国语言学家、文学评论家，代表作有《摹仿论》。

困难接踵而来，我很沮丧。尽管我知道自己有些许进步，但是要取得更大的进步谈何容易！

对我来说，语法并不难。“我想买这本书”和“I want to buy this book”差不多。像“本”这样的中文量词也不难，因为英语也有“A flock of geese”（一群鹅）、“a herd of cattle”（一群牛）或者“a pod of dolphins”（一群海豚），这些都是我们日常对话里经常出现的。我完全可以理解“a parliament of owls”（一群猫头鹰）是什么意思，尽管我自己以前从来没有用过这种表述。其实在英语里，一个“group”（组/群）后面完全可以随意加上任何你想表达的事物，比如汽车、大象、网球拍等等。

让我陷入汉语迷宫的是一长串同音异义词：它们发音相似，意义却不同。单单“jiàn”这个音就能留下无尽的猜测：是看见的“见”，军舰的“舰”，还是弓箭的“箭”呢？是践踏的“践”，飞溅的“溅”，还是山涧的“涧”呢？是指你的情人卑“贱”还是强“健”？而且，万一我们发音不准，或者是音调不对，那整个谈话就可能进入完全错误的方向，讨论的内容有可能从地理变为解剖！

笔画对于我来说也不是问题。正如数年前我在艺术史课上记住了著名的书法作品中的笔画，我可以记住汉字的笔画并进行区分。当然了，我读汉字肯定没有我读英语那么快，但我还是能看懂。我甚至去上书法课了，我的老师很棒，我也学会了如何鉴赏书法，但是就像在键盘上输入英文单词比手写要容易一样，输入中文也比写中文字更容易。

尽管我深深倾倒于书法的艺术魅力，我还是要靠“听”和“说”来学习中文。当我还是个学生的时候，我有很多机会去讲其他语言：这给了我频繁且有益的接触语言的机会。但是在中国，我是靠英语生活的。我的朋友、同事，不管是外国人还是中国人，都讲英语。短期内，我始终得不到机会去反复练习我的中文，使之变得更好。

就连理发这样的小事都变成了折磨。我一直磨蹭，直到我的刘海已经盖住了眼睛才不得不去。我抱着我的字典，鼓起勇气来到理发店。在那里，我一开口，痛苦就开始了。在世界的任何地方，不管是芝加哥还是成都，理发师都有个共性，那就是热衷于和客人聊天。刚来中国时，就算我紧盯着理发师的口型，仍听不懂她在说什么。当她转到我的侧面或者后面时，我就更加听不清了。没有视觉的辅助，我完全云里雾里。所幸大多数理发师都比较同情我，并且基本能剪出我想要的发型。

之后，慢慢地，我开始和人聊天，并且得到回应。2006年，中国的二线城市还鲜有外国面孔。因为我经常光顾菜市场，那些卖菜妇女们经常见到我，故而对我产生了好奇。她们对我买了什么菜尤其感兴趣，还会问我外国人是怎么做芦笋的——她们虽然卖这种菜，但是自己从来不吃。出租车司机会跟我聊车上放的歌曲，并且问我：新开的“宜家”有什么特别之处，为什么所有的外国人都喜欢去那里购物？我的朋友还模仿一个中文很流利的外国人说话，但所有的音调都是第四声。当我听到那个外国人讲话时，我意识到我朋友的模仿是多么的惟妙惟肖。我可以不用看歌词听懂一些邓丽君的歌。到2009年时，我终于可以不用随身携带字典，在一个没有几个人会说英语的小镇生活了，太好了！

我努力了三年便达到了汉语的中等水平，之后我们就回美国了。一回去，似乎就找不到继续学习中文的理由。我觉得我以后再也用不到中文了。芝加哥有个很大的中国城，那里的第一代或第二代移民也大都讲粤语，而非普通话。所以这期间我专注于其他事情，汉语逐渐荒废了。

意外的是，我丈夫在2011年需要去新加坡。虽然新加坡充斥着普通话和其他汉语方言，但是英语仍处于主导地位。我又开始学习汉语，想着可以在之前的基础上再接再厉。我们有很好的教材，学生的积极性也很高，但我总觉得不对劲：这个课程旨在帮助学生通过HSK（汉语水平考试），而不是学习如何真正运用汉语——这一点需要自我学习，但是究竟怎么做，我毫无头绪。我们苦背词汇、做阅读理解、参加考试，但没有机会在课堂或其他地方去说、去运用。对于我这样一个生活在新加坡的外国人来说，我再一次淹没在了全英语的环境中。我没有理由在一个周围人都讲英语的地方说中文，于是我退学了。真正掌握中文对于我来说，成了一件遥遥无期的事。

2015年，我们第二次回到中国。这次我们住在上海，人们都讲普通话。然而我们很快发现，在我们离开的这几年，中国变了，上海变了。在上海，很多年轻人都会说英语，而且说得很好。我完全可以只讲英语，就能在肯德基买到拿铁、在周边水果店买到水果、预订晚餐或者参加文学庆典。当然了，会中文可以让生活更容易。去理发店仍然不是很有趣，但最起码我已经不怕了。而且我终于可以让理发师明白我想要什么样的发型，也可以听懂他说的话。

现在，我们即将收拾行囊离开中国，我发现我的中文提高了。尽管没有我期待的那么多，但是已经足以满足我的日常所需。我会用中文的百度地图，使用双语的手机通讯录，给中国朋友发中英文夹杂的微信。在和中国人打交道时，我边听边学，并且试图重复他们的话。我不断在我的词卡里增添新词。最重要的是，我不再对自己欠佳的中文耿耿于怀，我学会了珍惜每一次使用中文的机会。每种语言都是不同的。对我来说，我已经掌握了学习中文的关键：那就是享受我在中国的生活。

作者简介：

Vicki Mayfield，美国籍，工商管理硕士。她是市场营销顾问，也是小说作家、业余摄影爱好者。她的丈夫于2015年至2016年担任上海外国语大学中东研究中心的顾问和访问教授。目前他们生活在芝加哥。

A Brush with Chinese: The Luckiest Accident in My Life

Ha Su Guen (South Korea)

Translated by George Fleming

When I was in junior and senior high school in Korea, I studied English. After university, I undertook postgraduate study in Germany, where I learned the local language. By contrast, I had had contact with neither Chinese nor Japanese, languages within my own East Asian cultural sphere. In fact, I was over sixty years old before I realized how overly Western my way of thinking was. On the other hand, I had relatively little idea about the situation of my own country. I was just reflecting on this depressing situation when my university launched an international exchange programme. As my own institution has a sisterhood agreement with Shanghai International Studies University, I then had the opportunity to come to Shanghai for a one-year exchange. I would be able to teach Korean language while learning about China's culture and its language, because although the latter two have had a substantial influence on both Korea and Japan, where traces can be found in the language, in fact the Korean language belongs to an entirely different family to Chinese. Linguistics researchers will all be aware of the fact that while the different cultures within one sphere may appear very similar, it is precisely the taking for granted of such surface similarity that leads to people making faux pas, even serious errors, in dealing with those from other countries. For instance, many believe that as a large proportion of Korean vocabulary is composed of Chinese loanwords, it therefore follows that Koreans should find learning Chinese very easy. In fact, the way a word is used can undergo tremendous changes over time and with the development of the host culture. Borrowing words wholesale when speaking another language can very well lead to misunderstandings — or even ridicule. When I reflect on these differences, I consider myself extremely fortunate to have been given this opportunity to embark on the long road to competence in Chinese, and to experience another culture. In the words of renowned linguistics researcher Wilhelm von Humboldt, "When we learn a new language, we learn far more than just a language: we learn, too, a deeper way of thinking that lies beneath it. Learning a foreign language allows us to understand the values that underpin it and thereby broaden our own perspectives. This is because the broadness of our perspective often depends on how much we understand of the world."

During my first semester in China, I could barely introduce myself in intelligible Chinese. I couldn't help worrying: how was I supposed to experience Chinese culture and ways of living if I couldn't understand the language? I came to realize that there was still something I could do, even if I could not. Firstly, I decided to get out and see more of life in Shanghai. Secondly, I would try the full gamut of Shanghainese cuisine. After all, travel and food are universal; you can experience these wherever you go. I had also wanted for a long time to make more local friends to talk to and understand their culture or traditions. But in order to do this, I would have to command at least a basic grasp of Chinese. This last goal appeared out of reach for the time being. I put it aside for my second semester.

Any Korean who has travelled to Shanghai or the surrounding area will know what I mean when I say there are almost no mountains here. In Korea, by contrast, 70% of the country is mountainous. There are mountains everywhere, which probably explains why the Koreans are such fans of mountain walking. I think it was the third week of my stay in Shanghai when I heard of a Mount She near the Songjiang campus of Shanghai International Studies University. I was also given to understand that Mount She was the highest peak in the vicinity. Eager to fulfill my special connection with the mountain, I took a cab there, ready for an adventure. However, when I got out of the taxi and saw "the highest mountain in Shanghai", I almost laughed. By Korean standards, the prominence that greeted me was at best a "hill". It was certainly not a *mountain*! The scene was really very funny, so I took a photo and sent it to my friends back home. I wanted to share the strange experience.

When you're living abroad, as long as you pay attention to your surroundings, you will discover many interesting places. Like the treasure hunts we used to play as children, you need a keen eye to spot the real-life treasures lurking around you. On the journey from the Songjiang campus to the Hongkou campus for my classes, I would always deliberately take a route through Luxun Park. I had a particular idea in mind: I wanted to see what Chinese parks were like. I was not disappointed. Shanghai's parks are different from Korean parks in many ways, and are all the more interesting for it. For example, the people in Luxun Park were engaged in a great variety of activities, which I found both odd and fascinating. I had never seen such things in Korea and thought it was very novel. I joined in with one of the groups to experience it for myself. There were old ladies dancing to music in one corner, while in another, people practiced their taichi in twos or threes. There was a young man playing an instrument and singing too. The place was so vibrant. Along the little paths in the park I saw small groups of young people chatting and laughing. It was a very happy and fulfilling scene. My only regret was that the language barrier hindered me from engaging with everyone. On one of the paths, several old people had opened out umbrellas and spread them on the ground. They had attached information about their sons or daughters, for whom they were scouting out potential partners. I was particularly struck by this behavior and think the memory will last a long time.

Shanghai's cuisine is not to be missed, either. Rather than the overly commercial, modern restaurants of the sort one can find anywhere in the world, I explored the local, traditional food markets. By coincidence, the accommodation that the university had arranged for me was close to many such small snack shops. In these were a multitude of vegetables and fruits, many of which I had never seen in Korea. I was still clumsy with Chinese money, so settling the bill was often tricky. When I was buying, at least, all I had to do was point, or say a simple "this one" or "how much?", and the staff would understand. Ordering, therefore, was a relatively straightforward affair. Because payment also meant having loose coins to hand, the bowl at home was always overflowing with coins. I set myself a target: I would try 200 types of Chinese food. If I could,

I would try all kinds of styles in a range of different restaurants. What's more, I succeeded. I once talked about this to a local acquaintance, and he said, "200 isn't nearly enough — try 300!"

Over the past few years in Shanghai, I have seen with my own eyes the differences between Chinese and Korean culture. These differences have led to many difficulties for me. Luckily, my students at the Korean faculty have assisted me many times. Sometimes, when I have to deal with a situation on my own, I remind myself of the golden rule: cast out all preconceptions. The most natural thing in the world back in Korea could be quite impossible here in China. When a situation arises, you must focus on reality and analyse what's going on. Nevertheless, even with the best preparations, the unexpected can be difficult to get a handle on. For example, one lunchtime the gas suddenly stopped working. I couldn't cook anything or take a hot shower. My first reaction was to assume that the boiler was broken, so I called the building management. They told me I hadn't paid the gas connection fee, so the gas company had cut me off. In Korea, the companies operate a system whereby you receive a bill at the end of every month. It is the opposite case in China, where one also pays a connection charge for electricity and water.

I felt that my poor command of Chinese was hampering my efforts to experience Chinese culture, so I threw myself into efforts to improve from my first semester. First of all, I applied to join the university's free beginners' Chinese course, which held one lesson a week. Of course, this was not nearly enough, so I made use of the Tandem method, which I had first heard about in Germany. Tandem involves two native speakers of different languages coming together and learning from one another in unstructured sessions to learn each other's language and culture. These sessions can take place face-to-face or in other ways such as over the phone, through email, or letter, and messaging over the Internet. Tandem leverages individual study, intercultural learning and partnering. It is also known as the "language exchange learning method". Because all the students on the Korean course lived in Songjiang, it was a challenge to find a Chinese person at the Hongkou campus who would be willing to learn Korean. In order to resolve the problem, I found a group of Korean students who were studying Chinese and created a language-partner group. Luckily, at the time the Hongkou campus offered classes in Korean as a second foreign language. I got in touch with the teacher of that course and thus got to know several of the Chinese students. We exchanged WeChat details and arranged to meet every week to learn from each other. The result was I gained two Chinese friends with whom to Tandem up long-term. I had laid a strong foundation for future fluency in Chinese. Having realized the importance of this method in learning a foreign language, I contacted both the Korean students at the Songjiang campus, and Korean students back home who were studying Chinese language, and put them in touch with each other via an online Tandem learning group. Everyone was really fired up about the idea: they could make friends and improve their foreign language at the same time: two birds with one stone. They proceeded to converse with each other in their foreign languages; when the message was lost, they could always switch back to their own language. They could also ask each other if they ran into problems. The Tandem group thus gave students a chance to try out the language they had learned in class, and to correct their mistakes. But most importantly, they made new friends!

About the author:

Ha Su Guen, South Korean, is a professor at Busan University of Foreign Studies. He taught at the School of Asian and African Studies at SISU from February 2016 to January 2017.

与中文邂逅，乃我今生之幸

河洙權（韩国）
王雪娇　译
梁晓雪　审校

我在韩国读中学的时候学习了英语，大学毕业之后，因为在德国留学的缘故，又学习了德语。然而，对于同处于东亚文化圈的汉语和日语却未曾接触过。直到年过花甲，我才突然意识到自己的思维方式过于西化，对于自己国家的情况反而知之甚少。正在我暗自嗟叹之际，学校新开设了一个国际交换项目，而我所在的大学和上海外国语大学又是合作院校，所以我就有了这个到上海交流一年的机会，可以一边教韩语，一边体验中国文化和学习汉语。虽说汉语以及中国文化对韩国和日本有很大的影响，在很大程度上这种影响也可以在语言上寻到踪迹，但韩语和汉语在根本上却属于完全不同的语系。研究语言学的人都深知，同一文化圈里不同民族的文化，虽然在表面上看起来有很多相似之处，但实际上这种自以为的“相似”往往会带来现实中的误解，甚至是错误。比如，很多人都认为韩语中有很多词汇来源于汉语，所以韩国人学起汉语来应该更快捷，殊不知同一个单词经历了历史变迁和民族文化的发展，很有可能已经不再适用于原来的语境，不分青红皂白地信手拈来很可能会引起误解甚至闹出笑话。所以，即使我很晚才踏上学习汉语的漫漫长路，也还是觉得能有机会去学习汉语、体验不同的文化是莫大的幸运。著名语言学者威廉·冯·洪堡曾说：“我们学习一门新的语言，不光是在学习语言本身，还包括学习语言背后所蕴含着的深层次思维。通过学习外语，我们能够了解到这种语言所包含的价值观，也可以因此丰富自己看待世界的角度。这是因为我们看待世界的广度往往取决于我们对世界了解的多少。”

刚来上海的第一个学期，我连一个像样的自我介绍都说不出来，于是不由得犯起愁来：在语言不通的情况下，我究竟该如何体验中国的生活文化氛围呢？思考的结果就是：即使语言不通，我也是可以做一些事情的。首先，我决定多体验一下上海的城市环境，到处走走。第二就是要尝遍上海的美食。毕竟旅行和美食是没有国界的。事实上，我还一直很期待能与一些当地人交朋友，与他们聊聊天，了解了解当地的风俗文化。但要达成这个心愿，我起码得懂一些当地的语言。看来这个愿望暂时是无法实现了，就把它作为我第二个学期的目标吧。

到过上海或者上海周边的韩国人都会明白我感到有点奇特的地方：在这里几乎看不到山。在韩国，70%的面积都是山地，可以说到处都是山，所以韩国人最喜欢的运动之一就是登山。来到上海的第三周，我听说上外松江校区附近有座佘山，而且还是上海近郊最高的山。于是，怀着对山的一种特殊情结，我独自打车来到佘山，开始了我的探索之旅。然而当我走下车，看到“上海最高的山”的瞬间，我不禁笑了。以韩国的标准来说的话，这个根本算不上山，顶多算个山丘嘛。由于实在太有趣，我就拍了照片发给家乡的朋友们，和他们一起分享这个有意思的经历。

在中国生活的日子里，如果仔细留意周围的生活环境，能发现许多有趣的地方。就像小时候玩“寻宝”游戏一样，蕴藏在生活中的“宝藏”也需要用“火眼金睛”去发掘。每次从松江校区到虹口校区上课时，我都会故意挑经过鲁迅公园的小路走，为的就是能满足一下自己的小“私心”，瞧一瞧中国的公园是长什么样子的。还别说，我发现上海的公园的确有很多和韩国公园不同、却十分有趣的地方。比如，让我感到既陌生又新奇的就是鲁迅公园里人们在做各种各样的运动。之前在韩国时，我从未见过这般情景，觉得十分新鲜，于是还亲自加入他们的队伍体验了一把。公园的一头有放着音乐跳舞的老太太们，另一头还有三三两两的人在打太极，还有一边弹奏一边唱歌的小青年，好不热闹。小路上还有三五结伴谈笑风生的年轻人们。看着这一切，我内心感到十分快乐和满足，唯一遗憾的就是语言障碍仿佛把我和他们的世界隔开了。公园小路上，老年人在撑开的伞面上贴上征婚启事，为子女征婚，这一场面也给我留下了深刻的印象。

还有一样千万不能错过的就是上海的美食。我没有选择那些已经商业化、世界各地都可以见到的现代化餐饮，而是挑选了当地传统的小吃市场。刚好学校给我安排的住所附近有很多这种小店，店里陈列了令人眼花缭乱的蔬菜和水果，有好多品种我在韩国都没有见过。由于我还不太会使用中国的钱币，所以结账时有点困难。但买东西的时候只要指一指，或简单地说“这个”“多少”，店家就能明白我的意思，所以购物还是进行得挺顺利的。由于买东西时总会有硬币找零，所以我家里的储蓄罐一直都是满满的。我给自己定了个目标，要吃够200种中国食物，可能的话还要去各种不同类型的店里品尝各样风味的食物。而且，我真的做到了！有一次我和在上海生活的熟人聊天时，他说：“200种哪够啊，你得吃够300种！”

在上海的这几年来，我目睹了中韩两国文化间的许多差异，也因此经历了不少的挫折。多亏了我的韩语系学生们，他们帮我解决了很多难题。有时候遇到不得不自己一个人处理的情况时，我就会在心里默默提醒自己：要抛开一切先入为主的想法。自己在韩国认为理所当然的事情在这里很可能行不通，因此遇事要直面现实，客观分析。但即使已经做好了心理准备，有时还是会被意料之外的情况弄得措手不及。比如，有一天中午家里的燃气突然断了，饭也不能做，热水澡也没法洗。那一瞬间我的反应是热水器坏了，于是给物业打电话询问，结果发现是没缴燃气开通费，燃气公司给切断了供应。在韩国，燃气缴费采用的是后付制，每个月先使用燃气，月末接到燃气公司的账单后去缴费即可。但在中国情况恰好相反，水电也要先缴一笔开通费。

由于语言沟通能力不足会影响我对中国文化的体验，所以为了提升自己的中文水平，我从第一学期开始就付出许多努力。首先，我申请了学校提供的免费中文入门课程，一周一次课。当然这是远远不够的。所以我决定亲身实践一下在德国留学时候学到的“Tandem互助学习法”。所谓Tandem互助学习法，指的是两个不同母语的学习者通过自主交流来学习对方的语言和文化。这种交流可以是面对面的交流，也可以通过其他手段进行，如电话、电子邮件（或者书信）、网上聊天等。它是一种建立在自主学习、跨文化学习和伙伴关系基础上的学习方法，也叫做“语言交换学习法”。由于韩语专业的学生都住在松江，所以要在虹口找一个想学习韩语的中国人还真不容易。于是我只好找了一些在中国学习汉语的韩国学生组成了一个学习互助小组。幸好当时虹口校区有设置二外韩语课程，通过韩语二外老师我认识了一些中国学生，互相加了微信，并约定了每周见面一起学习。由此，我有了两名固定的中国Tandem互助学友，为我进一步学习中文奠定了基础。意识到这是个学习语言的好方法后，我积极地给我松江校区的韩语学生和在韩国大学里学习中文的韩国学生牵线，让他们结成网上Tandem互助学习小组。学生对此都表现出相当地热情，既交到了朋友，又可以好好学习外语，真是一举两得。在学习中，中韩两国学生主要用各自的外语交流，当交流出现障碍时就可以借助自己的母语，有问题也可以相互请教。这样既可以把课堂上的知识学以致用，也可以及时修正使用不当之处，当然最重要的还是交到了新的朋友！

作者简介：

河洙權，韩国籍，釜山外国语大学教授，于2016年2月至2017年1月在上海外国语大学东方语学院任教。

Chinese and I

Gunsema Badueva (Russia)

Proofread by George Fleming

I had lived in China for many years before deciding last year that I would study Chinese. I had trouble committing myself to study of the language because I knew how difficult Chinese is. Living in an international metropolis, you can live perfectly easily without understanding the local language. However, if you want to understand the culture and psychology of its people, then getting to grips with their language is a must. I think this is the most important factor that pushed me to signing up for a Chinese course. Another reason was that when I travelled around China I would often have the following impression: even a rudimentary knowledge of the language made the trip a lot easier. I was better able to enjoy my beautiful surroundings and get more out of the experience. Although you can make yourself understood with gestures, you can't express exactly what you want to say, or what you want to find out about. I even had some ridiculous experiences such as ending up in places I had not planned to go to! That was the beginning of my Chinese study.

Shanghai International Studies University (SISU) has established beginners' and improvement Chinese language classes for its foreign experts. These classes have been an excellent opportunity to learn about ancient Chinese culture. Another advantage is that they are free.

Chinese is truly a difficult language to learn. If you want to remember the class material, you absolutely must revise after class and spend two to four hours a day consolidating your knowledge. However, not everyone is prepared to adapt to this lifestyle. I think this is precisely why, after a few lessons, we saw a significant drop in the numbers attending class. Although I have not been able to keep up with revision and practice, I still have a strong desire to speak Chinese: to use the language with my colleagues, students and friends, and to be able to understand what I hear without a translation.

Although Chinese seems relatively simple when you look at the grammar, Chinese experts remind me that you have to concentrate on the difficulties that are embedded in the language and are so hard to overcome. One of the greatest challenges is the tones. There are four of them, with thousands of words composed of different tones and syllables. It is enough to make you have a breakdown. Each Chinese character is like a work of art. It makes me shudder to think of having to write them all down and remember all their meanings! It would be great if I could commit even a hundredth of them to memory — although a thousandth would be an easier goal. In my opinion, studying Chinese characters can help my abstract thinking and improve my memory. However, it's a tough journey.

Wang Huihui, the teacher for the beginners' class, quickly came to be liked by everyone in the class. Frank, sincere and bubbly, Wang is a gifted teacher and could easily bridge the textbook examples and everyday language, in order to help us to more quickly apply our knowledge in life. Although we only have one class a week, I hope that her talent and our optimism in our studies can help us reach our goals. It is all a new experience for us that will enrich our lives here.

Although I cannot yet write the most correct or beautiful Chinese characters, my exercise book is ready, the course has started, and we are beginning to put words and sentences together. In front of us lies a long and difficult road to Chinese proficiency. Only the most persistent and patient students can overcome the obstacles ahead of them. Wish us success!

I am most grateful for the opportunity SISU has given me to study a new language, and to understand as much of Chinese culture as possible.

About the author:

Gunsema Badueva, Russian, has been working as an Associate Professor at the School of Russian and Eurasian Studies, SISU since September 2015.

我学汉语

Gunsema Badueva（俄罗斯）
王皓　译
梁晓雪　审校

我在中国已经住了好些年了，但决定开始学习汉语还是一年前的事。迟迟下不了决心学习汉语，是因为我知道这门语言非常难学。在国际大都市生活，就算不懂所在国的语言，生活也很方便。但要想了解这个国家的文化和大众心理，不懂语言是不行的——这大概是促使我去学习汉语最主要的原因。此外，我在中国旅游的时候，不乏遇到这样的状况：哪怕了解一点点的语言知识，就能让整个行程便利许多，能够更好地观赏风景，得到更多的情感体验。虽然手势语也能让人明白，但总归不能完全解释清楚你想说什么，以及此刻你想要了解的事情。甚至还发生过一些可笑的事情，比如，我到了原先根本没有打算去的地方。这也是我打算学习汉语的原因。

上海外国语大学（上外）为外国专家分别开设了汉语入门学习班和提高班，这为我们深入了解历史悠久的中国文化提供了极好的机会。这些学习班还有个好处，那就是全部免费。

汉语真的很难学。想要很好地掌握课上学到的知识，就一定要在课后复习，并且每天花2至4小时巩固这些知识。但不是每个人都准备好接受这样的学习方式。我想，正是因为这个原因，在几堂课之后，来上课的人少了许多。虽然我在实践中也没能很好地坚持复习巩固，但在我心中仍然有很强烈的愿望——说中文，用中文和同事们、学生们和朋友们交谈，不需要翻译就能明白我所听到的内容。

虽然从语法的角度而言，汉语并没有那么难，但汉语专家还是提醒我们要注意那些潜在的、通常难以克服的困难。最大的困难之一就是汉语的声调。汉字共有四个声调，几千个声调和音节不同的字几乎让我崩溃！每一个汉字都像是一幅艺术作品，但一想到要把它们都写下来并且记住全部含义就让我不寒而栗！我希望，在学习过程中能逐渐记住百分之一，哪怕是千分之一的东西就好了。在我看来，学习汉字还能够培养抽象思维并提升记忆力。但是，通往新知识的道路多艰辛啊！

入门学习班的汪慧慧老师很快就赢得了大家的喜欢。她性格坦率真诚，活泼开朗，善于教授知识，能很好地将课本材料和日常用语相结合，以便我们在课后能迅速地将知识运用到生活中去。虽然我们的课程一周只有一次，但是我希望，她的才能和我们对于学习的乐观精神能够帮助我们实现目标，用难忘的新体验丰富我们在中国的生活。

尽管我们暂时还不能完全正确地书写漂亮的汉字，但是书本已备好，课程已开始，我们已经能开始说一些词语和句子了。面前是提高汉语水平的漫长而又艰辛的道路，只有最顽强、最有耐心的学生才能战胜路上的困难！祝我们成功吧！

感谢上外提供的机会，让我能够学习新的语言，通过语言尽可能地去了解中国文化。

作者简介：

Gunsema Badueva，俄罗斯籍，自2015年9月起担任上海外国语大学俄罗斯东欧中亚学院副教授。

The Influence of SISU

Betty Barr (UK)

Proofread by George Fleming

One late afternoon this month, January 2018, I happened to be walking past one of SISU's gates when a man and a woman emerged from the campus. They took one look and cried, "Betty!" They had been my students twenty years ago! The man was from Ningxia and the woman from Xinjiang, two northwestern provinces in China, and they had come to SISU as middle school teachers to take a two-year course which led to a degree, a *benke*. In those years, SISU was one of five universities which jointly hosted a national project to upgrade the teaching of English in remote areas of the country.

From 1984 to 1988 there was a one-year Advanced Teacher Training

Course (ATTC) organized by the British Council based in the then English Department for college teachers of English. After all, it was not long after the Cultural Revolution and it was felt that college teachers of English from all over China needed help with their own language skills and, in particular, with their teaching methods. At the same time, Chinese counterparts were chosen to go to the UK for a year's study with the hope that they would return to teach on the course. I am still in touch with one of the students from those days, now retired from a college in Tunxi, Anhui Province.

Courtesy of Betty Barr

British Council Advanced Teacher Training Course in an outing to a park, 1984. Note the fashion!

From 1989 to 1991 a similar training course for Senior Middle School Teachers of English (SMSTE) was based in the then English Department II (which has now morphed into a Law School). This time the students were middle school teachers from the Northeast — Liaoning, Jilin and

Heilongjiang — and the Northwest — Gansu, Ningxia and Xinjiang. As mentioned above, it was a two-year course. The students had attended two-year courses in their own provinces but this course provided a *benke*, which could lead to promotion in their schools on their return.

The materials for the course were tailor-made, written by experienced British Council teachers, and, once again, the aim was to upgrade the teachers' own language skills and to introduce new ideas about their teaching methods. The "Communicative Approach" was a new term to most of them, who had been taught by traditional grammar-translation methods.

After that, from 1991 to 1994, I was fortunate enough to be involved in a third British Council project, Follow-up Research, also based at SISU. We visited as many former students as possible in an attempt to discover whether, on their return to their remote areas, they were, in fact, able to use the methods we had advocated. The results can be found in a small book we produced, *A Crane Among the Chickens*, the title using an old Chinese saying. One of our returned students lamented: "Sometimes when you try to share the ideas, they even turn up their noses at you, describing you as 'trying to be a crane among the chickens'."

It goes without saying that besides the serious research during those three years we had many adventures on our travels to the remote provinces. My Shanghainese husband, George Wang, accompanied me and we travelled mostly by public bus. When we arrived at Kashi (Kashgar) on a bus which was more than two hours late, it was heartwarming to find a student standing there waiting for us. During our time there we rented a jeep and travelled with him up a gravelly road high up into the spectacular Pamir Mountains on the border with Pakistan.

In the Northeast my former student, a rather serious Deputy Head of his middle school, took us one evening to a karaoke bar — my first experience of this form of entertainment — where a beautiful young lady sang and danced for us.

Back in Xinjiang, we stumbled off a dusty bus one late afternoon to be told that we would be going to a party that evening because there were visitors from Kazakhstan. My student's wife lent me an elegant dress and I appeared at the party to represent "the West". They were hoping to build up cross-border trade — a precursor of the present Belt and Road Initiative. I hope my presence helped to improve their economy!

The two students I met outside SISU's gate had been grading English papers for the College Entrance Examination. They are now teaching in middle schools in Shanghai suburbs. To me, this is an example of the influence of SISU not only in higher education through its own graduates but also in middle schools through these former middle-school-teacher students.

Courtesy of Betty Barr

Betty and her husband George Wang visiting former British Council Senior Middle School Teacher Training Course students in Jilin, around 1990

About the Author:

Betty Barr was born in Shanghai in 1933. She graduated from the Shanghai American School in 1949 and then attended Wellesley College, a very famous women's college whose graduates include Hillary Clinton and Soong Mayling. From 1973–1975 she was a teacher at the then Shanghai Foreign Language Institute (predecessor to SISU). Following that, she worked as an English teacher in Scotland. In 1984 she returned to Shanghai and then taught at our University until her retirement in 2002.

上外的影响

白丽诗（英国）

张宏雨　译

梁晓雪　审校

2018年1月的一个傍晚，我路过上外的大门，正巧碰到从校园里走出的一男一女。一看到我，他们就大呼一声："贝蒂！"原来，他们是我20年前的学生。男的来自宁夏，女的来自新疆，都是位于中国西北部的省份。当时，他们作为中学老师来上外进修本科，在这里学习了两年。那时候，上外与中国其他4所高校一起开展了这个国家级项目，目的是促进中国偏远地区英语教育的发展。

从1984年到1988年，英国文化教育协会在当时的英语系设立了为期一年的高级教师培训课程，为高校英语教师提供培训。毕竟，文化大革命刚刚结束不久，国内高校的英语老师都亟需提升自身的语言能力，尤其是教学方法。与此同时，中国选派了一批英语老师赴英国访学一年，以期提升他们的英语教学水平，回国后加入培训课程的教学队伍。这些老师当中，有一个我们至今还有联系，他曾在安徽省屯溪区的一所高校工作，现在已经退休了。

从1989年到1991年，英语二系（现在是法学院）为高中英语老师安排了类似的培训课程。这些英语老师有来自东北（辽宁、吉林和黑龙江）的，有来自西北（甘肃、宁夏和新疆）的。同样，这也是两年的课程培训。这些老师先在各自的省份参加为期两年的培训，之后再参加我们的课程。获得本科学历后，他们带着学到的新知识回到各自原先的岗位。

为这些老师提供的培训课程都是专门为学员量身定做的，教材由经验丰富的英国文化教育协会的老师编写，目的是提高这些老师自身的语言能力，并介绍新的教学方法。大多数国内教师熟知的是传统的语法翻译教学法，因而“交际教学法”对他们来说是一个崭新的概念。

之后，从1991年到1994年，我有幸参与了英国文化教育协会的第三个后续研究项目，也是在上外进行的。我们尽量采访参与过此项目的老师，以验证他们是否能将所学成果运用在实际教学中。我们将调查结果写成书出版，书名是《鹤立鸡群》，源于一句中国谚语。我们教过的一位学生曾叹惜道：“有时，你想和他人分享学到的新方法，而周围人会嗤之以鼻，说你只是想‘鹤立鸡群’。”

当然，在这三年时间中，除了认真严肃地调研之外，我们还得以探索很多偏远省份。我的丈夫王正文是上海人，他陪我一起去这些地方。我们旅行的主要交通工具是公共汽车。有一次，我们坐大巴去喀什，晚点了两个多小时，然而，当看到一个学生依然站在那里等候时，我们感到一股暖流涌上心田。之后的几天，我们租了一辆吉普车，在学生的陪同下翻山越岭，穿越铺满碎石的山路，驶向宏伟壮观的帕米尔山脉，直到巴基斯坦边境。

在东北的一个晚上，我之前的一个学生带我们去了一家卡拉

OK酒吧，他当时是一个中学的副校长，为人挺严肃。我还是第一次去这样的娱乐场所——在那里，有一位年轻漂亮的姑娘为我们唱歌跳舞。

有一天，我们坐车回到新疆，到达时已接近傍晚，我们刚跌跌撞撞地从满是灰尘的汽车上下来，就有人邀请我们去参加一个晚会，因为那天有从哈萨克斯坦来的客人。我学生的妻子借给我一条优雅的长裙，我穿上它代表“西方人”出席晚会。他们此次来访是希望能建立双边贸易，也就是我们现在“一带一路”要做的事情。希望我当时的出现有助于他们谈成交易！

我在上外门口遇见的这两位学生现在都是上海郊区中学的老师，他们来上外批阅高考试卷。在我看来，上外所作出的贡献不仅仅在于为高校培养出一代代优秀的大学毕业生，还在于为中学教育的发展培养出一批批优秀的中学老师。

作者简介：

白丽诗，1933年出生于上海，1949年从上海美国学校毕业，随后就读于希拉里·克林顿、宋美龄等人就读过的著名女子大学韦尔斯利学院。1973年到1975年期间，她在上海外国语学院（今上海外国语大学）任教，之后回苏格兰担任英语教师。1984年，她返回上外任教，直至2002年退休。